The Aztecs

The Peoples of America

General Editors
Alan Kolata and Dean Snow

This series is about the native peoples and civilizations of the Americas, from their origins in ancient times to the present day. Drawing on archaeological, historical and anthropological evidence, each volume presents a fresh and absorbing account of a group's culture, society, and history.

Accessible and scholarly, and well illustrated with maps and photographs, the volumes of *The Peoples of America* will together provide a comprehensive and vivid picture of the character and variety of the societies of the American past.

Already published

The Aztecs
Michael E. Smith

The Iroquois
Dean Snow

The Timucua
Jerald T. Milanich

The Tiwanaku: A Portrait of
an Andean Civilization
Alan Kolata

The Cheyenne
John Moore

The Moche
Garth Bawden

In preparation

The Cherokee
Gerald F. Schroedl

The Incas
Terence N. D'Altroy

The Nascas
*D. M. Brown and
Helaine Silverman*

The Navajo
Alan Downer

The Mayas
Donald S. Rice

The Sioux
Guy Gibbon

The Aztecs

Michael E. Smith

The right of Michael E. Smith to be identified as author of this work has been
asserted in accordance with the Copyright, Designs and Patents Act 1988.

First published 1996
Reprinted 1997 (twice)
First published in paperback 1998

Blackwell Publishers Inc
350 Main Street
Malden, Massachusetts 02148, USA

Blackwell Publishers Ltd
108 Cowley Road
Oxford OX4 1JF, UK

Library of Congress Cataloging in Publication Data
Smith, Michael Ernest, 1953–
The Aztecs / Michael E. Smith
p.   cm. — (The peoples of America)
Includes bibliographical references and index.
ISBN 1–55786–496–9
ISBN 0–631–20958–1 (Pbk)
1. Aztecs—History. 2. Aztecs—Antiquities. 3. Aztecs—Social life and customs.
4. Mexico—Antiquities. I. Title. II. Series.
F1219.73.S58   1996   972'.018—dc20   95–25889
                                                              CIP

British Library Cataloguing in Publication Data
A CIP catalogue record for this book is available from the British Library

Typeset in 11 on 12.5pt Sabon
by Graphicraft Typesetters Limited, Hong Kong
Printed and bound in Great Britain
by MPG Books Ltd, Bodmin, Cornwall

This book is printed on acid-free paper

To the memory of my mother, Esther O. Smith
and my stepmother, Carolyn S. Smith.

Contents

List of Figures

List of Tables

Preface

Is there perchance any truth to our words here?
All seems so like a dream, only do we rise from sleep,
only on earth do our words remain.
>> *Cantares Mexicanos (1985:f.5v), translated by*
>> *León-Portilla (1963:71)*

Words were important to the Aztecs, and we are fortunate today that many of their own words were preserved after the Spanish conquest. Also preserved were examples of the Aztecs's picture-writing as well as descriptions by Spanish conquerors and observers. These written sources have been available for four centuries, and many works on the Aztecs make use of them. But they are not the only window into the Aztec past; words are not all that remain on earth.

Paradoxically, the oldest information on the Aztecs is also the most recent to be discovered. I refer to the ruins of houses, temples, and towns that make up the archaeological record of Aztec civilization. Aztec archaeology is a relatively new field of study. Many exciting new discoveries over the past two decades have revolutionized our understanding of Aztec civilization, but until now most of this information has appeared only in technical reports and professional journals. A major goal of this book is to make these discoveries known to a wider audience. As a participant in this work, I try to communicate something of the excitement and significance of our research.

In the pages that follow, I draw heavily upon the results of fieldwork that I have directed at Aztec sites in the Mexican state of Morelos. I would like to acknowledge the following institutions and agencies for providing funding for that fieldwork: the National Science Foundation, the National Endowment for the Humanities, the Wenner-Gren Foundation for Anthropological Research, the National Geographic Society, the Heinz Charitable Trust, Loyola University of Chicago, the University at Albany (State University of New York), and the Institute for Mesoamerican Studies. My research in Mexico has been greatly facilitated by Mexican colleagues and officials, particularly Joaquim García-Bercena, Angel García-Cook, Lorena Mirambell, Mari Carmen Serra Puche, Norberto González C., and Hortensia de Vega Nova. I thank the following students who participated in the fieldwork for their contributions to its overall success: Patricia Aguirre, Martín Antonio, Robert Austin, Courtney Brown, Lisa Cascio, Elizabeth DiPippo, Ruth Fauman-Fichman, Timothy Hare, Kathleen Haynie, Kathryn Hirst, Ronald Kohler, Samantha Miller, Susan Norris, Joan Odess, Scott O'Mack, T. Jeffrey Price, Colleen Rhodes, David Shafer, Margaret Shiels, Jerrell Sorensen, Sharon Spanogle, Osvaldo Sterpone, Timothy Sullivan, Cheryl Sutherland, Deborah Szymborski, and Brian Tomaslewski. I also must thank my excellent field crews from the Morelos towns of Tetlama and Yautepec. My father, Dudley B. Smith, deserves thanks for providing pickup trucks for our fieldwork.

My understanding of Aztec civilization has benefitted greatly from interaction with my colleagues. Although these are too numerous to list, I do want to acknowledge an intellectual debt to the following scholars: Jorge Angulo, Carlos Barreto M., Frances F. Berdan, Richard E. Blanton, Elizabeth H. Boone, Elizabeth M. Brumfiel, Louise M. Burkhart, Robert M. Carmack, Thomas H. Charlton, George L. Cowgill, Ann Cyphers, Hortensia de Vega Nova, Susan T. Evans, Silvia Garza de González, Susan D. Gillespie, Norberto González C., Gary H. Gossen, David C. Grove, Rafael Gutierrez, Cynthia Heath-Smith, Frederic Hicks, Kenneth G. Hirth, Mary G. Hodge, Dorothy Hosler, John S. Justeson, Druzo Maldonado J., Deborah L. Nichols, Cynthia Otis Charlton, Jeffrey R. Parsons, Ana Maria Pelz, William T. Sanders, Juan Antonio Siller, Wanda Tommasi de Magrelli, Emily Umberger, and James Wessman.

I want to thank the following colleagues for providing comments on specific chapters: Louise Burkhart (chapters 8, 9, 11), Thomas H. Charlton (chapters 3–5), William E. Doolittle (chapter 3), Susan T. Evans (chapter 6), Mary G. Hodge (chapter 7), Dorothy Hosler (chapter 4), and Cynthia Otis Charlton (chapters 3–5). I am particularly grateful to the following readers who provided comments on many or all of the chapters: Elizabeth DiPippo, Cynthia Heath-Smith, Alan Kolata, Carolyn Smith, and Megan Snedden. The editing of Cynthia Heath-Smith has improved my prose greatly. I thank these colleagues for responding to my requests for help with illustrations: Frances F. Berdan, Elizabeth H. Boone, Louise Burkhart, Davíd Carrasco, Thomas H. Charlton, William E. Doolittle, Judith Friedlander, Mary G. Hodge, Dean Lambert, Eduardo Matos Moctezuma, Cynthia Otis Charlton, and Emily Umberger. I also wish to acknowledge the help of Dorothy Christiansen of the Special Collections Department, University Library, and Mark Schmidt of the University Graphics Office, University at Albany. I thank Marnie DiStefano, April Smith, and Heather Smith for their help with the preparation of the manuscript, and Ellen Cesarski and Kori Kaufman for help with drafting.

Last but not least, I owe the greatest debt to my wife, Cynthia Heath-Smith, and our daughters April Nicole and Heather Colleen. Cindy is a superb archaeologist who has contributed greatly to our fieldwork, and she is the best editor I know. She has also helped create a happy and stable home during our many moves between the U.S. and Mexico. April and Heather have assisted during some of the fieldwork described here, but more than that they help make the life of an archaeologist worthwhile and fulfilling.

Guide to Pronunciation and Spelling

In Nahuatl, the language of the Aztecs, most consonants are pronounced as in English, and vowels are pronounced as in Spanish. The major exceptions are:

h	pronounced 'hw' (Huitzilopochtli; macehualli)
qua, quo	pronounced 'kw' (quachtli)
que, qui	pronounced 'k' (Quetzalcoatl; pulque)
tl	pronounced like the English 'atlas' (Tlaloc), even at the end of a word, where it is unvoiced (Nahuatl; coatl)
x	pronounced 'sh' (Xipe Totec; Mexica)

1

The Aztecs of Mesoamerica

Next morning, we came to a broad causeway and continued our march towards Iztapalapa. And when we saw all those cities and villages built in the water, and other great towns on dry land, and that straight and level causeway leading to Mexico, we were astounded. These great towns and *cues* [temple-pyramids] and buildings rising from the water, all made of stone, seemed like an enchanted vision from the tale of Amadis. Indeed, some of our soldiers asked whether it was not all a dream. It is not surprising therefore that I should write in this vein. It was all so wonderful that I do not know how to describe this first glimpse of things never heard of, seen or dreamed of before.

Bernal Díaz del Castillo[1]

With these words Bernal Díaz del Castillo, a soldier in Hernando Cortés's conquering army, expressed his amazement at the Aztec capital city. When the Spaniards approached Tenochtitlan in 1519, it was one of the most populous cities in the world, the largest ever to flourish in the prehispanic New World, and far richer and more grandiose than any community the Spanish soldiers had ever beheld in their home country (figure 1.1). Expecting to find a simple, backward people, the conquerors were awed by the civilized nature of Aztec society. The kings and royal courts, the huge bustling marketplaces with their orderly layouts, the wealth of the nobility, the detailed scientific and technical knowledge of the priests and artisans, these and many other features of Aztec civilization filled the conquerors with wonder and awe.

Much about the Aztecs continues to amaze us today. When workmen in Mexico city accidentally uncovered a huge Aztec sculpture in 1978, the Mexican government quickly mounted one of the largest excavations in the country's history. What emerged from these diggings was the so-called "Templo Mayor,"

*Figure 1.1   Artist's reconstruction of the Templo Mayor and
the sacred precinct in the heart of Tenochtitlan
(After Marquina 1951:lámina 55)*

a huge temple-pyramid that had served as the sacred center of
the Aztec empire. The sculpture was an offering buried in front
of the pyramid. This pyramid (figure 1.1) and the thousands of
rich and exotic offerings uncovered in and around it are now
open to the public, and millions of visitors express their interest and appreciation every year.

Human sacrifice was a central ritual at the Templo Mayor,
as it was at most Aztec temple-pyramids. Each year thousands
of victims had their chests cut open, and their still-beating
hearts ripped out by knife-wielding priests, as throngs of spectators looked on. Today we find these bloody rituals horrifying
but morbidly fascinating. Yet the very same people who produced this sacrificial blood and gore wrote some of the most
beautiful and poignant lyric poetry ever recorded. Here is a
poem attributed to the philosopher-king Nezahualcoyotl of
Texcoco:

> Is it true that on earth one lives?
> Not forever on earth, only a little while.

Though jade it may be, it breaks;
though gold it may be, it is crushed;
though it be quetzal plumes, it shall not last.
Not forever on earth, only a little while.
(*Cantares Mexicanos*)[2]

Today we find this contrast intriguing – blood and sacrifice versus beauty and sensitivity.

As an archaeologist, I used to feel a different sort of fascination toward the Aztecs: why was there so little fieldwork at Aztec sites? Spectacular discoveries had been made for over a century at Maya sites in southern Mexico and Guatemala, but little effort was directed at the remains of the Aztecs. Nearly all of our information about the Aztecs came from ethnohistoric documents, but these left gaping holes in our reconstructions of Aztec society. Ironically, many of these gaps in the written record were topics for which the methods of modern archaeology were uniquely suited to study. If archaeologists could now provide detailed information on the agricultural systems, craft production, cities, houses, and rituals of other ancient civilizations, why were these methods not being applied toward understanding the Aztecs? This question had two answers: first, most scholars assumed that nearly all Aztec sites had been destroyed, either by the Spanish conquerors or by modern urban expansion; and second, those sites known to have survived were small and unassuming, unlike the large and impressive jungle cities of the Maya.

Happily my amazement was short-lived. Two breakthroughs – the excavations of the Templo Mayor starting in 1978 and the work of a group of Mexican and American archaeologists at smaller sites – showed that it was still possible to map and excavate Aztec sites, and the results of recent work have revolutionized our understanding of Aztec civilization. The Templo Mayor excavations are now complete, and a number of books and articles describe this work for specialists and non-specialists alike. Fieldwork at smaller Aztec sites continues unabated, but so far most of this research has been described only in technical reports and articles. Although archaeological fieldwork outside of Tenochtitlan has yet to turn up any finds as spectacular as the Templo Mayor, recent discoveries have led to exciting new views of Aztec social, economic, and religious life. My goal in writing this book is to draw upon both the ongoing archaeological study of Aztec sites and the continuing tradition of ethnohistoric scholarship in order to arrive at a more complete and comprehensive picture of Aztec society as it existed on the eve of Spanish conquest. As an active participant in Aztec archaeology, I hope to communicate something of the excitement and significance of our work and its contribution to a new understanding of Aztec life before 1519.

A Perspective on the Aztecs

My approach to Aztec civilization derives in large part from my perspective as an archaeologist. I take a wider and more inclusive view of the Aztecs, both geographically and socially, than most authors. For many, the term "Aztec" refers strictly to the inhabitants of Tenochtitlan (the Mexica people) or perhaps the inhabitants of the Valley of Mexico, the highland basin where the Mexica and certain other Aztec groups lived. I believe it makes more sense to expand the definition of "Aztec" to include the peoples of nearby highland valleys in addition to the inhabitants of the Valley of Mexico. In the final few centuries before the arrival of the Spaniards in 1519, the peoples of this wider area all spoke the Nahuatl language (the language of the Aztecs), and they all traced their origins to a mythical place in the north called Aztlan (Aztlan is the origin of the term "Aztec," a modern label that was not used by the people themselves).

The several million Aztecs were divided into twenty or so ethnic groups (such as the Mexica, Tepanecs, or Tlahuica). Although people identified themselves by their ethnic group and by the city-state in which they resided, they were tied together by a common language, origin myths, and cultural patterns. Ethnohistorian James Lockhart has found many cultural similarities among these peoples at the time of the Spanish conquest, and he uses the term "Nahuas" to describe the central Mexican Nahuatl-speaking peoples. My use of the term Aztecs parallels Lockhart's term for the period before 1519; after that I switch to "Nahuas" to describe these peoples following the Spanish conquest.[3]

This book also takes a more inclusive social perspective than most other works on the Aztecs. Much of the available written documentation of Aztec society is flawed by two biases. First, the lives and conditions of nobles are heavily emphasized, whereas the situation of commoners is given short shrift. Second, life in Tenochtitlan is described in detail, whereas rural life is almost ignored. These biases assure that any account of Aztec society based entirely on historical records will be incomplete.[4] At this point, however, archaeology comes to the rescue. Recent methodological and conceptual changes in the discipline now permit archaeologists to recover rather detailed information on the lives of commoners and the conditions of rural areas.

The archaeological study of the everyday lives of peasants and other commoners is a relatively new development in the history of the discipline. It is understandable that early archaeologists with an interest in the high civilizations – ancient Egypt, Sumeria, the Inca, Maya, and others – chose to devote their energy to the grand monuments of these cultures. For two centuries, archaeologists excavated pyramids, palaces, tombs, and temples, the highly visible remains of ancient power. They searched for artistic masterpieces to bring back to European or American museums. This style of fieldwork, which I call "monumental archaeology," still goes on today, but it has been supplemented by a newer approach, "social archaeology.'

Social archaeology develops its mission from a close interaction between archaeology and anthropology and draws its methods from the physical and biological sciences. This approach views archaeology as a social science whose goal is to reconstruct and explain the workings of past cultures. Pyramids and palaces were certainly important parts of ancient cultures, but so were peasant houses, foods and crops, merchants and markets, and other aspects of everyday life that the monumental archaeology approach omits. The social archaeology approach depends upon the principle that the everyday actions of ordinary people are important parts of any culture. These things can be reconstructed for the Aztecs or any ancient civilization if the appropriate methods and theories are used to guide archaeological fieldwork and analysis. One of the main tasks of this book is to bring the Aztec people – commoners as

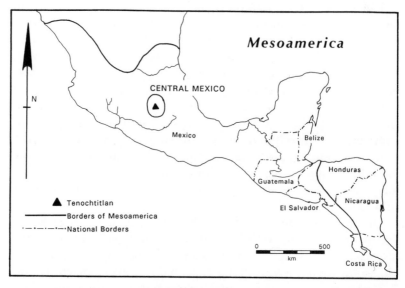

Figure 1.2   Map of Mesoamerica showing the location of central Mexico, the Aztec heartland (Drawing by Ellen Cesarski and Kori Kaufman)

well as lords – into the light of modern knowledge, and archaeology is the primary means for accomplishing this.

Mesoamerican Context

The Aztecs were a Mesoamerican civilization. Mesoamerica is the term for a distinctive cultural area that extends from north-central Mexico to Pacific Costa Rica (figure 1.2). Mesoamerica first took form with the initial spread of farming villages soon after 2,000 BC. By the year AD 1519, the area was composed of a large variety of peoples whose cultures resembled one another far more than they resembled other New World cultures. Even in the face of Spanish conquest and colonization, the native Mesoamerican peoples managed to maintain fundamental beliefs and practices. In Mesoamerica today a variety of native languages are still spoken; the most common are Nahuatl, Yucatec Maya (there are many Maya languages), Zapotec,

Mixtec, and Otomi. Nevertheless, the different Mesoamerican cultures share many characteristics, and key traits can be traced to their origin several thousand years ago.[5]

Early definitions of Mesoamerica focused on the identification of cultural traits unique to the area, which included economic features such as periodic markets, obsidian tools, plaster floors, and digging sticks, and religious traits such as human sacrifice, use of 13 as a sacred number, and a 260-day ritual calendar. Today, scholars are less interested in the compilation of lists of Mesoamerican traits and more concerned with the processes and mechanisms by which the diverse Mesoamerican cultures interacted with one another to maintain their cultural similarities and differences.[6]

Mesoamerican Environments

The hallmark of Mesoamerica as a setting for cultural development is its diversity. The area includes many different environmental zones, from steamy lowland jungles to cold, windy highland plains. This environmental diversity was matched by linguistic and cultural variation. Mesoamerican environments, which set the scene for the expansion of the Aztec empire, are best discussed in terms of elevation above sea level.[7]

The tropical lowlands Mesoamerica lies entirely within the tropical latitudes, and areas of low elevation tend to be hot and humid. Lands under 1,000 m in elevation are referred to by Mexican geographers as "tierra caliente" or the hot country. Rainfall is heavy in most lowland areas, producing either tropical forest vegetation (figure 1.3) or else savanna grasslands. Two Mesoamerican civilizations that evolved in tropical lowland environments were the Formative-period Olmec and the Classic-period Maya. The Aztecs were a highland civilization, yet they were dependant upon the tropical lowlands for a number of critical goods. Some of these goods were colorful feathers from parrots, quetzal birds, and other lowland birds (important in ritual and art), jaguar skins, cacao, tobacco, and jade.

Highland Mesoamerica Areas lying between 1,000 and 2,000 m above sea level are called the "tierra templada" or temperate

Figure 1.3　A Mesoamerican tropical forest at the Maya ruins of Tikal in Guatemala (Photograph by Michael E. Smith)

country. Many Mesoamerican civilizations, including the Mixtecs, Zapotecs, Tarascans, and highland Maya, flourished in this zone. Temperatures are more moderate than in the lowlands, with many areas averaging in the 70s (Fahrenheit) year round. Most places have enough rain to grow crops successfully. Rainfall is highly seasonal, with a wet season from June to October and a dry season from January to May. Much of the Mesoamerican highlands consist of steep mountains; human settlement was concentrated in river valleys with expanses of flat terrain. The southern portion of the Aztec heartland in central Mexico falls into this highland temperate zone.

The central Mexican plateau　Lands above 2,000 m in elevation are called the "tierra fria," or cold lands. This zone includes the central Valley of Mexico and adjacent valleys to the north, east, and west. Rainfall varies from levels adequate for farming to levels that will not support maize agriculture.

Average temperatures are much cooler than the other zones, and frost is a problem between October and March. The shorter growing season makes agriculture more risky than at lower elevations and limits the number and variety of crops that can be grown.

The Aztec Environment

Central Mexico, the home of the Aztecs, is a mountainous area, with much of the land surface taken up by steep wooded slopes. The highest mountain in Mexico, Pico de Orizaba (5,700 m elevation), sits at the eastern edge of the region. Human settlement in central Mexico has always been concentrated in the large highland valleys, whose fertile soils and abundant resources made them home to a series of complex ancient cultures beginning before 1,000 BC and leading up to Aztec civilization.

The Valley of Mexico

The Valley of Mexico was the heartland of Aztec civilization, and in 1519 it was home to approximately one million Aztecs. It is a large internally-drained basin ringed by volcanic mountains that reach over 3,000 m in elevation. Millennia of soil erosion from the mountainsides have produced deep, rich soils in the Valley and a system of shallow, swampy, saline lakes in its center (figure 1.4). These salty lakes furnished various types of food to the Aztecs, including fish, turtles, insect larvae, blue-green algae, and salt. The outcast Mexica peoples chose an island in the central lake (Lake Texcoco) to found their town Tenochtitlan, which later grew into the huge imperial capital. The southern arm of the lake system, Lakes Chalco and Xochimilco, was higher in elevation than Lake Texcoco and consequently less saline. The freshwater swamps of this arm proved to be ideal for the construction of *chinampas*[8] or raised fields, a highly productive form of agriculture used to feed the large Aztec population (see chapter 3).

Surrounding the lakes is a band of alluvial plains with deep,

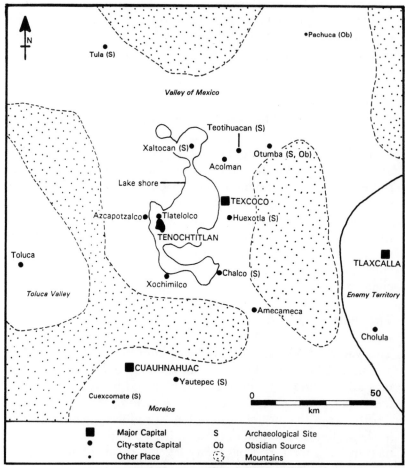

Figure 1.4   Map of Aztec central Mexico
(Drawing by Ellen Cesarski)

rich soils. Where springs or rivers could be tapped for canal
irrigation, the flat alluvium became a highly productive zone.
Most of the Aztec cities in the Valley (except for Tenochtitlan)
were located in this environmental zone. Beyond the flat alluvium are piedmont foothills that lead up to the volcanic mountains ringing the Valley of Mexico. The soils on these gentle
slopes are rich and easy to work using hand tools, but they are
shallow and prone to erosion. The Aztecs made use of stone

terrace walls to check erosion and create fields in this area. Few large settlements were located in the foothills, but this zone was crowded with dispersed rural houses of peasant farmers. A major outcrop of obsidian, the volcanic glass that was important to Aztec technology, is located in the foothills of Otumba in the Teotihuacan subvalley (see chapter 4).

The steep mountain slopes above the piedmont were not farmed and had little settlement. These areas were covered with a pine and oak forest exploited for wood for lumber, firewood, and charcoal production. Deer and various smaller mammals were hunted in these forests, although much of the game had been depleted by hunters of pre-Aztec cultures. A few shrines have been found on mountaintops above the treeline (4,000 m). In the southeast corner of the Valley the two towering volcanoes Popocatepetl (5,450 m) and Ixtacihuatl (5,290 m) are covered with snow year round.

Surrounding Valleys

The highland valleys and plains that surround the Valley of Mexico were home to the remaining two million Aztecs. The Toluca Valley to the west and the Puebla Valley to the east have environments similar to the Valley of Mexico. The lands north and south are considerably different.

Northern plains   Unlike the eastern, southern, and western borders, the northern edge of the Valley of Mexico does not have a steep mountain range to set it off from adjacent areas. The climate to the north becomes increasingly drier, and the northern border of Mesoamerica is soon reached. The agricultural potential of this area, now part of the Mexican state of Hidalgo, is poor and one of the major crops for the Aztecs of this region was the hardy *maguey* plant, cultivated for fiber and syrup. The Toltec capital Tula was located in this northern zone, as were several geological sources of obsidian.

East and west valley   The Toluca and Puebla valleys are at a similar elevation and have environments and climates comparable to the Valley of Mexico. Like the central Valley, the foothills were terraced and the alluvial areas irrigated during

*Figure 1.5   Typical central Mexican countryside (in southern
Puebla). The field in the foreground is planted in maize
(Photograph by Michael E. Smith)*

Aztec times. The Toluca Valley, to the west of the Valley of
Mexico, is a large, flat plain in the modern state of Mexico.
The headwaters of the Lerma River are in this valley. During
the Aztec period, Nahuatl speakers shared the valley with other
groups including Otomi and Matlatzinca speakers. The Puebla
Valley, east of the Valley of Mexico, is located in the modern
states of Tlaxcala and Puebla. Several Aztec city-states in the
northern part of this area (including Tlaxcalla and Huexotzinco)
successfully resisted attempts by the Triple Alliance (Aztec)
empire to conquer them and remained independent until the
arrival of the Spaniards.

The southern valleys   South of the Valley of Mexico, elevation
drops off more quickly and the valleys of the modern state of
Morelos and the southern part of Puebla lie about 1,000 m
lower than the other central Mexican valleys. A warmer climate permits cultivation of a number of tropical crops such as
cotton and many fruits. Otherwise, this area has similar environmental zones to the rest of central Mexico (figure 1.5). The
Aztecs built terraces on hillsides and irrigation canals in the

valleys, making Morelos one of the most fertile areas of central Mexico. Beyond the agricultural productivity of Morelos is its archaeological richness; Aztec sites are abundant and well-preserved here.

The Social Landscape

The natural environment of central Mexico is unique within Mesoamerica, and its qualities go a long way toward explaining why the area was a center for advanced civilizations for over two thousand years. The close juxtaposition of many diverse environmental zones encouraged communication and exchange among groups and enabled settlements to obtain readily a wide variety of goods. Unlike most highland areas in Mesoamerica, central Mexico has numerous flat valleys and plains. Rainfall is adequate for maize agriculture, though not abundant. This environment easily supported small agricultural populations for many centuries, but larger numbers of people, with more complex institutions such as cities and states, required higher levels of food production. Fortunately, many central Mexican regions could be made more productive with only modest investments of labor. Barren hillsides could be transformed into fertile plots by construction of terrace walls; valley plots could be improved with canal irrigation; and swamps could be turned into high-yielding farms by adoption of the ancient Maya technique of raised field agriculture.[9]

The Aztecs did in fact adopt all of these innovations in farming. They were carried out in response to two dramatic developments during the final centuries before Spanish conquest: an explosion of population and an expansion of city-states and empires across the region. One result of these changes in agriculture, demography, and politics was the spread of Aztec peoples across the face of the land. By the time the Spaniards arrived in 1519, central Mexico had been transformed into a social landscape filled with villages, towns, and cities set within a greatly modified agricultural countryside. Although I do not wish to invoke any sense of environmental determinism, it is clear that the unique characteristics of the central Mexican environment were crucial in order for this social and ecological transformation to occur.

Sources of Information

The Aztecs are long gone, yet we know quite a bit about them today. Our knowledge comes from two sources: ethnohistory, the study of written documents, and archaeology, the study of material objects or artifacts. At first glance, the use of this information seems straightforward. What could be clearer than a first-hand Spanish description of an Aztec town or ritual, or an archaeological interpretation of an Aztec temple or cooking pot? Yet as we look closer at the evidence, the picture begins to blur.

The conqueror Hernando Cortés sought to glorify his accomplishments by inflating the sizes of the towns he conquered, and he justified his destruction of Aztec culture by exaggerating its more savage elements. Similarly, a 500-year old pot does not have a label telling us whether it was used to store grain, to serve wine, or to cook human flesh. The archaeologist must infer its use and significance from fragmentary evidence.

In other words, scholars cannot simply leap from primary evidence – written or material – to believable interpretations of Aztec culture. We must consider the origin and nature of the evidence, we must apply rigorous methods to its study, and we must report the evidence and our methods objectively so that others may judge our interpretations on their merit.[10] Let us now take a look at the sources and methods used by ethnohistorians and archaeologists to create our understanding of Aztec civilization.

Ethnohistory

The use of documents and other written materials to study the anthropology of past cultures is known as ethnohistory. Ethnohistorians typically use the writings of explorers, soldiers, missionaries, diplomats, and others to reconstruct cultures at the time of contact with the west. Unlike many of the cultures studied by ethnohistorians, those of Mesoamerica were literate. For the Aztecs and other Mesoamerican peoples, the scope of ethnohistory is therefore broadened to include all written texts by and about these cultures. Ethnohistoric documents on the Aztecs can be divided into four types: native pictorial documents, reports of the Spanish conquerors, compilations of early colonial chroniclers, and Colonial-period administrative documents.

Native Pictorial Manuscripts

The Aztecs used one of the five known writing systems of ancient Mesoamerica; the others are Maya, Zapotec, Mixtec, and Epi-Olmec. Unlike Mayan writing, which could record anything that could be spoken, Aztec writing could only depict a limited repertoire of names and concepts. Most Aztec texts comprised pictorial images of persons, places, and things augmented with limited glyphic elements. Texts served as mnemonic devices – the readers (typically nobles, priests, and scribes) used the images as clues or keys and filled out the interpretation with their own personal knowledge. Manuscripts or codices (singular, codex) were written on bark paper or animal skins (see chapter 10). Only a few pre-Colonial examples have survived, but scribes continued to paint manuscripts in the Aztec style for several generations after the Spanish conquest, and several types of these still exist.

Pictorial histories depicted significant events in the history of a dynasty or city-state. In the most common form, a continuous series of year-glyphs was painted across the page, and depictions of events were drawn next to the year in which they occurred or were connected to the year by a line. Aztec history was related in oral form, with the historian using these manuscripts as a framework. The *Anales de Cuauhtitlan*, an early colonial, Nahuatl-language narrative that describes the events illustrated in a now-lost pictorial history, gives an idea of the content of these histories:

> 2 House [1481] was when the ruler Axayacatl died. Then Tizoc was inaugurated as ruler of Tenochtitlan. Also, there was an eclipse of the sun.
> 3 Rabbit [1482]. At this time the Colhuacan ruler called Tlatolcaltzin died. Then his son, called Tezozomoctli, was inaugurated as ruler of Colhuacan.

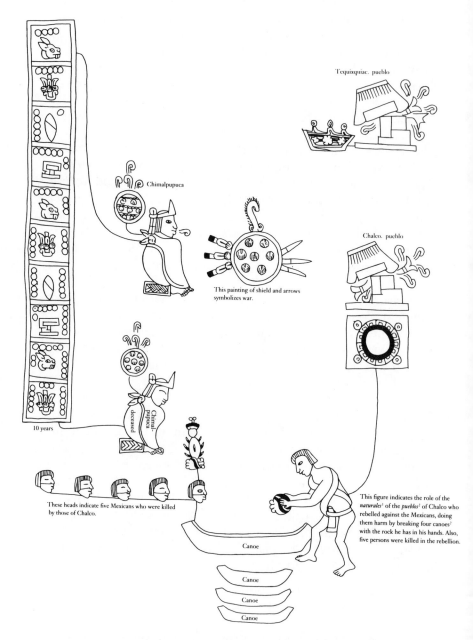

Tequixquiac, pueblo

Chimalpupuca

This painting of shield and arrows symbolizes war.

Chalco, pueblo

10 years

Chimal-pupuca deceased

These heads indicate five Mexicans who were killed by those of Chalco.

This figure indicates the role of the *naturales*[1] of the *pueblos*[2] of Chalco who rebelled against the Mexicans, doing them harm by breaking four canoes[2] with the rock he has in his hands. Also, five persons were killed in the rebellion.

Canoe

Canoe

Canoe

Canoe

Figure 1.6   A page from the pictorial history section of the Codex Mendoza *(1992:v.4:14; folio 4v) showing events during the reign of Chimalpopoca of Tenochtitlan*

Reading an Aztec Codex

This figure is a tracing of a page from the pictorial history section of the *Codex Mendoza* (1992:v.4:14; folio 4v). The ten years of the reign of Chimalpopoca of Tenochtitlan are depicted on the left side, starting with the year 4 rabbit (AD 1417) and ending with the king's death in the year 13 reed (1426). Chimalpopoca is shown with the attributes of kingship: he is seated on a reed mat and wears a crown. For the year 13 reed, he is shown with closed eyes, the symbol of death. Chimalpopoca's name glyph is on his left (his name means smoking shield: *chimalli* = shield; *popoca* = to smoke) and a glyph for warfare is on his right.

The two towns conquered by Chimalpopoca – Tequixquiac and Chalco – are depicted on the right with burning temples, the sign for conquest. This manuscript does not give the dates for individual conquests. Later, the people of Chalco rebelled by killing five Mexica from Tenochtitlan (shown at lower left with closed eyes and the Tenochtitlan glyph – a cactus on a rock) and destroying their canoes. The scribe who compiled the *Codex Mendoza* wrote descriptions of individual elements, in Spanish, on the manuscript. This information would have been supplied from memory by the historian who recited the chronicle. Figure 1.6 and all other images from the *Codex Mendoza* used in this book are tracings from volume 4 of Frances Berdan and Patricia Anawalt's edition of the *Codex* (*Codex Mendoza* 1992). The Spanish descriptions have been translated into English and printed in their original location.

4 Reed [1483]. At this time, in Tenochtitlan, the foundation was laid for the house of the devil Huitzilopochtli [i.e., the Templo Mayor], started by the ruler Tizoc.[11]

Another example, showing the typical sequence of year-glyphs, is found in the first part of the *Codex Mendoza* (figure 1.6 and box).

Ritual Almanacs helped priests to manage the ritual calendar, a sacred 260-day cycle (see chapter 10). These depictions of gods and rituals were used for divination and to keep records of ceremonies and cycles of time. *Tribute records* were lists of payments due by individuals to their lords and by city-states to the Aztec empire, and *maps* were records of land held by individual families.

For sheer quantity of information, the *Codex Mendoza* has been the most important Aztec pictorial document. This three-part manuscript was commissioned in the 1540s by the Spanish viceroy (Antonio de Mendoza) to show the king of Spain something of Aztec culture. The manuscript was painted in Aztec style, and then a scribe wrote short descriptions (in Spanish) of each element. The first part of the *Codex Mendoza* is a pictorial history showing the conquests of the Mexica emperors (figure 1.6). The second part is a record of the tribute paid by each province of the Aztec empire. These two sections are based on prehispanic manuscript formats and are similar to other pictorial histories and tribute records. The third part of the *Codex Mendoza* is an innovation without any known prehispanic antecedents – an account of the Aztec life cycle from birth to death.

The *Codex Mendoza* has had a colorful history. It contains a note from the scribe stating that he did not have sufficient time to complete the job to his satisfaction because the royal galleon was about to sail for Spain. French pirates hijacked the ship, and the *Codex* ended up in the possession of an aide to the French king. After a number of transfers, it came to rest at Oxford University, where it remains today.[12]

Reports of the Conquerors

Hernando Cortés and several of his soldiers recorded accounts of the conquest of the Aztecs. Bernal Díaz del Castillo, whose description of the approach to Tenochtitlan opens this chapter, wrote a particularly vivid description of his experiences. Cortés's lengthy reports to the king of Spain, Carlos V, were filled with information on the Aztecs.

As helpful as these documents are to modern scholars, they are biased in several ways and must be treated with caution. The Spaniards, Cortés in particular, were trying to justify and glorify their actions, and they slanted their accounts accordingly. Cortés gained greater glory by inflating the size of the armies he defeated, or the size of the cities he converted. Furthermore, Cortés and his army were criticized by priests and others for their wanton destruction of the Aztec people and their property, and he tried to justify his actions by portraying the Aztecs as terrible savages in great need of civilizing and conversion by the Spaniards. So long as these biases are taken into consideration, however, the lengthy reports of Cortés, Díaz del Castillo, and others are essential sources of information on the Aztecs.[13]

Accounts of the Chroniclers

The term chronicler refers to anyone who wrote a description of Aztec culture in the decades immediately following the Spanish conquest. This is a broad category that includes many authors and diverse types of written accounts. A brief look at four of the more important chroniclers – Durán, Sahagún, Alva Ixtlilxochitl, and Chimalpahin – gives an idea of the nature of these sources. The chroniclers provide some of the richest and most detailed accounts of Aztec culture.

Friar Diego Durán   The Dominican priest Diego Durán was born in Spain around 1537. He was brought to New Spain as a young boy and spent his youth in Texcoco and Mexico City before entering the priesthood in 1556. Durán travelled extensively throughout central Mexico, where he developed a curiosity about ancient Aztec culture. As research for his three books on the Aztecs, Durán read the earlier accounts of the conquerors, travelled widely to interview natives and Spaniards, and consulted Aztec pictorial manuscripts.[14]

Durán was quite energetic in seeking out knowledge on Aztec culture, and his respect for and objectivity towards Aztec customs and beliefs was unusual among his contemporaries. For example, he describes the practice of human sacrifice almost dispassionately and then goes on to discuss the famous racks of human skulls that were set up outside of temples:

> From pole to pole, through the holes, stretched thin rods strung with numerous human heads pierced through the temple. Each rod held twenty heads. These horizontal rows of skulls rose to the

height of the poles of the palisade and filled it from end to end. One of the conquerors assured me that they were so numerous that they were impossible to count, so close together that they caused fright and wonder. These skulls were all that remained of those who had been sacrificed . . . I asked whether they were set up flesh and all, and everyone said no; after the flesh had been eaten, only the skull was brought to the temple. Some were left with their hair on, and they remained until the hair fell off.[15]

Friar Durán interviewed Mexica nobles and consulted pictorial histories to write the most complete historical account of the Mexica people.[16]

Friar Bernardino de Sahagún   Sahagún was born in Spain in 1499 and travelled to New Spain as a Franciscan monk in 1529. He helped found the College of Santa Cruz in Tlatelolco, where he instructed young Mexica nobles in Spanish and Latin and in turn learned Nahuatl from them. Like Durán, Sahagún was keenly interested in the precontact culture and strived to learn as much as he could about Aztec history, customs, and especially religion. He began to collect systematic information on these topics, employing a team of Indian assistants and artists. They interviewed surviving Mexica nobles, asking the same questions of a series of different informants. Answers were cross-checked, and informants were reinterviewed to settle conflicting accounts and to amplify previous replies. All the interviews were conducted in Nahuatl, which helped to ensure that Sahagún's account preserved much of the Aztec point of view.

Friar Sahagún produced several distinct, yet overlapping, written accounts of Aztec culture. The most informative, today called the *Florentine Codex: General History of the Things of New Spain,* is a lengthy chronicle written in Nahuatl. Although Sahagún made a hasty Spanish translation of the manuscript, the original Nahuatl version is more complete. It was written in twelve books, some of the titles of which are as follows: *The Gods, The Ceremonies, Rhetoric and Moral Philosophy, Kings and Lords, The People,* and *Earthly Things.* Each book was accompanied by numerous drawings illustrating major points. The *Florentine Codex* has been translated into English and published in a bilingual (Nahuatl and English) edition. The work of Bernardino de Sahagún stands as the most detailed and systematic first-hand account of Aztec culture. I make numerous references to Sahagún's writings in the pages that follow, and many of his illustrations are reproduced in this book.[17]

Alva Ixtlilxochitl and Chimalpahin These two chroniclers, descendants of Aztec nobles and kings, recorded historical accounts of their native towns. Fernando de Alva Ixtlilxochitl (1578–1650) was a mestizo (a person of mixed native and Spanish origins) whose ancestors were kings of Texcoco (his namesake Ixtlilxochitl ruled from 1409 to 1418). He was educated at Sahagún's Colegio de Santa Cruz and wrote his first chronicle, in Spanish, in 1600.[18] His description of the expansion of the Triple Alliance (Aztec) empire provides a non-Mexica point of view of the empire's history to balance the better-known Mexica versions, and gives scholars insight into the nature of Aztec native historical accounts.[19]

Domingo de San Antón Muñón Chimalpahin Quauhtlehuanitzin (1579–1660) was a descendent of a minor branch of the nobility of Amecameca, a city-state in the southeast corner of the Valley of Mexico that was subject to Chalco. He was a caretaker at a Christian church and was in contact with Alva Ixtlilxochitl and other native historians of the early seventeenth century. Chimalpahin wrote several histories of Chalco and Amecameca, in Nahuatl, that cover events from the time of the Toltecs until 1612.[20] These documents are valuable for their historical chronicle of these areas and for their portrayal of the Aztec view of histories and settlements.

Durán, Sahagún, Alva Ixtlilxochitl, and Chimalpahin were only four of the many sixteenth-century chroniclers. Other notable examples are the priests Acosta, Mendieta, Motolinía, and Torquemada; the Aztec noble Alvarado Tezozomoc; and the Spanish administrator, Zorita. Taken as a group, the works of the chroniclers are our single most extensive source of information on the Aztecs. Recently, however, ethnohistorians have begun to recognize two serious drawbacks to these accounts. First, the chroniclers describe overwhelmingly the lives and activities of lords and nobles with scant attention to the commoners. Second, most of their descriptions are very generalized and written as if they apply to all parts of the Aztec realm, whereas we now realize that there was considerable variation between regions in customs, beliefs, and social conditions. For example, the chroniclers described Aztec cities as huge, complex urban centers, using the imperial capitals Tenochtitlan and Texcoco as their models. Yet recent research on other Aztec cities shows them to be far smaller and simpler than the imperial capitals. Just how widely can we generalize descriptions of the Mexica of Tenochtitlan to other Aztec peoples and places? There is a growing dissatisfaction with the work of the chroniclers as descriptions for all Aztec peoples and areas, and this sentiment has led to an increased use of the fourth type of ethnohistoric document.

Colonial-period Administrative Documents

Once the conquest of the Aztecs was completed in 1521, central Mexico became a province of the Spanish empire called New Spain. The Spaniards ran their empire in a highly bureaucratic fashion, and countless written reports were produced on topics ranging from fruit trees to Aztec land tenure to strategies for converting the natives to Christianity. These documents were stored in archives in Mexico and Spain, where many still remain for scholars to study. Fortunately, a large number of the most informative examples have been transcribed and published, and some have been translated into English.

Documents on the civic administration of New Spain are numerous. Wills, deeds, baptismal and death records all provide information on household and family organization. Many of the most informative records are those written by Nahuas in Nahuatl, using the Spanish alphabet. The Aztecs quickly learned to use the Spanish legal system, and lawsuits with extensive written documentation proliferated. These suits often involved detailed information-gathering actions, and the results are a treasure trove of useful information on local conditions in many areas of central Mexico soon after the Spanish conquest.[21]

The most systematic attempt at gathering information on New Spain and the other Spanish provinces was a questionnaire prepared by the crown in 1577 and sent to all colonial administrators. Fifty questions were included on a variety of topics, from the ancient customs of the area to the natural environment and resources to the Spanish occupants. The often lengthy replies to this questionnaire, called *Relaciones Geográficas*, fill nine books today and furnish detailed pictures of several hundred Aztec towns in the years 1579 to 1581.[22]

Excerpts from the *Relación Geográfica* from Huaxtepec, a town in the modern state of Morelos, give an idea of the information to be found in these documents. The reply was submitted on September 24, 1580, by Juan Gutiérrez de Liébana, mayor of Huaxtepec and other towns.

> *Question 14:* To whom were they subject when they were heathens; what power did their rulers have over them; what did they pay in tribute; what forms of worship, rites, and good or evil customs did they have?
>
> *Reply:* They say that in this town, although they recognized Montezuma the Elder and his successors as king, they did not pay tribute beyond participation in his campaigns . . . They had another local lord whom they obeyed and recognized as king . . . called Tultecatl tecuhtli. When the king would go out of his house, no one dared look at him except those who accompanied him . . . For affairs of state, they had two officials like judges who ascertained and verified what had happen when crimes occurred . . . And they say that they had only one idol in the town's public market, called Ichpuchtli Quilaztle . . . to this idol, every 20 days they sacrificed a child, the offspring of slaves they had captured in war.[23]

In addition to the written replies, many of the *Relaciones* are accompanied by maps of the towns and their dependent villages (see chapter 7). Unfortunately, not all Aztec towns are covered by these reports, and some examples that were submitted have since been lost. For towns that do have a surviving report, it is one of the first places ethnohistorians turn for information on local conditions.

Archaeology

The contributions of archaeologists to Aztec studies are quite recent. For decades archaeologists bypassed Aztec sites on their way to the spectacular jungle ruins of classic Maya civilization.

A few surviving Aztec pyramids at sites such as Tenayuca (in Mexico City) and Teopanzolco (in Cuernavaca, Morelos) were excavated and restored, but most Aztec sites had little to offer fieldworkers whose focus was on the great monuments of ancient civilizations. In the late 1970s, when the ideas of social archaeology began to bring a more scientific approach to the discipline, archaeologists took another look at the potential of Aztec sites.

Today archaeologists design their fieldwork with clear research problems in mind. Previously, archaeologists would select a site simply because it had large mounds or was conveniently located and then would excavate it to see what turned up. Sometimes the results were spectacular; sometimes they were meager. Now, we focus on a particular problem and use that to structure the research. We select which sites to study and what methods to use in order to answer specific questions about the past. This change makes fieldwork much more efficient and productive. When this approach is coupled with the latest technical advances in dating methods, fieldwork, and artifact analysis, it allows archaeologists to reconstruct many aspects of Aztec society in great detail.[24] A number of examples of projects that follow the problem-oriented social archaeology approach are discussed in the chapters that follow. My discussion of Aztec archaeology here is organized by the types of methods employed.

Regional Survey

The goal of regional survey is to locate archaeological sites across the landscape. A team of archaeologists walks over the entire surface of an area, using maps and areal photographs to plot the locations of sites and features. This method is particularly useful in arid and semiarid environments, such as most of central Mexico, where the surface of the ground can easily be seen. Most of rural central Mexico has been plowed for many years. Although plowing destroys the upper portion of archaeological sites, it also brings buried artifacts to the surface where the survey crew can find them. The team members spread out in a line and walk forward with their "nose to the ground." Sites are identified by either the presence of mounds (usually the ruins of temples or residences) or more commonly by a scatter of potsherds, obsidian tools, and other artifacts.

Once a site is found, the survey crew measures its size, makes a map, and takes one or more collections of artifacts from the ground surface. Regional surveys provide information on the number and size of sites in each temporal period and the locations of sites in relation to the natural landscape and to each other. These data are then analyzed to produce population estimates and reconstructions of settlement patterns for each period.

The use of regional survey in highland Mesoamerica was pioneered by William T. Sanders in the Teotihuacan subvalley of the Valley of Mexico in the 1960s. As part of this research, Sanders located many Aztec sites, and he used ethnohistoric sources to interpret Aztec settlement patterns. His methods of regional survey were then applied to other parts of the Valley of Mexico by Jeffrey R. Parsons, Richard E. Blanton, and in later fieldwork by Sanders himself. By 1975, several thousand square kilometers had been surveyed, resulting in the identification of nearly four thousand archaeological sites.[25] A major discovery of these projects was a population explosion that took place during the Late Aztec period. The implications of this growth are discussed in chapters 2 and 3.

Intensive Site Surface Studies

At many sites, artifacts are numerous on the surface of the ground, or the foundations of houses and temples may still be visible. Many Aztec sites are characterized by not being deeply buried. In these cases, the mapping of structures and features and the systematic collection of surface artifacts allow archaeologists to reconstruct the ancient activities and lifeways at a site. The surface collections taken during regional survey are usually inadequate for this purpose. Intensive site surface studies typically take hundreds or even thousands of separate artifact collections for thorough coverage of the site (figure 1.7).

Intensive site surface research at Aztec sites was pioneered by Elizabeth M. Brumfiel at the city-state center of Huexotla. Brumfiel took 1,243 artifact collections from the surface of the site and studied changing patterns of resource use, commerce,

Figure 1.7   Archaeologists collecting surface artifacts from a 2 by 2 meter square in a corn field at the Aztec city of Yautepec (Photograph by Michael E. Smith)

and craft production between the Early Aztec (AD 1150–1350) and Late Aztec periods (1350–1520). She later applied this method to the sites of Xico and Xaltocan, and I used a similar but less intensive approach at Yautepec (see chapter 8). The most spectacular results from intensive site surface research come from the city-state center of Otumba. Thomas H. Charlton, Deborah L. Nichols, and Cynthia Otis Charlton took 1,150 artifact collections that documented extensive craft production activity, including the manufacture of obsidian tools, pottery figurines and incense burners, textiles, and several types of jewelry. This unexpectedly high degree of craft specialization has changed our views of Aztec urbanism and economics; the Otumba research is discussed in more detail in chapter 4.[26]

Excavation

Beginning with the uncovering of the Templo Mayor in 1978, excavations at Aztec sites have added tremendously to our

Figure 1.8 Excavation of an elite residence at the Aztec city of Yautepec. The flat white surfaces are lime plaster floors. This ruin is in a schoolyard today; the modern basketball courts are visible in the background (Photograph by Michael E. Smith)

knowledge of Aztec culture. The Mexican government project at the Templo Mayor, directed by Eduardo Matos Moctezuma, has produced the most dramatic results. Beyond documenting the history of building and rebuilding of the central temple of Tenochtitlan, these excavations have yielded new information on imperial rituals, tribute from distant lands, and the cosmic symbolism of the Aztec empire.[27]

Outside of the Templo Mayor project, two types of excavations have been done at Aztec sites: large-scale exposure of houses and domestic contexts, and small, problem-oriented test-pit operations. House excavations are crucial for the reconstruction of Aztec economic and social patterns (figure 1.8). Except in the largest cities, houses were widely separated and people simply threw their trash out back. By excavating these trash middens, we can learn of domestic activities and living conditions of individual Aztec households. Susan T. Evans excavated several houses at the rural village of Cihuatecpan in the Teotihuacan Valley, and I have dug houses at a village (Capilco), a town (Cuexcomate), and a city (Yautepec) in Morelos. Hortensia de Vega Nova and colleagues have been excavating an Aztec royal palace in Yautepec.[28]

A number of recent projects have used test excavations to investigate specific issues at Aztec sites. For example, Jeffrey R. Parsons and colleagues tested the *chinampa* agricultural fields in the southern Valley of Mexico to learn how and when these features were constructed. At Otumba, Charlton, Nichols, and Otis Charlton followed up their intensive surface collections at craft workshops with test excavations to better document economic activities at the site. Similarly, Brumfiel used test pits to amplify her intensive surface collections at Xaltocan, and Mary G. Hodge excavated test pits in Chalco to investigate economic and social changes. At Yautepec, I used test excavations to look for buried houses (some were successful, some not), to see whether early Spanish churches were built on top of Aztec temples (they were not), to test (successfully) my earlier reconstruction of the borders of Aztec Yautepec, and to look (unsuccessfully) for evidence of Aztec irrigation canals.[29]

Analysis and Interpretation

Artifacts do not speak to us directly. They must be analyzed, and the results must be interpreted. This is the tedious side of archaeology. It is fun and exciting to excavate sites, but then we are faced with the long task of classifying, studying, and describing the artifacts and architecture. The fruits of five months of excavation at Cuexcomate and Capilco (nearly half a million artifacts, mostly potsherds) required my wife and me to spend four years in the laboratory studying artifacts plus several additional years of computer analysis and write-up.

Beyond the basic classification and description of artifacts, new technological analyses have revolutionized the discipline. We routinely use methods such as radiocarbon dating or obsidian hydration dating to determine the ages of artifacts and deposits, and new techniques of chemical analysis permit artifacts to be traced to their often distant points of origin. Some of the advances made possible by these methods are discussed in chapters 4 and 5.[30]

Nearly all of our interpretations of archaeological remains depend upon inductive logic, also called reasoning by analogy. For example, I have interpreted small bowls with tripod supports as tools used in the spinning of cotton thread based on an analogy with modern cotton hand-spinning techniques. When modern Mayan Indian women spin cotton, they use a small bowl to control the twirling spindle. The small Aztec bowls resemble modern spinning bowls, so I argued by analogy that the ancient artifacts functioned in a similar manner. An analogy is a hypothesis, so the next step was to test this interpretation with independent data. Several lines of evidence converge to support this hypothesis: pictorial sources from the Early Colonial period such as the *Codex Mendoza* show women spinning cotton using a small bowl; the artifacts show traces of abrasion where the spindle has worn away the interior surface of the bowl; and these artifacts are found in domestic contexts where we know from other evidence that spinning took place.[31]

This example shows the importance of modern (and historical) analogues for our interpretation of many aspects of Aztec culture. Thus our knowledge of the Aztecs comes not only from ethnohistory and archaeology but also, indirectly, from Mesoamerican ethnology, the study of modern and historic cultures. Two other branches of modern anthropology – physical anthropology and linguistics – also contribute greatly to Aztec studies. Physical anthropologists study the skeletal remains of the Aztecs in order to determine their sex, age, health and nutrition, and sometimes cause of death. Linguists have contributed greatly to our knowledge of Nahuatl and its historical development in Aztec and more recent times. Several other disciplines also make important contributions to Aztec studies. Art historians have clarified many aspects of Aztec art, religion, cosmology and iconography, and geographers have provided new information on the physical environment, farming systems, and settlement patterns.

Aztec Studies Today

If any overarching theme can be identified within the recent boom of research on Aztec civilization, it is an explicit focus on people. Ethnohistorians and archaeologists are reconstructing the activities of families, social groups, and villages while they explore the social conditions of the people who lived in all parts of the Aztec world. Whereas many earlier scholars restricted their studies to lords, temples, gods, and cities, the advances of social archaeology and recent ethnohistory now give us access to peasants, workshops, and villages. Themes that were unheard of two decades ago, such as women's roles, farming methods, domestic crafts, and standards of living, are now topics of active research.

Modern anthropology, the study of human cultures and their variations over space and time, provides the best framework for our emerging understanding of Aztec civilization, and I use an anthropological approach to structure the narrative that follows. Chapter 2 sets out the historical outline of Aztec culture, from its predecessors through the Spanish conquest. Chapters 3 through 10 discuss specific aspects of Aztec culture, beginning with settlement (chapter 3), followed by economics (chapters 4 and 5), social organization (chapter 6), politics (chapter 7), urbanism (chapter 8), religion (chapter 9), and intellectual and aesthetic life (chapter 10). Chapter 11 recapitulates the glory of the final century of Aztec civilization and tells the story of the Spanish conquest, followed by chapter 12, an account of the legacy of the Aztecs today. I begin my account in central Mexico before the Aztecs arrived on the scene.

2

The Rise of Aztec Civilization

So great were the feats and exploits of the Aztecs, so full of
adventure, that those who are not acquainted with these exploits and with these people will enjoy hearing of their ancient
customs and of their origins and descendants.

Friar Diego Durán[1]

The evolution of Aztec civilization is partly a rags-to-riches
story of the sudden rise of the Nahuatl speakers from obscurity
to power and partly a chronicle of continuity in the cultural
achievements of central Mexican civilizations. These two themes
were important elements in Aztec native historical accounts,
and they loomed large in the Aztecs' own sense of identity and
heritage. The rags-to-riches theme centers on the Mexica people, following them from their origin as a simple nomadic tribe
in the northern desert, through the founding of Tenochtitlan,
and on to their rise to power as the lords of the Aztec empire.
Native historical accounts of this story suggest that the rise of
Aztec civilization was due to the genius and accomplishments
of the Mexica and their leaders.

In contrast to the rags-to-riches story, the theme of cultural
continuity stresses the debt that the Aztecs (Mexica and others)
owed to both their Toltec ancestors and the still earlier
Teotihuacan culture. The last in a series of advanced urban
civilizations, the Aztecs inherited much of their culture from
these earlier peoples. Although the progress of the Mexica
people may make a more exciting story, most scholars today
find the theme of cultural continuity provides a more satisfac-
tory account of cultural evolution in Postclassic central Mexico.
The rise of Aztec civilization was due less to the genius and
success of one small group (the Mexica) than to the larger
social forces that had shaped the rise and fall of central Mexican civilizations over the centuries.

In this chapter I trace the historical course of the Aztec peoples from their predecessors at Classic-period Teotihuacan (AD 200–750) up to their conquest by the Spaniards in 1519. But first I review the archaeological and native historical timetables through which Aztec history is written.

Timetables

The central Mexican archaeological record goes back thousands of years to the small bands of early hunters and gatherers who flourished at the end of the Pleistocene ice age. Maize and other Mesoamerican food crops were first domesticated between 5,000 and 7,000 BC, but agriculture did not become the main form of subsistence until around 2,000 BC. During the next two millennia, a period archaeologists call the Formative or Preclassic, central Mexico was the setting for small villages and towns, a few of which grew into centers of modest-sized chiefdoms. Chalcatzingo in Morelos, for example, became an influential chiefdom during the Middle Formative or Olmec period. Around 100 BC two of these towns – Cuicuilco in the southern valley of Mexico and Teotihuacan in the northern Valley – became large and powerful enough to be called states. The eruption of the Mt. Xitle volcano in the first century AD buried Cuicuilco under a thick mantle of lava, and soon after Teotihuacan grew into the largest urban center in Mesoamerica.[2]

The era of Teotihuacan ascendancy in central Mexico is known as the Classic period (AD 0–750). The burning of Teotihuacan around AD 750 ushered in a time of decentralized city-states called the Epiclassic period (AD 750–950). The final six centuries of Prehispanic cultures are known as the Postclassic era (AD 950–1519), which archaeologists divide into Early, Middle, and Late Postclassic periods (figure 2.1).

The Early Postclassic period (AD 950–1150) is sometimes called the Toltec period, since it corresponds to the flourishing of Toltec culture. The story of the Aztecs themselves begins with the arrival of Nahuatl-speaking peoples in central Mexico at the start of the Middle Postclassic period (AD 1150–1350). The Early Aztec phase is the term archaeologists use to describe Middle Postclassic sites in the Valley of Mexico, and I

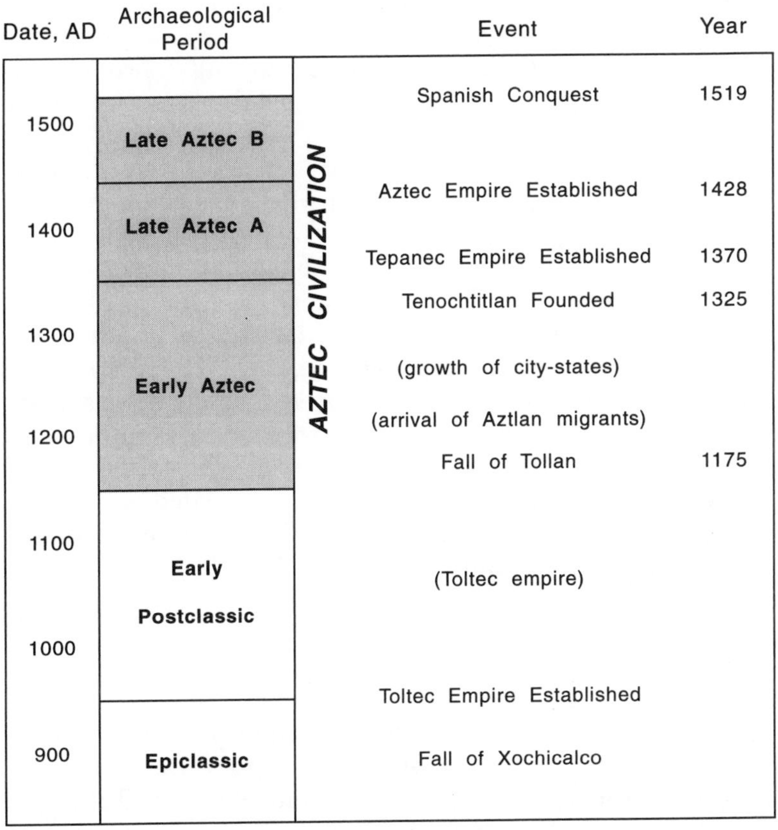

Date, AD	Archaeological Period		Event	Year
1500	Late Aztec B	*AZTEC CIVILIZATION*	Spanish Conquest	1519
1400	Late Aztec A		Aztec Empire Established	1428
			Tepanec Empire Established	1370
1300			Tenochtitlan Founded	1325
1200	Early Aztec		(growth of city-states)	
			(arrival of Aztlan migrants)	
			Fall of Tollan	1175
1100	Early Postclassic		(Toltec empire)	
1000				
900	Epiclassic		Toltec Empire Established	
			Fall of Xochicalco	

*Figure 2.1   Archaeological and native historical chronologies
for Aztec civilization (Drawing by Michael E. Smith)*

use this term for the Middle Postclassic period throughout the
Aztec realm. During this crucial epoch most Aztec towns, cities, and dynasties were first established.

The Late Aztec period, part of the wider Mesoamerican Late
Postclassic period (AD 1350–1520), includes the growth of
Tenochtitlan and the formation and expansion of the Triple
Alliance empire. In some regions of central Mexico, archaeologists have subdivided the Late Aztec period into two subperiods
(referred to here as Late Aztec A and Late Aztec B) covering
the intervals before (1350–1430) and after the formation of

the empire (1430–1520). In other regions, including the Valley of Mexico, only a single archaeological phase is in use, which can make fine-grained study of change difficult. Chronological refinement is topic of active research by archaeologists working on the Aztecs.[3]

The native historical timetable for Aztec civilization begins with the Toltecs, but the early part of the historical record is not very reliable. There are fewer native historical sources, and their content is more obviously mythological in character than later documents. For the final century of Aztec civilization, there are numerous independent native historical accounts that can be cross-checked to gauge their accuracy. The expansion of the Aztec empire after 1430 is covered in great detail, and most scholars believe that much of the historical information is correct. The extent to which the archaeological and native historical records can be compared and correlated is a topic of continuing research, but most authorities agree on the outline of Aztec history presented in figure 2.1.

Predecessors

The Aztecs were heirs to a long tradition of complex urban civilizations and owed a great cultural debt to the earlier peoples of Teotihuacan and Tula. The inhabitants of Tula – the Toltecs – figured heavily in Aztec native history, but the more ancient peoples of Teotihuacan were a mystery to the Aztecs. A brief review of these earlier peoples sets the scene for the rise of Aztec civilization.

Teotihuacan

The great Classic period metropolis of Teotihuacan flourished between AD 150 and 750 in the northeastern Valley of Mexico. At its height between 450 and 650, Teotihuacan's 150,000 inhabitants, spread over 21 square km, made it one of the largest cities in the world.[4] The city was laid out according to a strict grid pattern, organized around a central north–south avenue called the "Street of the Dead" (figure 2.2). The massive Pyramid of the Sun stood adjacent to the central avenue,

*Figure 2.2   Air photo of the ruins of Classic-period Teotihuacan
(Photograph courtesy of Compañía Mexicana de Aerofoto)*

with the smaller Pyramid of the Moon at the northern end of
the street. Most people lived in large walled apartment compounds, which were tightly packed together, with only narrow
alleys and passages between them. The city's rulers and elite
class had larger and more elaborate residences along the Street
of the Dead.

During the Classic period, Teotihuacan's renown and influence spread over all of Mesoamerica. Within its immediate
hinterland in the Valley of Mexico, the city's rulers maintained
a tight grip on economic activities and peoples' lives. Outside
of the valley, Teotihuacan's armies conquered nearby peoples
and forged one of the earliest empires of Mesoamerica. Beyond
the reach of its empire, Teotihuacan engaged in trade relationships with many parts of Mesoamerica, and the city was viewed
as an important sacred center by peoples as far away as the
Maya lowlands in Guatemala.

Teotihuacan's prosperity and success came to an end in the

seventh and eighth centuries when the city was burned and largely abandoned for reasons still unknown. A remnant population continued to live on the site of the Classic city throughout the Prehispanic era, and there was an Aztec town located at the edge of the old city. But by the time the Aztecs came to power, the city's center had lain in ruins for centuries. To the Aztecs, the city was a mystical and sacred place, the birthplace of the gods, and they named the ruins Teotihuacan, which means "city or place of the gods" in Nahuatl. The modern popular names of the main pyramids (sun and moon) and the "Street of the Dead" are translations of the Aztec terms. We do not know what the city or its buildings were called in the Classic period, nor what language(s) were spoken there.

A number of Aztec traits can be traced back to Teotihuacan. The Aztecs were the only other Mesoamerican culture to build a city as large as Teotihuacan, or to create a zone of economic and political influence as extensive as Teotihuacan's. Teotihuacan's planned grid layout was duplicated at Tenochtitlan. The origins of a number of Aztec religious traits can be traced to Teotihuacan as well. Among these traits are human sacrifice as a state-sponsored ritual, and the worship of a feathered serpent god (the Aztec god Quetzalcoatl) and a goggle-eyed deity (the Aztec Tlaloc). Nevertheless, the Aztecs adapted these older gods to their own purposes. Tlaloc, for example, was a peaceful rain god to the Aztecs, whereas his goggle-eyed predecessor at Teotihuacan was a more militaristic state god.[5]

Tula and the Toltecs

The fall of Teotihuacan initiated a period of warfare and disruption throughout central Mexico.[6] A series of large and impressive fortress-cities, protected by walls and ditches, were founded at Xochicalco, Cacaxtla, and Teotenango. Stone carvings and painted murals emphasized military themes and sacrifice. These warring cities flourished between AD 750 and 950 (the Epiclassic period; see figure 2.1), after which time they were largely abandoned. Then in the succeeding Early Postclassic period (AD 950–1150), the city of Tula grew into the first center large and powerful enough to warrant the title of successor to the great Teotihuacan. Modern understanding of Tula's role in Mesoamerican history is made difficult, however, by contradictions between native historical descriptions and the results of archaeological fieldwork. The Aztecs referred to the capital of the Toltecs as Tollan, a term meaning great metropolis. Scholars have linked the Tollan of the native histories to the ruined city at the site of Tula in the modern state of Hidalgo. To the Aztecs, Tollan was a fantastic city of mythical proportions and qualities, and the Toltecs almost superhuman in their accomplishments. They were said to have invented most of Mesoamerican culture, including all of the arts and crafts, writing, and the calendar. The Toltecs were the wise, healthy, and rich lords of a far-flung empire ruled by semidivine kings.

Archaeology paints a different picture, however. Mesoamerican crafts, writing, and the calendar originated long before the Toltecs arrived on the scene. Although Tula was the largest city in central Mexico at the time, it was far smaller and more modest than either Teotihuacan or Tenochtitlan. Tula had a population of about 50,000, covering approximately 13 square km. The central ceremonial core had two large pyramids, two impressive ballcourts, and other civic buildings arranged around a large public plaza (figure 2.3). There is no archaeological evidence for a Toltec empire, and in fact, Toltec artifacts are notable for their absence outside of Tula itself.[7] At Tula, exotic trade goods are far rarer than at either Teotihuacan or Tenochtitlan. Although Tula must have been an important local urban center, the scale and luxury of the city certainly do not accord with the lavish imaginings of the Aztecs. The end of Toltec civilization came about with the abandonment of Tula in the mid to late twelfth century, although like Teotihuacan, the city continued to have a minor occupation through Aztec times.

The symbolic importance of Tollan and the Toltecs to the Aztecs cannot be overestimated. Aztec rulers traced their genealogy, whether actual or invented, back to the Toltec kings, and this semimythical dynastic origin was a major source of political legitimacy to Mesoamerican kings, both Aztec and non-Aztec, at the time of Spanish conquest. The Aztec emperor Motecuhzoma (sometimes called "Montezuma" in English) sent a party to dig for precious relics at Tula, and Toltec objects were revered as sacred icons by the Aztecs. Although the Aztec

Figure 2.3   Air photo of the ruins of the central ceremonial district of Tula, the Early Postclassic Toltec capital (Photograph courtesy of Compañía Mexicana de Aerofoto)

kings traced their history to the Toltecs, the Aztec peoples themselves looked to a different source for their origins.

The Aztlan Migrations

According to native historical accounts, the Aztecs migrated into central Mexico from an original home in a place called Aztlan. Some scholars believe that Aztlan was a real place and argue over its exact location (opinions range from just north of the Valley of Mexico to the southwestern United States). Others argue that Aztlan was a mythical place with no precise location on the map. The term Aztlan, meaning "place of the herons," is the origin of the word "Aztec," a modern label that was not used by the ancient peoples themselves. Whether or not there ever was a place called Aztlan, scholars agree

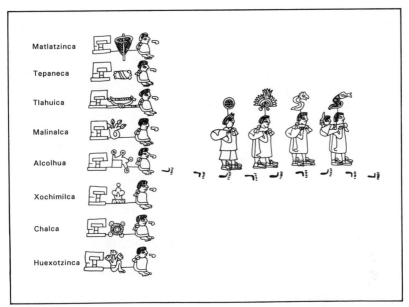

Figure 2.4   The seven Aztec tribes leaving their homeland of Aztlan to migrate south to central Mexico (After the Tira de la Peregrinación *1944; drawing by Ellen Cesarski)*

that the Aztec peoples migrated into central Mexico from the north.[8]

Setting out from Aztlan, the migrants visited Chicomoztoc, or "place of seven caves." A number of sources describe seven tribes at Chicomoztoc although they disagree over the identity of these tribes. When all of the native histories are compared, no fewer than seventeen ethnic groups are listed among the original tribes migrating from Aztlan and Chicomoztoc. One version of the seven tribes account is the *Tira de la Peregrinación* (also known as the *Codex Boturini*), illustrated in figure 2.4. The name glyphs of the groups are translated on the left side. The southward migration of these groups took several generations to complete. The migrants were led by priests, and they stopped periodically to build houses and temples, to gather or cultivate food, and to carry out rituals.

The historical accounts of the Aztlan migrations may vary widely in the content of their lists of the migrating groups and the precise order in which they travelled, but there is consistency in the overall timing of three contingents of migrants. The first groups to arrive in central Mexico settled throughout the Valley of Mexico. The groups that formed part of this initial contingent were the ancestors of the major Nahuatl ethnic groups to be found in the Valley of Mexico in the sixteenth century; they included the Acolhua, Tepaneca, Culhua, Chalca, Xochimilca, and several other groups.

The second contingent of migrants arrived to find the Valley of Mexico settled, so they moved on to occupy the surrounding valleys of central Mexico. These groups included the Tlahuica of Morelos, the Tlaxcalteca and Huexotzinca of Tlaxcala and Puebla, the Matlatzinca of the Toluca Valley and the Malinalca of Malinalco. Historical dates for the arrival of the Aztec migrants fall around AD 1200 for the Valley of Mexico groups and around 1220 for the groups in the surrounding valleys. The last to arrive, around AD 1250, were the Mexica, who found all of the good land occupied and were forced to settle in an undesirable, desolate area of the Valley of Mexico called Chapultepec, "grasshopper hill" or "place of the grasshopper." Far more details are available about the Mexica migration than about the other groups simply because more Mexica-based histories have survived. These sources tell us that the Mexica were guided by their patron god, Huitzilopochtli, whose image was carefully carried from Aztlan to the Valley of Mexico. We know the names of the places where the Mexica stopped on their journey, and some of the events that happened along the way.

Native historical descriptions of the Aztlan migrants contain contradictory information on the cultural sophistication of these peoples. In some accounts they are said to have lived in caves, made their living by hunting with bows and arrows, and wore animal skins for clothing. These traits describe peoples known as Chichimecs (barbaric peoples from the north), and the Mexica and other groups claimed to have been Chichimecs before they settled down and became civilized in central Mexico. The Chichimec notion was a major part of the rags-to-riches theme of Aztec origins.

Contrasting with this picture of the migrants as barbaric Chichimecs are descriptions of complex economic and cultural activities such as the planting of maize, the construction of temples, and the use of the ancient Mesoamerican 52-year calendar. Nomadic hunter/gatherers of the north Mexican desert did not have these practices, which suggests that the migrants had experience with Mesoamerican civilization long before they arrived in central Mexico. The presence of these contradictory traits among the Aztlan migrants is part of the dual conception of the cultural origins of the Aztecs, who believed themselves descended from both savage Chichimecs and civilized Toltecs.

The north-to-south movement of the Aztlan groups is supported by research in historical linguistics. The Nahuatl language, classified in the Nahuan group of the Uto-Aztecan family of languages, is unrelated to most Mesoamerican native languages. Whereas the other major Mesoamerican language families – Mayan, Oto-Mangueyan, and Mixe-Zoquean – had deep roots going back millennia, Nahuatl was a relatively recent intrusion into Mesoamerica.[9] The Uto-Aztecan languages originated in northern Mexico or the southwestern United States, and Nahuatl was brought to central Mexico by peoples moving south. Linguists argue over the exact timing of the arrival of Nahuatl speakers in central Mexico, but most agree that this must have occurred sometime after the collapse of Teotihuacan and before the rise of the Aztecs. Since the descendants of the named Aztlan groups were Nahuatl speakers in 1519, it is reasonable to assume that the Aztlan migrants spoke Nahuatl when they first arrived in central Mexico several centuries earlier. Whether they were the initial speakers of Nahuatl in central Mexico is uncertain, but once the Aztlan migrants arrived, the Nahuatl language spread rapidly through both migration and cultural contact. As the political and economic influence of the Aztec empire expanded, Nahuatl became the language of diplomacy and trade. By the time of the Spanish conquest, Nahuatl had spread far beyond its initial stronghold in the fertile valleys of central Mexico.

The Growth of Aztec City-States

New Towns, New Dynasties (1150–1350)

The Aztlan migrants arrived in central Mexico during the Early Aztec period (figure 2.1). The countryside was far from empty

and the settlers avoided existing settlements to found their own
sites.[10] Most of the indigenous non-Nahuatl-speaking peoples
were eventually assimilated into Aztec culture, although some
groups, such as the Otomi, managed to retain their separate
ethnic identity within Aztec civilization. Many of the new settlements were successful and grew rapidly into towns or cities
with regional political and economic significance. Nearly all of
the major Aztec cities and towns extant at time of Spanish
conquest were founded during this time period.

Central Mexico became the arena for a dynamic system of
interacting city-states. The rulers of these small polities were
petty kings called *tlatoque* (sing. *tlatoani,*) who endeavored to
establish genealogical links to the Toltec kings through marriage ties with their descendants or through invention. Like
systems of city-states in other ancient cultures, the polities of
Early Aztec central Mexico interacted intensively with one
another in both friendly and antagonistic fashions. Alliances
between dynasties and trade between city-states were accompanied by warfare and aggression.

The native histories are full of accounts of battles among the
city-states. During the first century or so after initial settlement, small-scale warfare among the new city-states was frequent, but because of shifting alliances and the small scale of
most conflicts, no individual polity succeeded in establishing a
tributary empire. Among the more active and influential polities at this time were the cities of Azcapotzalco, Coatlinchan,
Culhuacan, Tenayuca, and Xaltocan in the Valley of Mexico,
and Cuauhnahuac, Tollocan, Cholula, and Huexotzinco in surrounding areas.[11]

During the Early Aztec period a common Aztec culture
emerged among the new settlers of the central Mexican highlands. The use of the Nahuatl language and the acknowledgement of a common Aztlan origin were at the foundation of this
widespread culture. The intensive interactions among city-states,
particularly through trade and noble marriage alliances, kept
far-flung peoples in touch. An important component of this
widespread culture was religious ritual. Although individual gods
and ceremonies varied slightly from region to region, a common core of ritual and belief united most of the central Mexican peoples. This religion received concrete material expression

*Figure 2.5 An Early Aztec twin-stair pyramid at Teopanzolco,
a site in the city of Cuernavaca, Morelos (Photograph by
Michael E. Smith)*

in a distinctive new style of temple pyramid. In contrast to
earlier Mesoamerican pyramids with a single temple on top
and a single stairway up the side, the pyramids built by the
Early Aztec peoples had twin temples and double stairways.
Impressive examples of such pyramids have been excavated
and restored at the Early Aztec sites of Tenayuca in the northern Valley of Mexico and Teopanzolco, in the modern city of
Cuernavaca, Morelos (figure 2.5). This style was later adopted
by the Mexica for the central temple of Tenochtitlan, the Templo
Mayor.[12]

Native historical accounts provide increasing detail about
political events in the Valley of Mexico in the thirteenth and
fourteenth centuries. In the context of an unstable city-state
system, the story of the Mexica peoples stands out since the
vast majority of the surviving native histories come from the
Mexica tradition.

Mexica Outcasts (1250–1325)

By the time the Mexica arrived in the Valley of Mexico around 1250, most of the land was already claimed by the city-states of the earlier immigrants groups.[13] The Mexica settled initially in Chapultepec, a hill adjacent to a swamp, because the land was empty and barren. Nearby groups, such as the Tepaneca and Chalca, were wary of the newcomers. A young warrior named Copil, son of a Mexica sorceress who had been exiled during the migration, stirred up opposition to the Mexica among their neighbors. War broke out and the allied armies forced the Mexica to flee Chapultepec (although they did manage to kill Copil and throw his heart into the swamp).

The Mexica convinced the reluctant king of Culhuacan to let them settle in an isolated, snake-infested part of his realm called Tizaapan. Culhuacan was an ancient town southeast of Chapultepec that had been settled by both Toltecs and Aztlan migrants, and the Culhua nobles and peoples considered the Mexica newcomers barbaric. The Culhua ruler Coxcoxtli said to his advisors that for the Mexica, Tizaapan "is good, for they are no true people, but great villains, and perhaps they will perish there, eaten by the serpents, since many dwell in that place."[14] Rather than perish, the Mexica flourished on a diet of snakes and lizards, prompting Coxcoxtli to later exclaim to his court, "See what rascals they are; have no dealings and do not speak to them." The king's attitude soon changed as the Mexica became good subjects and neighbors of the Culhua. The Mexica began to trade in the Culhuacan market and soon were intermarrying with the Culhua people. The Culhua called on the Mexica to come to their aid in a fierce battle with the Xochimilca, and the arrival of Mexica troops turned the tide in favor of the Culhua. This victory was important, for it previewed the later military success of the Mexica as vassals of the Tepanecs.

The Mexica managed to turn the Culhua against them, however. According the semi-mythical accounts of native history, their god Huitzilopochtli ordered the Mexica to obtain a Culhua princess to be worshipped as a goddess. The Culhua king agreed and sent them his favorite daughter. Some time later, he and the other Culhua lords were invited to witness ceremonies and sacrifices to the new Mexica goddess. On Huitzilopochtli's orders the Mexica had killed and flayed the princess, and a Mexica priest donned her skin to dance in public (a common Aztec ritual practice, see chapter 9). When the Culhua king saw what the Mexica had done, he ordered his nobles and troops to attack, and the Mexica were driven from Tizaapan by force. This was all part of the god Huitzilopochtli's divine plan, however.

The Mexica fled into the wilderness of swamps that ringed the salty lakes of the Valley of Mexico, where they wandered for weeks. Huitzilopochtli appeared in a vision to one of the priests and told the Mexica that they would soon find their promised homeland, in a place where an eagle lived atop a tall nopal cactus. This was a sacred place, for the cactus had grown from the heart of Copil after his death in the Mexica's first battle. When the Mexica saw the eagle and cactus on a small island in the swamp, they were overjoyed and proceeded to found the site of Tenochtitlan, "place of the cactus fruit," in the year 2 House, AD 1325.[15]

The fourteenth century was a time of rapid and far-reaching transformation among the Aztecs. One of the most striking changes was an unprecedented population explosion. Many new settlements were founded, existing villages grew into towns, and towns grew into cities; the overall population of central Mexico increased by a factor of five or more. Major modifications were made to the landscape in order to intensify agricultural production to feed the growing number of people (see chapter 3). Another dramatic change was the emergence of the first true empire since Teotihuacan. In the native historical record, these changes are best documented for the Mexica and their city, Tenochtitlan.

Tenochtitlan's First Century (1325–1428)

Tenochtitlan's location on a small island in the middle of a swamp may seem inauspicious, but actually it had numerous advantages for the Mexica. The salt marshes provided abundant wild plant and animal resources to feed people until agricultural fields could be constructed and begin to produce.

Highly productive *chinampas* or raised fields were built on land reclaimed from the swamp as soon as methods were devised for keeping the salty waters of Lake Texcoco apart from the fresh waters of Lakes Chalco and Xochimilco. A system of dikes and canals accomplished this purpose, and gradually the cultivated fields turned the outskirts of Tenochtitlan into a lush green ring around the inner city. Commerce with other towns in the valley was facilitated by the use of canoes and boats; at the same time, the limited access to the city provided protection against military attack.

To build their city, the Mexica obtained construction materials through the market system in exchange for swamp delicacies such as fish, frogs, ducks, and algae. Once the Mexica were able to settle in one place, their numbers began to increase rapidly. Soon the other communities in the Valley of Mexico came to regard the Mexica as equals. During this time, two city-states had begun to expand their reach through conquest: the Tepanecs of Azcapotzalco on the western shore of Lake Texcoco and the Acolhua of Texcoco on the eastern shore. The Mexica, not powerful enough to resist these two incipient empires, allied themselves with the Tepanec ruler Tezozomoc and became tribute-paying subjects. For the most part, their tribute consisted of military service. Tezozomoc was a shrewd leader who put the military abilities of the Mexica to work as part of his imperial plans. From the mid-fourteenth century until the formation of the Aztec empire in 1428, the Mexica fought under the Tepanec banner and helped Tezozomoc forge the first significant empire since Teotihuacan.

The Mexica were becoming an increasingly powerful polity and in 1372 they sought a *tlatoani* of their own to provide leadership and legitimacy. They looked to Culhuacan for help, in spite of their earlier alienation of the Culhua king, because of the prestige of the ancient Toltec dynasty there and the past cooperation between the two peoples. There were four simultaneous royal dynasties at Culhuacan, and one of the Culhua kings gave his daughter in marriage to a high-ranking Mexica. Their son *Acamapichtli* became the first Mexica *tlatoani*. Acamapichtli led the Mexica for 19 years (1372–91) and then passed the throne to his son Huitzilihuitl, whose mother was also a Culhua princess.

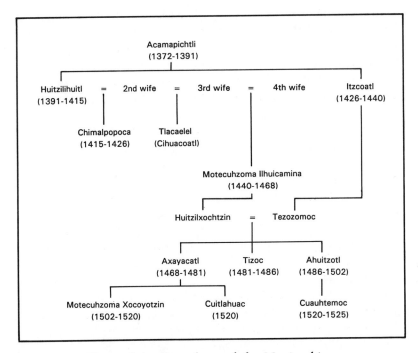

Figure 2.6   Genealogy of the Mexica kings
(Drawing by Ellen Cesarski)

Huitzilihuitl, who ruled from 1391 until 1415 (figure 2.6), presided over one of the most important periods in Mexica history. Under his popular leadership, people from all over the Valley of Mexico came to live in Tenochtitlan, and the city expanded greatly. The Mexica became highly skilled as soldiers and diplomats in their dealings with neighbors. One of Huitzilihuitl's major accomplishments was the establishment of successful marriage alliances with a number of powerful dynasties. Marriage alliances were an important component of diplomacy among Mesoamerican states. Lower ranking kings would endeavor to marry the daughters of more powerful and important kings. A marriage established at least an informal alliance between the polities and was a public acknowledgement of the dominant status of the more powerful king. Aztec nobles practiced polygamy, and as time went on, the dynasties of important polities became closely intertwined. Huitzilihuitl planned a strategy to improve his own standing and the political fortunes of the Mexica by marrying princesses from several of the more powerful central Mexican dynasties.

Huitzilihuitl successfully petitioned Tezozomoc himself for the hand of his daughter. She bore a son, Chimalpopoca, who later succeeded Huitzilihuitl as Mexica *tlatoani*. Chimalpopoca's mother died young, and Huitzilihuitl turned to the powerful dynasty of Cuauhnahuac for another wife. The Cuauhnahuac *tlatoani* ruled a large domain in what is now the state of Morelos, south of the Valley of Mexico. He was said to be a great sorcerer, who used magic to protect his daughter from suitors. He initially refused Huitzilihuitl's petition, asking how his daughter could lead the luxurious life to which she was accustomed in the rustic, swampy town of Tenochtitlan.

According to legend, the Mexica king, following an idea that came to him in a dream, filled a hollow arrow shaft with precious jewels and shot the arrow into the Cuauhnahuac palace where it fell at the feet of the princess. She found the jewels, and soon the couple were wed.[16] This marriage formed the first Mexica royal alliance with a state outside of the Valley of Mexico, and a son of this union, Motecuhzoma Ilhuicamina, would later become one of the great Mexica kings, Motecuhzoma I. In addition to his diplomatic success, Huitzilihuitl also led the Mexica to victory in a number of military campaigns, but the conquered towns became subjects of the Tepanec capital Azcapotzalco, not Tenochtitlan.

Huitzilihuitl died in 1415 and was succeeded by his son *Chimalpopoca*, who reigned for 11 years. During this time Tenochtitlan continued to grow in size and prosperity. In the northern part of the island, the separate town of Tlatelolco was also growing. Around this time merchants from Tlatelolco began to offer goods such as parrot feathers and jewels for sale in their market. These exotic luxuries signalled a growing economic prosperity and the presence of enough nobles (the consumers of such items) to make the sales worthwhile. The Tlatelolco market later evolved into the largest in the empire (see chapter 5).

At the same time that Chimalpopoca was continuing to help the Tepanecs to expand their domain, the Acolhua of Texcoco were expanding in the eastern Valley to become the only true rivals of the Tepanec empire. When a new Acolhua king,

Ixtlilxochitl, challenged Tezozomoc, war broke out between the two states. The Mexica played a major role in the fighting, which resulted in the death of Ixtlilxochitl and victory for the Tepanecs. To reward the Mexica for their services, Tezozomoc granted them the city-state of Texcoco as a tributary subject. For the first time the Mexica had tribute-paying subjects of their own. This was not the only relationship between the Mexica and the Acolhua, however. Ixtlilxochitl had married Chimalpopoca's half-sister, and their son Nezahualcoyotl became the new Acolhua king. These events cemented a special relationship between Texcoco and Tenochtitlan that was to continue until the Spanish conquest.

The death of Tezozomoc in 1426 initiated a series of events that would lead to the formation of the Aztec empire two years later. In the struggle over succession to the Tepanec crown, the Mexica backed Tezozomoc's chosen heir Tayauh. Tayauh's brother Maxtla, a member of an anti-Mexica faction, usurped the throne, however. Soon after, Chimalpopoca was killed under suspicious circumstances, and the Mexica council chose Itzcoatl, brother of Huitzilihuitl (figure 2.6), to be the new *tlatoani*.

Itzcoatl, an experienced soldier and forceful leader, was determined to stand up to Maxtla and the Tepanecs. By now Tenochtitlan was a large and prosperous city, and the Mexica had attained a reputation as the fiercest warriors among the Aztec peoples. The Mexica government was strengthened by Itzcoatl's personality and his use of two able and experienced ministers, Motecuhzoma Ilhuicamina and Tlacaelel. Motecuhzoma was Itzcoatl's nephew, and succeeded Itzcoatl as *tlatoani*. He was an outstanding general, diplomat, and advisor. Itzcoatl created another advisory office, the *Cihuacoatl* ("woman serpent"). Tlacaelel, Motecuhzoma's half-brother by still another of Huitzilihuitl's marriage alliances, was its first occupant. This triad of strong leaders – Itzcoatl, Motecuhzoma, and Tlacaelel – were in large part responsible for the creation of the Aztec empire.

The Empire of the Triple Alliance, 1428–1519

The establishment of the Triple Alliance empire in 1428 ushered in the final century of Aztec civilization. This period, the

Late Aztec B archaeological phase, witnessed the greatest accomplishments of the Aztecs. The story of the foundation of
the empire began in 1426 with the escalation of hostilities
between the Mexica and the Tepanecs. To counter the growing
threat of the Mexica, Maxtla tried to blockade Tenochtitlan,
and he demanded increasingly high amounts of tribute from
the Mexica. At the same time, Maxtla continued to harass the
Acolhua, forcing Nezahualcoyotl to flee his palace in Texcoco.
The Acolhua king escaped over the eastern mountains to the
Puebla-Tlaxcalla area, where he lobbied the kings of Tlaxcalla
and Huexotzinco to come to his aid against the Tepanecs.
Meanwhile, Motecuhzoma and Tlacaelel were marshalling
support for a Mexica rebellion in the Valley of Mexico; their
best aid came from dissident Tepanecs in the town of Tlacopan.
   War soon erupted, and in 1428, the combined forces of
Tenochtitlan, Texcoco, Tlacopan, and Huexotzinco managed
to defeat the Tepanecs of Azcapotzalco. The Huexotzinca returned to their home over the mountains, and the other three
polities formed a military-economic alliance. They agreed not
to wage war on one another and to cooperate in wars of
conquest against other towns. The tribute generated by these
conquests was to be divided, with two-fifths to Tenochtitlan,
two-fifths to Texcoco, and one-fifth to Tlacopan. This accord,
known as the Triple Alliance, would soon rule the largest empire
ever forged in ancient Mesoamerica.
   The first task of the new alliance was to secure control over
the Valley of Mexico. The towns in the southern part of the
Valley had avoided taking sides in the Tepanec war, and Itzcoatl
turned his attention to this area. He first conquered Coyoacan
(an old Tepanec town), and then Xochimilco and Cuitlahuac
in the *chinampa* district. The construction of *chinampas* (raised
fields) in the freshwater lakes of Chalco and Xochimilco had
begun in Early Aztec times, and by 1430, these productive
farm plots covered nearly the entire lakebeds (see chapter 3).
This district was the breadbasket of the Valley of Mexico, and
its conquest gave the allies access to a large supply of tribute
in foodstuffs.
   Next, Itzcoatl and Nezahualcoyotl initiated expansion of the
empire outside of the confines of the Valley of Mexico. Their
first targets – Cuauhnahuac and Huaxtepec in the modern

state of Morelos – offered a number of enticements. These towns were located just over the Ajusco mountain range south of the *chinampa* zone in an area with abundant rainfall and a semi-tropical climate. Like the Valley of Mexico, Morelos was the home of a dense Aztec population organized into city-states and reliant upon intensive agricultural practices. Conquest of this rich area was the logical first step toward forging a tribute empire beyond the Valley of Mexico.

During his reign, Itzcoatl began a process of glorifying the Mexica at the expense of earlier Aztec groups, and he burned many historical books written earlier. In the words of Miguel León-Portilla, "With the intention of suppressing the 'lies' of history, Itzcoatl directed himself to the creation of a history which would give an appropriate background to the future glory of the Aztecs [Mexica]."[17] As the Aztec empire expanded during the 91 years between the fall of Azcapotzalco and the arrival of Hernando Cortés, the Mexica increasingly assumed a dominant role, to the point at which some scholars refer to the empire as the "Mexica empire." The formal tribute-sharing arrangement remained in effect to the end, however.

In 1440, soon after the Morelos campaign, Itzcoatl died and *Motecuhzoma Ilhuicamina* assumed the Mexica throne. Scholars refer to him as Motecuhzoma I to distinguish him from his great-grandson Motecuhzoma Xocoyotzin, ruler of the empire when Cortés arrived in 1519. During his 28 years in office, Motecuhzoma I proved to be one of the two most successful Mexica leaders in furthering the expansion of the empire. Before Itzcoatl's victories in Morelos could be followed up, however, one remaining holdout in the Valley of Mexico had to be conquered. For decades the city-state of Chalco had resisted all conquerors – Tepanec, Acolhua, and Mexica (see figure 1.6) – but after a long and arduous war, Chalco finally fell to the combined armies of Motecuhzoma and Nezahualcoyotl.

The defeat of Chalco and a subsequent program of political consolidation within the Valley of Mexico occupied the first decade of Motecuhzoma I's rule. The Mexica emperor undertook a series of measures to reduce the threat of rebellion among subject city-states and to ensure the continuity of Mexica rule. Selected kings were replaced by Mexica puppets, new administrative positions were established, and a comprehensive imperial tribute system was initiated. The Mexica installed their own people as tribute collectors, effectively bypassing the existing city-state dynasties. The long-term effect of this strategy of political consolidation was to promote imperial control over the core area and to contribute toward the rising power and influence of the Mexica at the expense of their Acolhua allies.

Motecuhzoma began major construction on the great temple of Tenochtitlan, and he issued a new legal code that widened the gap between nobles and commoners. Some of its provisions are as follows:

1   The king must never appear in public except when the occasion is extremely important and unavoidable . . .

3   Only the king and the prime minister Tlacaelel may wear sandals within the palace . . .

5   The great lords, who are twelve, may wear special [cotton] mantles of certain make and design, and the minor lords, according to their valor and accomplishments, may wear others . . .

7   The commoners will not be allowed to wear cotton clothing, under pain of death, but can use only garments of maguey fiber . . .

8   Only the great noblemen and valiant warriors are given license to build a house with a second story; for disobeying this law a person receives the death penalty.

9   Only the great lords are to wear labrets [lip plugs], ear plugs, and nose plugs of gold and precious stones . . .

13 All the barrios [*calpolli*] will possess schools or monasteries for young men where they will learn religion and correct comportment.

14 There is to be a rigorous law regarding adulterers. They are to be stoned and thrown into the rivers or to the buzzards.

15 Thieves will be sold for the price of their theft, unless the theft be grave, having been committed many times. Such thieves will be punished by death.[18]

At the same time that he was enlarging the social gulf between nobles and commoners, Motecuhzoma allowed talented commoners to rise to positions of influence by creating a new title, *quauhpilli* (eagle lord). This status, a kind of nobility of achievement, was awarded to the most successful soldiers in the army.

In the years 1450–54 a serious drought hit the Valley of Mexico. For several years running crops failed, and famine was widespread. The royal granaries were opened to feed the public, but the stored food lasted only a few years. By 1454 chaos gripped the Aztecs. Thousands died, and people wandered the countryside looking for any scrap of food to eat. The Totonac peoples of the Gulf Coast were unaffected, and they took advantage of the famine, bringing grain to the Valley of Mexico in order to purchase slaves. Finally, in 1455, the rains fell again, crops were successful, and the process of rebuilding took place.

Beginning in 1458, Motecuhzoma I and Nezahualcoyotl of Texcoco set out on a series of military campaigns that would expand the empire far beyond the Valley of Mexico. Previously conquered city-states such as Cuauhnahuac (home of Motecuhzoma's mother) were reconquered, and then the Mexica and Acolhua forces subdued the rest of Morelos, the Gulf Coast area, and parts of the modern state of Oaxaca. It is interesting to compare historical accounts of these campaigns. The Mexica histories describe the conquests as carried out largely by Motecuhzoma's forces, with minor help from Nezahualcoyotl, while histories from Texcoco describe the wars as major Acolhua victories, with some help from the Mexica. Taken together, the sources suggest that the Mexica and Acolhua were more-or-less equal partners in the empire at this point. The two kings conquered vast areas of Mesoamerica for the empire. Their victories, together with modest gains made by the next Mexica king, Axayacatl, constituted the first of two great cycles of imperial expansion (figure 2.7).

In 1468, Motecuhzoma I died and was succeeded by *Axayacatl*. This young prince, whose grandfathers were Motecuhzoma I and Itzcoatl, was selected by a council consisting of the top nobles in Tenochtitlan, Nezahualcoyotl, and the king of Tlacopan. Much of his 13-year reign was occupied with the consolidation of the conquests achieved by his predecessor. Some towns had to be reconquered, and it took time to work out the logistics of a tribute system that covered thousands of square kilometers of the new empire. Three important battles occurred during the reign of Axayacatl: victories over Tlatelolco and Toluca, and defeat at the hands of the Tarascans. A dispute developed between Tenochtitlan and its twin city Tlatelolco, resulting in the conquest of the latter. Axayacatl installed a

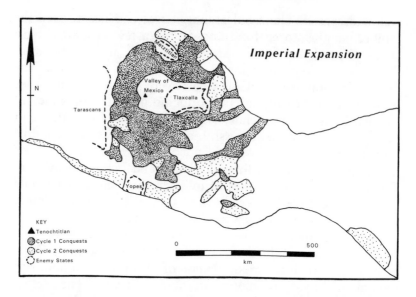

Figure 2.7   Cycles of expansion of the Triple Alliance empire (Data from Berdan et al. 1996; drawing by Kori Kaufman)

military governor to rule Tlatelolco in place of the formerly independent *tlatoani*. The Tlatelolco marketplace had developed into the largest in Mesoamerica, and the professional merchants (*pochteca*) who ran the market started working for Axayacatl (see chapter 5).

Axayacatl's only major addition to the empire was the Toluca Valley, a broad expanse immediately west of the Valley of Mexico. This was a multiethnic area where Nahuatl speakers descended from the Aztlan migrants mingled with speakers of Matlatzinca, Otomi, and other languages. The Toluca Valley was of great strategic importance to the Aztecs since it formed a buffer between the Valley of Mexico and the Tarascan empire of western Mexico.

The Tarascans lived in what is now the state of Michoacan, just west of central Mexico. In many ways the Tarascan empire resembled the Aztec empire. Tarascan oral tradition also told of ancestors who were relatively recent immigrants to their home area. They, too, settled in a highland basin with a large lake in the center, the Patzcuaro Basin. There, processes of population growth and cultural evolution led to the development of city-states and then to the expansion of an empire headed by a powerful dynasty.[19]

By the 1470s the Tarascan armies were approaching the central Mexican highlands, and Axayacatl prepared to do battle from a base in the Toluca Valley. In 1478 or 1479, some 24,000 Aztec soldiers went up against 40,000 Tarascans, resulting in an Aztec loss of 20,000 men either killed or taken prisoner. Axayacatl himself was seriously wounded in the battle. The remaining Aztec forces limped back to Tenochtitlan, and the Aztecs never again dared to engage the Tarascans in a major direct confrontation.

Axayacatl died in 1481 and was replaced by his brother *Tizoc*. Tizoc proved to be a weak ruler and a poor military leader. He added little new territory to the empire, although this did not prevent him from commissioning a major sculpture, the so called "Tizoc stone," that depicts him conquering numerous towns. Tizoc died, perhaps assassinated, in 1486 and another brother, *Ahuitzotl*, was crowned. By this time the title of the Mexica king had changed from simply *tlatoani* to *huehuetlatoani* or "supreme king." The Acolhua *tlatoani* Nezahualpilli, son and successor of the great Nezahualcoyotl, apparently had lost some of his power to the Mexica, although officially the empire was still run by the Triple Alliance. Ahuitzotl's extravagant coronation was soon followed by another major state celebration upon completion of the Templo Mayor in 1487.

One of Ahuitzotl's first tasks was to suppress a rebellion by the Huaxtec peoples of the Gulf Coast. Rebellions were a common occurrence in the Aztec empire because of the indirect nature of imperial rule. Local dynasties were left in place as long as they cooperated with the Triple Alliance and paid their tribute. In many cases, the positions of rulers of provincial city-states were actually strengthened by their participation in the empire since these rulers could call on the empire for aid in the event of local troubles. Periodically, a provincial king would decide that he was strong enough to withhold tribute payments from the empire. This is what the sources refer to as "rebellion." The Triple Alliance would respond by dispatching an army to threaten the errant king and, if necessary, reconquer the city-state. As a result of repeated resistance and rebellion, many towns reappear in the conquest lists of multiple emperors. For example, Cuauhnahuac, initially conquered by Itzcoatl, had to be reconquered successively by Motecuhzoma I and Axayacatl.[20]

The unstable nature of the Aztec empire should not be taken as an indication that imperial expansion was random or haphazard. The Mexica and Acolhua followed two deliberate strategies in planning and implementing their conquests. The first strategy was economically motivated. The Aztecs wanted to generate tribute payments and promote trade and marketing throughout the empire. The Mexica rulers sponsored *pochteca* (professional merchants), imposed tribute in non-local goods (so that provincial towns had to engage in commerce to obtain their imperial tribute), and protected market towns and trade routes. The second strategy dealt with enemy frontiers. The Aztecs established client states and outposts along imperial borders to help contain their enemies (see chapter 7).

Ahuitzotl began a new cycle of imperial expansion, guided by these two strategies. He brought the Valley of Oaxaca and the Soconusco coast of southern Mexico (Xoconochco) into the empire for their economic value. Major trade routes ran through the Valley of Oaxaca, and Xoconochco, the most distant province of the empire, was an important source of tropical lowland products such as cacao and feathers. Ahuitzotl pursued the frontier strategy by carrying out conquests and establishing client states along the Tarascan border. He built a fortress at Oztoma, along the southern part of the Tarascan frontier, and sent colonists from the Valley of Mexico to guard it and to settle the immediate area.

Ahuitzotl was a popular king who personally led his armies into battle. He rewarded achievement in warfare with promotions in status, astutely using the *quauhpilli* category established by Motecuhzoma I. Talented commoners could advance socially this way, and government positions were opened up to members of this new class. Ahuitzotl's reign was a time of unparalleled prosperity and growth in Tenochtitlan, accompanied by major territorial expansion in the empire. Ahuitzotl increasingly took over the duties of running the empire from the other Triple Alliance kings, and by the end of his reign, the

Mexica state was clearly dominant over the others in power, prestige, and influence.

Ahuitzotl died in 1502 and was succeeded by his nephew, the son of Axayacatl, *Motecuhzoma Xocoyotzin*. Motecuhzoma II was a seasoned general who had participated in many of Ahuitzotl's wars of conquest. His style of rulership was virtually the opposite of Ahuitzotl's. Motecuhzoma II eliminated the status of *quauhpilli* and reserved all important military and government positions for members of the Mexica hereditary nobility. He replaced all of Ahuitzotl's officials and had many of them killed. Instead of ruling through the pride and cooperation of talented officials, Motecuhzoma II controlled his court through terror. Some scholars have seen these actions as steps toward the creation of an absolute monarchy among the Aztecs.[21]

Just as Axayacatl's reign was concerned with the consolidation of his predecessor's conquests, his son Motecuhzoma II's imperial activities centered around the consolidation of Ahuitzotl's conquests. Some of the distant towns had to be reconquered, and Motecuhzoma II continued his predecessors' long-standing war with Tlaxcalla. Like the Tarascan empire, the states of the Tlaxcalla area remained unconquered enemies. The ancestors of the Tlaxcallans had come from Aztlan, but these city-states grew apart culturally from the other Aztec peoples. The Aztec armies were never able to defeat the Tlaxcallans, but the empire did manage to surround the area and reduce its commerce with the outside world. Motecuhzoma II fought a number of battles with the Tlaxcallans in which the Aztecs appeared to have had the upper hand, but victory proved elusive.

According to historical accounts, Motecuhzoma II's reign was plagued by omens of disaster and doom, which appeared to the king, to his priests, and to the public. In 1519, these omens proved all too real in the form of an invading Spanish army under the leadership of Hernando Cortés. The empire was at the height of its glory when it was destroyed by Cortés. Some writers, citing the slowdown of imperial expansion under Motecuhzoma II, have asserted that Aztec culture and the empire had begun a process of decay and decline before 1519, but that was not the case. Motecuhzoma II's relatively modest additions to the empire were simply part of the rhythm of Aztec imperial expansion, in which major conquests were followed by consolidation of control. There were two great cycles of imperial growth (figure 2.7). In the first, Motecuhzoma I added many new areas to the empire and then Axayacatl consolidated these gains. In the second cycle, Motecuhzoma II performed the role of consolidating the territory brought into the empire by Ahuitzotl. By the year 1519 this was the second-largest empire in the ancient New World (the Inca empire of South America covered more territory), and there were few if any signs of decline or decay.

3

People on the Landscape

In those times these hills and valleys were populated with thousands of souls who lived, following their custom, in many scattered hamlets, a short distance from one another.

An early Spanish observer[1]

The arrival of the Aztlan migrants and the subsequent development of Aztec civilization transformed the central Mexican countryside from the thinly-populated backwater of Toltec times into a densely-settled landscape. On the eve of Spanish conquest, the Aztecs had more people, more cities, and larger cities, than any other ancient culture of the New World. This large population was not the result of a gradual build-up over many centuries, rather it was a single dramatic surge that took place between 1200 and 1500. In part, the Aztec population explosion can be attributed to the arrival of the Aztlan migrants at the beginning of this time period, but two other factors were also responsible. First, central Mexico was emerging from five centuries of abnormally dry conditions (AD 600–1100), and rainfall increased significantly.[2] This led to a dramatic improvement in agricultural productivity, and the resulting increased food supply helped set off the population surge. Second, once the Aztec migrants settled in and established their city-states, political and economic conditions encouraged people to have larger families.[3]

The large size of the population influenced many aspects of Aztec society and culture. Although it is no longer fashionable among archaeologists to attribute cultural change and evolution solely to "population pressure," it is difficult to escape the conclusion that the Late Aztec population explosion brought about a series of fundamental changes throughout central Mexican society. The most obvious of these are in the realm of food and agriculture. As their numbers grew, the Aztecs had to adjust their diet by finding new sources of food. They were also forced to increase their farming efforts to produce enough food. This process, known as agricultural intensification, led to a massive modification of the landscape as canals, dams, terraces, and crop beds were constructed all over central Mexico.[4]

The Late Aztec demographic surge also changed the nature of both urban and rural settlement in central Mexico. More cities were founded, and cities grew larger than in earlier times. At the same time, non-urban settlement dispersed across the countryside to the point where people were living almost everywhere (see the quotation at the start of the chapter).

How Many Aztecs?

Just over one million people were living the Valley of Mexico when Hernando Cortés and his army arrived in 1519, and another two to three million Aztecs dwelt in the surrounding valleys of central Mexico. How have modern scholars arrived at these estimates?

Counting back from Colonial Census Figures

The Aztecs kept several types of census-like written records to keep track of land holdings and tribute obligations (chapter 10), but too few have survived to be of much help in determining the total size of the Aztec population. First-hand accounts by Spanish soldiers and missionaries who saw the Aztecs before they were devastated by smallpox and other diseases are another potential source of information. Unfortunately, these are difficult to use because their descriptions of population sizes vary wildly. For example, Hernando Cortés estimated the size of the Tlaxcaltecan army at 100,000 soldiers, whereas his soldier Bernal Díaz counted the same army at 40,000 soldiers.[5] These men were hardly dispassionate observers since both writers were trying to justify and glorify the Spanish conquest of the Aztecs. Even if such estimates could be trusted, first-hand observations exist for only a few cities and armies, far from complete coverage of the Aztec population.

After the conquest of Mexico in 1521, Spanish administrators began to collect information on their new Nahua subjects. Systematic census-taking began soon after the conquest in some areas, but it was not until 1568 that the entire area of central Mexico was subjected to a comprehensive and standardized census whose findings are known today. In the half century between the Spanish conquest and the 1568 census, however, the Aztec population dropped precipitously owing to the introduction of European diseases (see chapter 11). In 1568, there were 410,000 non-Spanish occupants of the Valley of Mexico and 970,000 in central Mexico as a whole.

Several studies have attacked the problem of measuring the size of the Aztec population in 1519 using these accurate but late Spanish census figures. There are quite a few scattered pieces of information that relate to the sixteenth century demographic loss, but it is almost impossible to piece these together into a single continuous picture of population loss in any single town or area. All demographic studies of this time period must rely upon a series of assumptions and estimates that are difficult to verify. Table 3.1 lists the most influential estimates of the Aztec population. The size of Native American populations before European conquest and colonization is a contentious issue that has been debated hotly by historians and archaeologists of the 1980s and 90s. Of the several studies of the historical demography of early colonial central Mexico, William T. Sanders uses the most reasonable assumptions and the widest range of information, and Thomas Whitmore employs the most sophisticated methods (computer simulation). For these reasons, most scholars favor their estimates over the very high figures of Woodrow Borah and Sherburne Cook.[6] Although the lower estimates in Table 3.1 are the more reasonable ones, these still show a very high Aztec population size and density. These were the highest population levels of any Prehispanic time period. Modern population in the Valley of Mexico did not surpass Aztec levels until the mid-twentieth century. The overall population density of 160 persons per square kilometer, which includes uninhabited areas such as the lakes and steep hillsides, is a very high figure for a preindustrial society.

Counting Sites

William Sanders's estimate, based on documentary evidence, of one million inhabitants in the Valley of Mexico, is corroborated

*Table 3.1   Documentary estimates of the Aztec
population in 1519*

	Borah and Cook	Sanders	Whitmore
Valley of Mexico			
(area: 7,260 km^2)			
Total Population			
(in millions)	2.96	1.16	1.59
Population Density			
(persons / km^2)	410	160	220
Aztec Central Mexico[a]			
(area: 20,810 km^2)			
Total Population			
(in millions)	6.40	3.33	(4.56)[b]
Population Density			
(persons / km^2)	310	160	(220)[b]

[a] "Aztec central Mexico" includes most of the Nahuatl-speaking areas of central
  Mexico except for the Toluca Valley, whose 1568 population is not reported in
  the same format as the other areas.
[b] Whitmore only reports figures for the Valley of Mexico. I have extended his
  estimate to the area of central Mexico using his population density figure for the
  Valley of Mexico.
Sources: Borah and Cook (1963), Sanders (1970), Whitmore (1992)

by results from the Valley of Mexico Archaeological Survey
Project. These archaeological population estimates were produced as follows. Based upon the archaeological principle of
analogy, the directors of the survey hypothesized that ancient
settlements in the Valley of Mexico resembled modern traditional settlements. They carried out studies of the modern settlements and classified them into types such as dispersed village,
nucleated village, nucleated town, and hamlet. The settlements
composing each type share characteristics such as population
density and settlement layout.

Information on the modern settlements was then applied to
the ancient sites located in the regional survey. The size of each
archaeological site was measured for each of the time periods
during which it was occupied. Sites were then assigned to
types (again, for each time period) based upon information
such as the density of artifacts, the number and arrangements

Table 3.2 Aztec archaeological sites and population levels in the Valley of Mexico

Category	Number of Sites	
	Early Aztec	Late Aztec
Type of Site		
Hamlet	258	986
Small Village	15	265
Large Village	4	89
Regional Center	14	41
Supraregional Center	0	2
Ceremonial Precinct	1	59
Special Use Site	1	57
Indeterminate Type	105	137
Total Sites	398	1,636
Total Population	175,000	920,000

Source: Sanders et al. (1979:184–185, 215)

of mounds, and the size of the site. The population of a site in a given time period was estimated by multiplying the population density figure for that type (as determined from the modern settlements) by the total area of the site in that period. The results of this operation for the Early and Late Aztec periods are listed in Table 3.2, and they are portrayed in the maps of Figure 3.1. These findings provided the first indication of the Aztec population explosion mentioned above, and they are among the most important results yet achieved by archaeologists working in central Mexico.[7]

The high Late Aztec population estimate produced by archaeological survey, 920,000, is consistent with the results of the historical demographic research summarized above. The survey results show that the large Late Aztec population was achieved through a rapid growth during a few centuries rather than a gradual sustained increase over many centuries. The Late Aztec period witnessed a great dispersion of population to all corners of the central Mexican highlands. The large size of

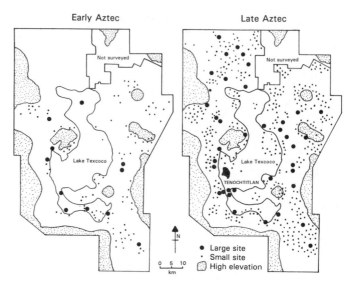

Figure 3.1 Population growth in the Valley of Mexico from the Early Aztec to the Late Aztec period. The dots labelled "small sites" show areas where such sites are numerous; there are far too many small Late Aztec sites to mark each one on a map of this scale (Based upon Sanders et al. 1979: maps 17, 18; drawing by Ellen Cesarski)

the population raises several questions, including: what foods did the Aztecs eat, and how did they grow enough to feed three to four million people in highland central Mexico?

The Aztec Diet

Staple Foods

Like all Mesoamerican peoples before and since, the Aztecs depended heavily on maize, or corn (*Zea mays*), for their sustenance.[8] Maize is a remarkable plant whose domestication made possible the evolution of Mesoamerican civilizations. Maize exists in many different varieties, adapted to specific local conditions of soil and climate, and it can grow nearly

Figure 3.2   Mother teaching her thirteen-year old daughter to make tortillas (Codex Mendoza 1992:v.4:125; folio 60r)

everywhere in Mesoamerica except for the cold high mountains. Indeed, the northern boundary of Mesoamerica as a culture area is usually defined as the northern limits of rainfall-based maize cultivation. A highly productive plant, with caloric yields among the highest of any major world food crop, maize is also high in protein. Animal sources of protein were in short supply in ancient Mesoamerica, so maize was an essential component of the diet.

Maize was eaten in a variety of forms. Most common was the *tortilla*, a round, flat, toasted bread that has been a staple of Mesoamerican cuisine from the Classic period through the present. Tortillas were prepared by first soaking the shelled corn in an alkali solution (water with limestone, ashes, or another source of calcium hydroxide); next grinding the corn into a flour on a *metate* or grinding-stone; then, shaping the tortillas by hand; and finally, cooking them on a clay griddle called a *comalli*. Instruction in tortilla-making was one of the fundamental lessons mothers taught their daughters (figure 3.2). Tortillas could be eaten fresh from the griddle, or they could be stored for later use, including meals eaten away from home by farmers, merchants, soldiers, or other travellers. Also popular were *tamales*, a more ancient, steamed food. Coarse maize dough was shaped into balls, often with some beans, chiles, or sometimes meat in the center, then wrapped in maize leaves and steamed in a large clay pot. Other forms in which the Aztecs ate maize were *atole*, a thin gruel of fine maize flour in water flavored with chiles or fruits; *pozole*, a soup or stew containing large maize kernels (hominy); and *elote* or corn on the cob.

Maize figured prominently in Aztec religion and thought. A number of deities were devoted specifically to maize and its growth (for example, *Centeotl*, whose name means "corn god," and *Chicomecoatl*, the goddess "seven serpent"), and many rituals were carried out to propitiate these deities. Farmers requested a successful harvest by addressing the maize seeds formally before planting. Women thanked the maize before preparing it to eat, a practice that survives in the folk ritual of Mesoamerican peasants today. The symbolism of maize permeated Aztec thought, and people were often compared to the maize plant. For example, a person who had achieved honor was said to have "reached the season of the green maize ear."[9]

Beans were second only to maize in the Aztec diet. Like tortillas, they were served at every meal. Tomatoes, avocados, and several varieties of squash were also common, and squash seeds were eaten in several forms. A large variety of chili peppers gave spice and flavor to food. The seeds of the domesticated chia and amaranth plants were ground in the same manner as corn and eaten in several ways. The Aztecs shaped amaranth dough into small figures of the gods and ate them on ritual occasions. Amaranth leaves were also eaten as greens, and chia seeds were pressed to extract the oil.

Nopal, the prickly pear cactus, was cultivated in the Valley of Mexico for its sweet succulent fruit and paddle-shaped leaf, which was a popular vegetable once the spines were removed. The *maguey* plant, a member of the *Agave* family, was cultivated for a number of uses. The fresh *maguey* sap was a nutritious beverage and, when allowed to ferment, became *pulque* or *octli*, the only alcoholic drink known to the Aztecs. *Maguey* and *pulque* were sacred to the Aztecs and had their own deities. A number of other products were derived from parts of the *maguey* plant: rope, textiles, nets, bags, and sandals were made from its coarse fibers, sewing needles from its spines, and medicines from the sap (see chapter 4).

Animal Foods

Dogs, turkeys, and the Muscovy duck were the only domesticated animals in ancient Mesoamerica. All were used for food, but they made only a minor contribution to the Aztec diet. This contrasts sharply with the ancient civilizations of the Old World which exploited a variety of domesticated animals for food, fiber, and work as draft animals. The Aztecs also fished and hunted wild game, but again these sources of food were limited. After more than a millennium of urban civilizations with high populations, central Mexico no longer had significant reserves of game that could be used by the Aztecs. Archaeologists do find the bones of fish, deer, rabbit, iguana, dog, turkey, and other animals in Aztec domestic trash deposits, but rarely in dense concentrations. Meat from large animals was a minor part of the Aztec diet.

Early Spanish observers noted the widespread use of insects among the Aztecs, including ants, grasshoppers, maguey worms, and *jumil* bugs. Insects are high in protein, tasty, and could often be harvested in large numbers. The Aztecs also gathered great amounts of blue-green spirulina algae (*Spirulina geitlerii*) from the surface of the lakes. This algae, known as *tecuitlatl*, is extremely high in protein, grows rapidly and abundantly, and is easy to gather with fine nets. Bernal Díaz del Castillo said of it, "the fisherwomen and the men ... sell small cakes made from a sort of weed [algae] which they get out of the great lake, which curdles and forms a kind of bread which tastes rather like cheese."[10] The Spanish soldiers and priests had a low opinion of the palatability of this algae, but it was much prized by the Aztecs. The Aztecs also gathered a wide variety of wild plants for food and medicinal purposes.

Nutritional Status

The nutritional status of the Aztecs has been debated for a number of years. Some authors, pointing out the low level of animal protein in the Aztec diet and the large size of the population, argue that the Aztecs (or at least the commoners) must have been severely malnourished. In an extreme version of this argument, the unlikely suggestion has been made that the Aztecs resorted to cannibalism on a large scale to make up protein and calorie deficiencies.[11] The notion that the Aztec diet was poor has been countered by analyses of the composition of Aztec foods, which show that for the most part the diet was nutritionally adequate. Whether or not sufficient *quantities* of food were produced in central Mexico to meet the needs of the burgeoning Aztec population, however, is a more difficult question to answer.

Maize was the key to the nutritional success of the Aztec diet. Most traditional diets around the world depend on low-protein staple grains (such as wheat or rice) to provide the bulk of the calories but must be supplemented by animal foods to provide sufficient protein. As mentioned above, maize is relatively high in protein for a grain, but by itself it is not a complete protein since it does not supply all of the essential amino acids that the human body needs. The ancient Meso-americans worked out two cultural practices that, when combined, provided them with a complete protein source and greatly reduced their need for meat.

For a food to be a complete protein (i.e., an adequate source of protein for human metabolism), it must supply all eleven of the essential amino acids. Animal flesh is a complete protein, which is why most cultures rely on meat for their protein needs. Maize is high in most of the essential amino acids, but several, including lysine and tryptophan, are chemically bound and not available if the maize is eaten unprocessed. Soaking the shelled kernels in an alkali solution both frees the tryptophan and adds calcium to the mixture.[12] Beans are high in lysine. When eaten together with lime-soaked maize, one has a complete, plant-derived protein source. The Mesoamerican preference for maize and beans at every meal has a solid nutritional basis.

How did these practices originate and become fixed cultural patterns? We can only speculate. Mesoamerican farmers, in the past and today, let the maize dry out and harden in the field before harvesting it in order to store it for the coming year. The hard kernels must be soaked in water to soften them before grinding. Somehow, it was discovered that adding chemical lime to the soaking water, most likely in the form of lime-stone, improved the maize. I have asked modern Mesoamerican peasant women why they soak the maize before cooking it, and their answer is that the tortillas don't taste right if the maize is not lime soaked. The Aztec ancestors of these women five centuries ago probably would have said the same thing.

Other components of the Aztec diet provided important nutrients as well. For example, chili peppers are high in iron, riboflavin, niacin, and vitamins A and C; chia has high amounts of calcium, phosphorus, and iron; beans are high in niacin; and many of the wild herbs and spices used by the Aztecs are high in calcium and vitamin A. Without the benefit of modern nutritional knowledge, early Mesoamerican peoples managed to work out an adequate diet that suited their environment, and by the time the Aztecs arrived, these patterns were deeply ingrained cultural practices.

The Aztec diet provided adequate amounts of protein and other key nutrients, but were their farmers able to produce enough to feed a population of several million? An important concept here is "carrying capacity," or the total population that a particular environment can support, given the types of crops and farming methods in use. Because the measurement of ancient carrying capacity combines many difficult estimates (e.g., human nutritional requirements, the nature of past environments, ancient crop yields, the technology and organization of labor used in farming and hunting), the whole endeavor is somewhat controversial. Nevertheless, the available evidence suggests that the Aztec population had reached or exceeded the carrying capacity of central Mexico. The Aztecs could easily feed themselves in good years, but when yields were poor, owing to low rainfall, early frosts, or other periodic environmental fluctuations, the Aztec agricultural system did not produce sufficient food to feed adequately the entire population.[13] During the final century of Aztec society, a number of famines and years of poor harvests were reported, and the famine of 1450–54 was disastrous. How did the growing Aztec population attempt to meet its subsistence needs?

Farming Systems

Agricultural Intensification

The intensification of agricultural practices was one of the most direct responses to the Late Aztec population explosion. It is also one of the most archaeologically visible responses.

Agricultural intensification refers to changes in farming in which additional energy is invested in agriculture in order to secure higher yields from a given unit of land. Nonintensive or extensive agricultural methods, such as slash-and-burn farming or simple rainfall cultivation, are not highly productive in terms of yield per area, but they are energetically efficient because they do not require large investments of human labor. Extensive agriculture is adaptive where the population density is low and high yields are not necessary to meet subsistence needs. More intensive agricultural methods, such as heavy weeding, fertilization, or irrigation, provide greater amounts of food per area under cultivation, but require that a lot more work be expended in farming.

The intensification of agriculture is a process that goes hand in hand with cultural change. As cultures evolve and their populations grow, they require more food from the land, which forces farmers to intensify their methods. The development of social stratification and the state also stimulates intensive agriculture. Farmers must produce enough to meet the tribute and tax demands of the government and elite class as well as their own subsistence needs. All ancient civilizations relied upon one or more forms of intensive agriculture.[14] In the Aztec case, simple rainfall agriculture was supplemented by terracing, irrigation, raised fields, and houselot garden cultivation. None of these intensive methods were new; they all dated back to earlier Mesoamerican civilizations. What was unique about Aztec agriculture was the *degree* of intensification, which transformed the countryside from its natural condition into a cultivated cultural landscape with little empty or wild land left.

Friar Sahagún described the activities of the Aztec farmer as follows:

> The farmer . . . is bound to the soil; he works – works the soil, stirs the soil anew, prepares the soil; he weeds, breaks up the clods, hoes, levels the soil, makes furrows . . . He sets the boundaries; . . . he works [the soil] during the summer; he takes up the stones; he digs furrows; he makes holes; he plants, hills, waters, sprinkles; he broadcasts seed; he sows beans, provides holes for them . . . fills in the holes; he hills [the maize plants], removes the undeveloped maize ears, discards the withered ears . . . gathers the maize, shucks the ears, removes the ears . . .[15]

*Figure 3.3   Farmers planting maize with a digging stick
(After Sahagún 1950–82:bk.10:fig.70; drawing by Ellen Cesarski)*

Rainfall cultivation that involved some fallowing of the land was called *tlacolol*. The basic agricultural tool was a flat, wooden digging stick called a *coa*, which was used to turn over and perforate the soil (figure 3.3). At the start of the Early Aztec period, most farmers practiced extensive rainfall cultivation. As populations grew and city-states expanded their control, more intensive methods were applied. Not every field could be transformed by intensification, however, and rainfall cultivation continued to be used in many parts of central Mexico.

Farming the Hills

Central Mexico is mountainous, but the Aztecs put the gently sloping hillsides to good use. They constructed many miles of stone terrace walls to create level planting surfaces and turned otherwise unusable hillslopes into productive farm fields. Remnants of ancient stone terrace walls are found throughout the Aztec territory, and in some areas, Aztec terraces have been maintained or rebuilt and are still in use today. The Aztecs built three types of terraces, each adapted to different environmental conditions: hillslope contour terraces, semi-terraces, and cross-channel terraces.[16]

The most common type of terrace had stone walls that ran

Figure 3.4   Aztec agricultural terraces at Cerro Texcotzinco in the Valley of Mexico. These terraces, used in the 1400s, were irrigated with water from a spring; the saddle between the hills at top right is an aqueduct that carried the water (Photograph by William E. Doolittle; reproduced with permission)

parallel to the contour of the slope (figure 3.4). The stones were piled up by hand, and the terrace behind the wall was filled in by digging into the hillside or by relying on natural soil erosion from uphill. Today the archaeological remnants of Aztec terrace walls are rough stone alignments rarely having more than a single course or layer of stones. In comparison with the better-known Inca agricultural terraces of the Andes Mountains, Aztec stone terraces were smaller and built of rougher stones with simpler masonry techniques. Whereas the carefully-constructed Inca terraces often extended in parallel rows for hundreds of meters, Aztec terraces were much shorter and irregular. They do not show the hand of central planning.

On more gentle slopes the Aztecs used low terrace walls made from long lines of *maguey* plants grown close together. Archaeologists call these "semi-terraces." The *maguey* plants held soil erosion in check, creating level planting surfaces on which maize and other crops could be cultivated. The maguey

*Figure 3.5   Aztec check-dams (cross-channel agricultural terraces)
at the site of Cuexcomate (Photograph by Michael E. Smith)*

themselves could be exploited for fiber and *pulque*. Cross-channel terraces or check-dams (figure 3.5) were built across streambeds in the bottoms of ravines, perpendicular to the stream. As the water flowed over the walls, silt and other sediments carried by the stream were deposited naturally behind the stones to create a level surface. As deposition continued season after season, farmers gradually built the walls higher and the new field surfaces expanded greatly in area. Although check-dams were built in small increments over a period of years, the end result could be an impressive stone terrace wall holding back a large level field. Excavations of check-dams at the site of Cuexcomate, in the state of Morelos, revealed walls over two meters high, which were constructed over a long period of time and used for many decades (see discussion below).

Farming the Valleys

Irrigation was another method of intensive agriculture used by the Aztecs.[17] In contrast to terracing, which opened up previously unusable land to cultivation, irrigation was applied to already-farmed valley soils to make them more productive. This was done by extending the rainy season (i.e., watering fields before the onset of the summer rains) and by providing additional water to crops during the growing season to supplement the natural rainfall. Although irrigation technology had a long history in central Mexico (it was very important at Teotihuacan), the Aztecs built canal systems that were both larger and more sophisticated than earlier endeavors.

By the time of the Spanish conquest, nearly all available sources of fresh water in central Mexico had been tapped for irrigation. Although archaeological remains of canals and dams are scarce, Spanish administrative documents mention the use of irrigation throughout sixteenth century central Mexico. In many areas, small-scale irrigation systems were the norm. Dams diverted water from springs or small rivers into simple ditch canals that brought the water to nearby fields. In a variation called floodwater irrigation, small dams spread the frequent rainy-season flash floods onto nearby fields.

In some areas the Aztecs built larger and more technologically advanced irrigation systems. For example, a major segment of the Cuauhtitlan River in the northwest Valley of Mexico was diverted and channeled to provide water to a large area of fields. The river channel itself was deepened, widened, and straightened, and the results are impressive even today (figure 3.6) A series of canals were built leading off the river to the fields. In the eastern part of the valley, a complex irrigation network was built in the area of Mount Texcotzinco. Springs were tapped to feed canals, some of which were up to ten kilometers in length. The longest canals were built of stone and the channels were lined with plaster. Aqueducts carried the canals over ravines and other low points.

Aqueducts were also used to bring water to the city of Tenochtitlan. The swampy island had a limited supply of drinking water, so an aqueduct was built to carry fresh water over the lake from springs at Chapultepec on the mainland. These elaborate hydraulic works were some of the most impressive accomplishments of Aztec technology. This hydrological knowledge was also applied to a third form of intensive agriculture, the *chinampas*.

Figure 3.6 Aztec embankment built to contain the new channel of the Cuauhtitlan River in the Valley of Mexico (Photograph by William E. Doolittle; reproduced with permission)

Farming the Swamps

Raised fields, or *chinampas*, were an ancient Mesoamerican technology for turning swamps into highly productive fields.[18] Large straight ditches were dug to drain away excess water. Between the ditches, long narrow artificial islands were built up to form planting surfaces (figure 3.7). Mud and muck from the lake bottom were piled up, along with vegetation and other organic matter, and the fields were held together with wooden stakes driven into the lake bottom. Trees were also planted to help stabilize the fields. The resulting plots were very productive. The muck and organic matter served as fertilizers and the roots of the maize and other crops drew on abundant groundwater from the naturally high water table. The fields were piled high enough to prevent the roots becoming waterlogged, and fertility was maintained by periodically adding more vegetation and rich muck scraped from the canals. Farmers used canoes to travel on the canals between the fields.

Figure 3.7   Aztec chinampa *still used today to cultivate maize
(Photograph by William E. Doolittle; reproduced with permission)*

Plants were germinated in seedbeds built on floating reed
rafts, and these were pulled by canoe to individual *chinampa*
plots for replanting. These floating seedbeds have given rise to
the modern term "floating gardens," used mistakenly to refer
to the *chinampa* fields themselves. Their high fertility and their
location in the frost free southern Valley of Mexico allowed
three or four crops to be grown annually on the *chinampas*.
This made them the most intensive and productive of all
Mesoamerican agricultural practices.

The Aztecs built *chinampas* throughout Lakes Chalco and
Xochimilco, the two lakes that formed the southern arm of the
Valley of Mexico lake system. Archaeological surveys that were
carried out in this area before the recent urban expansion of
Mexico City located many square kilometers of long narrow
ridges arranged in an overall grid pattern indicative of Aztec
chinampa cultivation. According to early colonial documents,
chinampas also were built on the outskirts of Tenochtitlan.
The system survives today in a few areas of the southern
lakebed, particularly in the modern towns of Xochimilco and

Mixquic. The *chinampas* have historically provided vegetables for the Mexico City market, but recent environmental degradation, caused by pollution, urban expansion and a lowered water table, is having a negative affect on their economic viability. The *chinampa* towns have developed into tourist attractions, and for a fee one can travel through the old canals on boats. Although raised field agriculture was practiced throughout Mesoamerica and South America in prehispanic times, the fields were abandoned before or soon after Spanish conquest in all areas except for the southern Valley of Mexico. These modern *chinampas* provide crucial insights on this important ancient technique of intensive agriculture.

Farming in Town

Much of the land devoted to terracing, irrigation, and raised field cultivation was located either away from settlements or adjacent to them. The Aztecs also practiced the intensive cultivation of gardens within their villages, towns, and cities. In most settlements, each family had a substantial garden plot adjacent to the house, which was used to grow some maize, fruits, herbs, medicines and other useful plants. These houselot gardens, called *calmil*, were intensively cultivated in that they were fertilized with domestic refuse, actively weeded and carefully tended by family members.

Susan T. Evans's archaeological study of the village of Cihuatecpan suggests that much of its surface area was taken up with *calmil* cultivation that used *maguey* semi-terraces on the gently sloping terrain.[19] This intensive garden cultivation may be one reason for the dispersed nature of most Aztec settlements, from villages to cities.

Household Enterprise or State Control?

Was the state involved in the management of Aztec intensive agriculture? This is an important question in the study of ancient civilizations, for some scholars have suggested that intensive agricultural methods such as irrigation could only be managed by centralized bureaucratic states, whereas others have argued that independent households could take care of their own intensive agriculture without interference from the state.

Aztec terrace agriculture was similar to terrace systems in many parts of the world today where construction, maintenance, and cultivation is carried out on the household level.[20] The labor of individual families or cooperative groups of a few families was sufficient to build terraces, and most farming was probably done on a small scale by the individual owners of the terraces. The intensive cultivation of terraces and the need for continual maintenance on the walls made it advantageous for farmers to live close to their plots. This contributed to the great dispersion of rural settlement across the landscape during the Late Aztec period. Houselot *calmil* gardens were also organized on a household basis.

Unlike rainfall agriculture or terracing, which are organized on the household level in most societies, irrigation systems normally require cooperative labor for their construction and maintenance and some form of central authority for their management.[21] Irrigation networks must be planned carefully from the start. Considerable labor goes into digging canals and building dams. Canals silt up frequently, and clearing them out is a regular and time-consuming task that goes beyond the abilities of individual households. A common political authority is usually needed to establish water rights and schedules and to settle the numerous disputes that inevitably arise in the operation of any irrigation system. This authority does not have to be the state, however, since in many modern systems the body regulating irrigation is a lower-level local organization.

In Aztec central Mexico, irrigation was most heavily used in the area of the modern state of Morelos. The size and shape of the major Late Aztec states in this area suggest a link between irrigation and state organization.[22] A series of north-south river valleys were extensively irrigated, and the major states, such as Cuauhnahuac, Yautepec, and Huaxtepec, were each confined to individual valleys. Each state could control its own irrigation system without having to rely upon the good-will of upstream competitors for water. The capital cities of each of these domains were located near the northern or upstream edges of their territory. Irrigation was important to the people of Morelos, and the size and layout of city-states reflected this importance.

The organizational requirements of raised field cultivation

were intermediate between those of terracing and irrigation. The initial construction of a system of raised fields required planning and a considerable investment of labor, but once they were built, *chinampas* were easily farmed and maintained by households. Some archaeologists see the hand of the state in the regular grid-like arrangement of chinampas in Lakes Chalco and Xochimilco, but documentary sources on the *chinampas* at the edge of Tenochtitlan describe small plots of several fields farmed by individual households who lived among their fields.[23]

In sum, some of the intensive agricultural methods used by the Aztecs required organization and control by a central authority, perhaps local lords or city-state bureaucrats, but other methods were almost certainly organized and operated entirely at the scale of the individual farm household.

Rural Settlement

Settlement Patterns

Most of the several million Aztecs in central Mexico were peasants – rural cultivators who farmed land controlled by lords. Rural settlements took a variety of forms, depending upon the local environmental setting, the type of agriculture practiced, and the nature of local social organization. When the Aztlan migrants first arrived in central Mexico, their new settlements were small and scattered widely across the landscape. As far as we know, no large cities existed in the Valley of Mexico during the Early Aztec period. As the population grew, small groups moved into the swampy backwaters of Lakes Chalco and Xochimilco and constructed the earliest *chinampas*. Then, during Late Aztec times, large numbers of people moved onto the lakeshore plain and built irrigation systems, and into the foothills, where they constructed terraces. These farming systems had a major impact on the nature of rural settlement patterns.

Archaeological surveys indicate that much Late Aztec settlement was dispersed. The remains of individual houses and house groups are widely scattered across the landscape, particularly in areas where terrace agriculture was practiced. The

Late Aztec settlement of the Buenavista hills, an alluvial fan in western Morelos, it typical. This ancient geological formation of long gently sloping ridges extends out for several miles from the Ajusco mountain range to the north. Late Aztec house foundations, which are visible on the ground surface, are scattered along the ridgetops. The sloping sides of the ridges are covered with the remnants of stone terrace walls, and checkdams are present in the ravines between the ridges. As one moves along the narrow ridge tops, the density of houses increases periodically, clustering around small groups of mounds, which were probably elite residences and/or small temple-pyramids. Between the mound groups, house density drops off but never to the point where there are large empty areas.[24]

Not all Aztec farmers lived in these dispersed settlements. Nucleated villages and towns were also common, particularly in the *chinampa* zone of the southern Valley of Mexico. In these settlements, houses were packed more closely together, and the communities had clearer boundaries. Towns and some larger villages contained distinctive buildings that had administrative and religious functions. These buildings might include the residence of a village headman or a lord, a temple, or other special structures. Large villages, towns, or areas of dispersed settlement often corresponded to a *calpolli*, a social and territorial unit that helped regulate land tenure and tribute payment (see chapter 6).

Excavations at Cuexcomate and Capilco

Archaeological fieldwork at the rural sites of Cuexcomate and Capilco in western Morelos provides a case study to illustrate some of the topics covered in this chapter. My wife, Cynthia Heath-Smith, and I directed mapping and excavations at these sites in 1985 and 1986 in a project designed to gather information on social and economic conditions among Aztec peasants.[25] Although ethnohistoric sources provided rich data on the lives of Aztec nobles and urban-dwellers (see chapter 6), little was known about the Aztec peasantry. We selected these sites for study because they were not deeply buried, and the foundations of individual houses were visible on the ground surface. Archaeologists have found that the best information

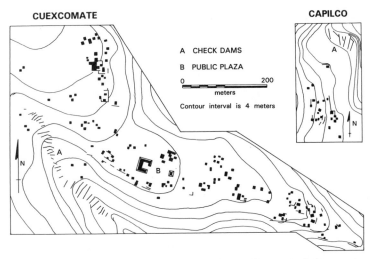

*Figure 3.8   Maps of Cuexcomate and Capilco, rural Aztec sites
in Morelos. The black squares are houses (Drawing by
Michael E. Smith)*

on social and economic organization comes from the excavation of houses, and conditions at Cuexcomate and Capilco
made them ideal sites. We could begin to excavate houses
immediately, without wasting a lot of time and effort locating
buried structures. The sites are located in a rural area today
and, at the time of fieldwork, were little disturbed by modern
settlement or activities.

Capilco is a small site with 21 house foundations, and
Cuexcomate is a larger site with over 150 houses and other
structures, including temples, storehouses, and ritual dumps
(figure 3.8). One of our first tasks was to estimate the populations of these sites. Since we were unable to excavate all 164
houses at the two sites, we used the technique of random
sampling to select a sample of houses at each site. At Capilco,
eight of the 21 houses (38 per cent) were selected in a simple
random sample, while at Cuexcomate 21 out of 143 houses
(15 per cent) were chosen in a stratified random sample.[26]

For each house in the two samples, two test pits were dug: one
in the structure to date its construction, and one in a nearby
midden (trash deposit) to recover information on domestic

Table 3.3 *Population and site areas of Cuexcomate and Capilco*

Site	Time Period		
	Early Aztec 1200–1350	Late Aztec A 1350–1440	Late Aztec B 1440–1550
Capilco			
Population	28	72	116
Site Area (hectares)	.14	.60	1.15
Cuexcomate			
Population	0	237	803
Site Area (hectares)	0	9.94	14.58

Source: Smith (1992a)

artifacts and living conditions. Through a combination of dating methods, we determined in which periods each house was occupied. We used a detailed sequence of temporal phases based upon the types of pottery present. The latter part of the Early Aztec period is represented at these site in the Temazcalli phase (AD 1200–1350), and the Early Cuauhnahuac (AD 1350–1440) and Late Cuauhnahuac (AD 1440–1550) phases correspond to the Late Aztec A and B periods (figure 2.1).

The use of random sampling to choose the 29 houses to excavate permits us to extrapolate characteristics of the houses in the samples to the total collection of houses at Capilco and Cuexcomate. For example, two of the eight houses (25 per cent) tested at Capilco had occupation during the Early Aztec phase. We therefore inferred that 25 per cent of the 21 houses at the site, or five houses, were occupied in Early Aztec times. The numbers of houses were then converted into population estimates using average family size figures from early colonial census documents from various towns in Morelos.[27]

Patterns of house occupation show a dramatic growth of population across the three phases (table 3.3). Although these results pertain only to the two sites, they suggest that the demographic explosion reported for the Valley of Mexico was also taking place in adjacent areas such as western Morelos. When we applied the demographic patterns from Capilco and

Cuexcomate to nearby sites in western Morelos, it became obvious that by the Late Aztec B phase, the regional population far exceeded the carrying capacity of rainfall agriculture. This burgeoning population needed intensive agricultural methods to survive, and in the hilly landscape of western Morelos terraces and check-dams were the logical choices.

When we mapped these sites, we noticed check-dams at both sites. Although the remains of ancient check-dams and hillside terraces had been reported from various parts of central Mexico, no one had excavated these features to establish their age, construction methods, or use. At Capilco, we excavated two of the seven check-dams, and we dug three of the 36 check-dams that crossed a seasonal stream bed just southwest of the occupation zone at Cuexcomate (figure 3.8). The Cuexcomate features were much larger and better-preserved than at Capilco.

We were able to piece together the history of one extensively excavated check-dam at Cuexcomate by using a combination of methods, including stratigraphic analysis, pollen studies, soil chemistry, grain-size analysis, and radiocarbon dating.[28] Its construction was begun sometime in the fifteenth century. A stone wall was built and the upstream side quickly filled up with sediments carried by flash floods. After a period of active use, a flood breached the wall and carried away much of the accumulated deposit. The wall was repaired, and a long period of use followed, during which sediments gradually built up, and the wall was enlarged several times one row of stones at a time. A radiocarbon date of AD 1476 was obtained from a deposit early in this period of gradual expansion. Unfortunately our pollen results were equivocal and do not permit us to state which crops were grown on this or other check-dam fields. The dam was probably abandoned soon after the Spanish conquest, when the occupants of Cuexcomate (those who did not succumb to disease) were forced to move to another community.

Although we had noted the remnants of a few stone terrace walls on hillsides around Cuexcomate and Capilco, they did not seem to cover a large area. The soils are very rocky, and today large and small stones are scattered all over the ground surface, in pastures and plowed fields alike. One of the student excavators first noticed that the sloping flanks of the ridge

surrounding the settlement of Cuexcomate had many subtle
stone alignments that could only be the bases of ancient terrace
walls.[29] The crew had been walking all over these features for
months without noticing their existence. We mapped and excavated some of the stone alignments, but soil erosion on the
hillsides has been severe since the site was abandoned, and
preservation of the terraces is quite poor. The surviving terrace
walls consist of rough lines of stones, only a single course high,
often resting directly on bedrock.

The Rural Landscape

The peasants who farmed the hills, valleys, swamps, and villages of rural central Mexico were essential participants in the
Aztec social order. Their efforts provided food and other products such as cotton to supply the tens of thousands of people
who did not farm for a living. The nobility lived off the work
of these peasants, as did craft specialists and other inhabitants
of cities. Not all Aztec peasants were full-time farmers, however. Women produced textiles for trade and tribute, in addition to their other domestic tasks, and many men took up
part-time crafts such as pottery, making stone tools, or rope
making.

The Aztec countryside did not consist solely of isolated farming families; small home-based cottage industries thrived in
many areas, and a large number of lords lived in small towns
or country estates. Peasants were well integrated into an extensive system of marketplace trade, and they had access to goods
from all over the empire. In short, the Aztec countryside was
a thriving and complex social landscape, not a rural backwater
of impoverished peasants. The next two chapters describe how
agricultural production was complemented by craft industries,
and how a thriving system of markets and merchants served to
distribute goods throughout the rural and urban settlements of
Aztec central Mexico.

4

Artisans and their Wares

The last sign, the twentieth, called Xochitl, means Flower . . . and was a sign which was associated with masters and craftsmen. Thus it was said that those born under it were to be painters, metalworkers, weavers, sculptors, carvers – that is to say, [workers in] all the arts that imitate nature.

Friar Diego Durán[1]

In a complex society like that of the Aztecs, the producers of goods played an important role. Work was heavily specialized, and a relatively small group of people was relied upon to manufacture most of the goods that people used in their homes, temples, and workplaces. There were two types of craft industries in Aztec central Mexico – utilitarian and luxury – and the nature and organization of work in each of these sectors had very different implications for the lives of both producers and consumers. Utilitarian goods such as reed sandals or pottery vessels were produced by part-time artisans, who worked in their homes and sold in the marketplace. Luxury items such as gold jewelry or stone sculptures were fashioned in the workshops of full-time artists who worked directly for elite patrons.[2]

Utilitarian Crafts

Early Spanish observers had little to say about Aztec utilitarian objects such as kitchen utensils or household tools and even less about how these items were produced. Archaeologists, on the other hand, can say much about these objects because the bulk of the artifacts recovered from most sites are the detritus of mundane, daily activities. Furthermore, the production of utilitarian items often left clear traces in the archaeological record. Increasingly those who study ancient civilizations, including the Aztecs, are turning their attention to issues of utilitarian craft production and specialization.

Obsidian

Obsidian cutting tools are among the finest achievements of Mesoamerican manufacturing technology. Obsidian is a naturally-occurring, black volcanic glass which is available in several highland areas of Mesoamerica. Although brittle and easily broken, obsidian can fracture into pieces with extremely sharp edges. In fact, microscopic studies have shown obsidian blades to have the sharpest edges of any known tool, ancient or modern. The edge of a well-made prismatic blade can be sharper than a surgeon's scalpel. No wonder that the earliest Mesoamericans, many millennia before the Aztecs, selected obsidian as the material of choice for the manufacture of stone tools. By Aztec times, the technology of obsidian-working had been perfected and stoneknappers could produce a wide range of domestic and industrial tools.[3]

Obsidian tools are the second most abundant type of artifact found at Aztec residential sites, surpassed only by ceramic vessels. Every Aztec household maintained a collection of implements used for a variety of purposes. Prismatic blades, long thin parallel-sided flakes with a characteristic prism-shaped cross-section (figure 4.1), were most common. These versatile tools were used chiefly as knives, but hafted onto wooden handles, they also served as sickles and razors. Prismatic blades were often shaped into new tools, including drills, scrapers, and arrow points. Other common obsidian tools were bifacially flaked knives and projectile points, scrapers, and simple unmodified flakes that could be used for a number of cutting jobs.

Implements of obsidian also were used outside of the home. The Spanish conquerors first encountered obsidian in Aztec swords. The *maquahuitl* sword consisted of a stout wooden shaft with opposing rows of prismatic blades (see chapter 7). These swords were sharp enough to decapitate a man. The more mundane industries such as carpentry and woodworking, textile production, basketry, and farming also utilized obsidian tools.

Figure 4.1   Obsidian blade-core and four prismatic blades from Aztec houses at Yautepec (Photograph by Michael E. Smith)

The technology of obsidian tool production began at the mines. The Aztecs were fortunate to have several nearby obsidian sources, both in the Valley of Mexico and in the mountains just north of the valley.[4] The Otumba source, located in the Otumba city-state in the Teotihuacan Valley, and the Pachuca source, just north of the Valley of Mexico, were the most important to the Aztec industry. Because of its chemical composition and crystal structure, Pachuca obsidian was better suited for prismatic blade technology than most other obsidians. The stone was mined from pits and shafts using basalt tools, although in some areas boulders had eroded from the ground and were easily picked up.

Obsidian knapping is a "subtractive" technology in that, during the process of tool-making, waste flakes are removed or subtracted from a core. Each stage of the process – from quarry to finished tool – produces a distinctive type of waste material, which allows archaeologists to reconstruct the various tool-making activities that took place at a site. The presence of initial shaping flakes at quarry sites indicates that excess material usually was chipped from the mined chunks at the quarry prior to carrying the obsidian back to the knapper's home or workshop. At the workshops, most nodules were used in one of two basic technologies: biface production or prismatic blade production. A biface tool is flaked on both its upper and lower surfaces. Biface production is an old technology that has been used throughout the world for tens of millennia. Prismatic blade production is far more difficult and has a more limited distribution.

To make prismatic blades, the obsidian first was worked into a rough, cylindrical macrocore, which then was refined into a symmetrical blade-core through careful chipping. The upper, flat surface of the blade-core was ground with a basalt tool to roughen it in preparation for blade making. The actual blades were removed from the core through the application of steady force to a small area on the edge of the core. This step, known as pressure flaking, was the most difficult part of the whole process. The force required is greater than a person's arm-strength, and it must be applied evenly at just the right place on the core. It took archaeologists many years of experimentation to figure out how the Aztecs and other Mesoamerican peoples accomplished the removal of blades.[5] After many blades had been produced from a core, the exhausted core was either discarded or else fashioned into a new tool; figure 4.1 shows one of these exhausted cores.

The high degree of skill required to produce prismatic blades suggests that blade making was done by specialists. Since all households used the tools, the demand for these blades must have been enormous. Also, they broke easily. Nevertheless, a skilled blade maker could produce some 200 blades from a single core in a short period of time, so the number of specialists was not necessarily high. It is likely that many obsidian workers, at least in the rural areas, were part-time specialists who used their obsidian work to supplement farming activities. Archaeological excavations confirm that blade production was carried out in only a few places. The city of Otumba, located next to the Otumba obsidian source, had several obsidian blade workshops that supplied the surrounding area (see below). On the other hand, the rural sites Capilco and Cuexcomate (see chapter 3) were not located near an obsidian source, yet their inhabitants had ready access to blades and other tools. More than 12,000 obsidian artifacts were recovered from the excavations at these sites (mostly blade fragments), but there was virtually no evidence for the production of cores or blades. These farmers bought their blades, already-made, in the marketplace.

Pottery

Aztec kitchens were equipped with a variety of pottery vessels for cooking, preparing, and serving food. Each family probably owned one or two painted water jars; several flat tortilla griddles (*comalli*); cooking pots of various shapes and sizes for beans, sauces, and other foods; a pot to soak maize in; a rough-bottom tripod grinding dish for chiles and tomatoes; a salt jar; and various plates, bowls, and cups for meals. In addition to kitchenware, pottery was used for religious items (figurines and incense burners); tools (spindle whorls and special bowls to support the spindle during the spinning of cotton thread); and a range of small objects, of uncertain uses, that include stamps, disks, bells, balls, tubes, whistles, and miniature cookpots (figure 4.2). With all of these breakable objects in common use, it is not surprising that broken pieces of pottery, or sherds, are by far the single most abundant type of artifact at Aztec sites.

Aztec pottery was produced by hand. For most objects, the clay was shaped over a mold made of fired clay and then baked in open fires or in kilns. Unfortunately there is little direct archaeological evidence of pottery manufacture among the Aztecs. Unlike subtractive technologies such as obsidian tool making additive technologies like potting leave far less debris for the archaeologist to find. Although molds for figurines, incense burners, and spindle whorls have been recovered from Otumba, Yautepec, and other sites, no Aztec kilns or firing areas have been found, in spite of excavations at a number of sites.

Several lines of indirect evidence provide clues to the

Figure 4.2　Small ceramic objects recovered from excavations of houses at Cuexcomate and Capilco. These are tobacco pipes (upper left), miniature cookpots (upper right), bells (lower left), and whistles (lower right) (Photograph by Michael E. Smith)

techniques of pottery production. For example, sherds from jars sometimes show horizontal join-marks where two halves of a vessel – each formed in a convex mold – were joined together. Small cavities in the body of Aztec orangeware sherds indicate the addition of plant fibers (reeds or grasses) to the clay as temper to improve its workability. A pink tint in many of these sherds, caused by the presence of salt in the moist clay, suggests some potting near the saline lakes. In chapter 5, I discuss chemical analyses of Aztec sherds and the insights they provide into ceramic production.

Ethnohistoric sources contain bits of information on the Aztec pottery industry. In his descriptions of occupations, Sahagún lists two types of potters: a general "clay worker," who made many different types of vessels, and a "griddle maker," who specialized in tortilla griddles or (*comalli*):

> The griddle maker [is] one who moistens clay, kneads it, tempers it with [soft pieces of] reed, makes it into a soft paste . . . He makes griddles; he beats [the clay], flattens it, polishes it, smooths it; he

applies a slip. He places [the unfired pieces] in the oven; he feeds the fire, makes the oven smoke, cools the oven.

He sells hard-fired [griddles] which ring, [which are] well tempered, [as well as those which are] poorly fired, smudged, blackened, discolored, poorly made, inferior, sounding as if cracked – cracked in firing.[6]

From this passage, two things may be inferred. One, a griddle maker was a specialist who made only one type of vessel, which indicates a division of labor within the overall pottery industry. Two, some potters sold their own wares in the market, a common pattern among the artisans described by Friar Sahagún. Many questions, however, remain unanswered. Did most towns and villages have some potters, or did a few large production centers supply all of central Mexico? How large were individual workshops? Were potters full-time or part-time specialists? Some tentative answers are suggested below and in chapter 5, but archaeologists continue to search for more evidence concerning the manufacture of Aztec pottery.[7]

Cotton Textiles

Cotton cloth had many uses in Aztec Mexico. Much of it was made into clothing for men (loin cloths and capes) and women (skirts and huipils or pullover shirts). Cloth also was used for bedding, bags, awnings, decorative hangings, battle armor, adornments for statues of the gods, and shrouds for the dead.[8] Cotton textiles served as items of exchange, most commonly in the form of the *quachtli,* a long narrow folded cloth or cape. *Quachtli* served as currency in the markets, were exchanged as gifts among the nobility, and formed the dominant item of tribute payment at all levels. Commoners used them to pay nobles and subordinate city-states to pay the Aztec empire.

Cotton cloth had symbolic importance in addition to its practical uses. Clothing and capes came in both plain and highly decorated styles. Fancy, colorful types were reserved for important nobles or priests, and a special kind of decorated cape was worn exclusively by the Mexica kings. Among the Mexica, only nobles were permitted to wear cotton clothing; commoners wore clothing of *maguey* cloth or animal skins. Thus cotton symbolized the privileges of nobility.

Women made cotton cloth in the home. From ethnohistoric documents, we know that spinning and weaving were viewed as women's work and that all Aztec women, from the lowliest slave to the highest noblewoman, engaged in cloth production. Cloth production was a fundamental part of female gender identity. Newborn girls were presented with miniature spinning and weaving tools to symbolize their later adult activities (see chapter 6). Women worked at these tasks off and on, throughout the day, interspersed with their other domestic activities. Textile production began with the cleaning and combing of the raw cotton. The cleaned cotton was spun by hand into thread, and the thread was twisted into yarn. In the *Codex Mendoza*, an illustration of a women teaching her daughter to spin cotton shows the method and tools that were used (figure 4.3, top). The fibers were drawn out and twisted onto a twirling wooden spindle or distaff. A round ceramic weight, the spindle whorl, gave the spindle momentum and provided a base on which the thread rested. Because cotton fibers are short, the spinner had to use care to control the spindle. A small bowl kept the base of the twirling spindle from sliding out of control.

Two of the spinning tools depicted in figure 4.3 – the spindle whorl and the small bowl – were made of fired clay. These artifacts survive as direct archaeological evidence for Aztec cotton spinning (figure 4.4). Spindle whorls have been found at almost every excavated Aztec house in central Mexico, which supports the statements in ethnohistoric sources that all women – nobles and commoners, rural and urban – spun thread in their homes.

Once the thread was twisted into yarn, it was dyed if necessary. A variety of plants and insects were crushed and then boiled with water by specialists to extract dyes. The residue was removed in cake form and sold to consumers in the market. Women reconstituted the dyes, soaked the yarn, and then fixed the colors with a mordant. Cloth was woven on a backstrap loom. A woman hooked one end of the loom over a tree branch or pole and attached the other end to a harness that wrapped around her back. She leaned back to weave, using her posture and position to adjust the tension of the loom (figure 4.3, bottom). Unfortunately, the cross-pieces, shuttles,

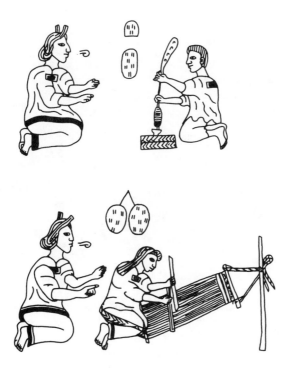

Figure 4.3   Girls being taught by their mothers to spin and weave cotton. Top: a seven-year old learns to spin (Codex Mendoza 1992:v.4:123; folio 59r); bottom: a fourteen-year old learns to weave with a backstrap loom (Codex Mendoza 1992:v.4:125; folio 60r)

and other parts of the loom were made of wood or bone, and few of these have survived at Aztec archaeological sites.

Cotton is a warm-country crop that does not grow at the chilly, high altitude of the Valley of Mexico. Families in the Aztec heartland obtained raw cotton from warmer areas through the market, and cotton was probably somewhat expensive when compared with the fibers of the locally-grown *maguey* plant. Most households in the Valley of Mexico produced more *maguey* cloth than cotton cloth. In areas of lower elevation, like Morelos, the situation was reversed: cotton was cultivated

Figure 4.4   Ceramic cotton-spinning tools from the Aztec village of Capilco. Compare these bowls and spindle whorls to those illustrated in the Codex Mendoza *(figure 4.3, top) (Photograph by Michael E. Smith)*

in great quantities, but the fiber-producing species of *maguey* did not grow well in the warmer, moister climate. Fortunately for archaeologists, the ceramic spindle whorls used to spin cotton and *maguey* are easily distinguished by size. At Aztec houses excavated in Morelos, the small, cotton-spinning whorls are ubiquitous, but very few of the large, *maguey*-spinning whorls are found. In the Valley of Mexico, *maguey* whorls are preponderant.

The Maguey Industries

The *maguey* plant[9] is a remarkable cultigen whose leaves and sap the Aztecs used for many products (figure 4.5). The sixteenth-century Spanish naturalist Francisco Hernández described its benefits as follows:

Figure 4.5 A maguey *plant at the Aztec city of Otumba
(Photograph by Michael E. Smith)*

This plant has almost innumerable uses. The plant itself serves as firewood and for fencing fields . . . its leaves serve to cover roofs, as roof tiles, as plates or dishes, to make paper, and to make thread for footwear, cloth, and all kinds of garments . . . They make nails and tacks from the thorns, with which the Indians formerly perforated their ears in order to mortify their flesh when they worshipped demons . . . From the juice that drips out into the plant's central cavity when the interior leaves are cut out with stone knives, they make wine, honey, vinegar, and sugar.[10]

The two major *maguey* industries were production of fiber and of *pulque* or wine. To make fiber, the long fleshy leaves or *pencas* were cut off the plant and the flesh was loosened by soaking the leaves in a solution or by roasting them in a pit. The fibrous flesh was then scraped from the outer membrane of the leaf with an obsidian scraper and allowed to dry. The dried fibers were spun tightly to make thread or twisted coarsely to make rope or twine. A coarse fiber, with long filaments, *maguey* thread was spun by hand onto a spindle outfitted with a large, heavy ceramic whorl. Unlike cotton, *maguey* fiber was drop-spun, a method in which the twirling spindle hangs in the air, spinning freely. The thread was woven into clothing and other textiles on a backstrap loom similar to that used for cotton cloth.

Pulque or *octli*, the only alcoholic beverage drunk by the Aztecs, was made from the fermented sap of the *maguey* plant. When a plant reached maturity, its center was cut out to leave a cavity. The sides of the cavity were then scraped with an obsidian scraper to stimulate the flow of sap into it. The collector extracted the sap by sucking it into a hollow gourd, and then emptied it into a ceramic jar. The sap was brought to the workshop, where it was emptied into large fermentation vats. The plants had to be scraped and emptied two or three times daily for a period of several weeks to six months, and each *maguey* plant provided two to four liters of sap each day. The sap, called *aguamiel* today, could be drunk both fresh or in its fermented form, *pulque*; it was also used for medicinal purposes.

Although archaeologists have not located *pulque* production workshops at Aztec sites, they have identified the obsidian tools used to scrape the plant for sap extraction. These tools are widely distributed at Aztec sites in the Valley of Mexico, which suggests that *pulque* production was carried out in many local areas. Among the Aztecs, the drink was used in rituals, and drinking to intoxication was strictly prohibited by law. Old people, however, were permitted to indulge as a reward for their long lives. *Pulque* is still a popular beverage among central Mexican peasants today; its alcoholic content is similar to that of beer or wine.

Copper and Bronze Tools

The technology of metallurgy was introduced into Mesoamerica from Andean South America.[11] The ancient ancestors of the Incas had developed sophisticated methods for working gold, silver, and copper, including the ability to produce tools of bronze alloys, several millennia prior to the Spanish conquest. Around AD 700, seaborne traders or artisans introduced the techniques of copper metallurgy to west Mexican cultures. Later, around

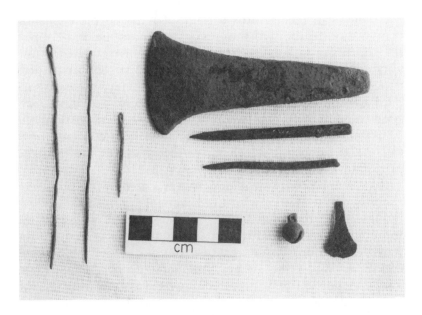

*Figure 4.6   Bronze tools from Aztec houses in Yautepec. There
are three sewing needles, an axe, two punches or awls, a bell,
and a tweezer (Photograph by Michael E. Smith)*

AD 1200, the methods of bronze-working were introduced
into west Mexico, again from a South American place of origin. Bronze is an alloy consisting primarily of copper with
limited amounts of tin or arsenic that improve its strength and
workability. The smelting of bronze is a more complex technology than copper-working, requiring greater skills and higher
temperatures. This technology flourished in west Mexico, and
by the Late Aztec period, metalsmiths had perfected a repertoire of techniques for fashioning copper and bronze objects.
Cold hammering, hot hammering, open-mold casting, and lost-
wax casting were used to make a variety of products, including
both ritual/elite items such as bells, rings, tweezers, and ornaments, and utilitarian tools such as sewing needles, chisels,
awls, axes, and fishhooks (figure 4.6). Some of these techniques originated in South America and others were developed
independently by west Mexican peoples.
Experimental research by Dorothy Hosler has shown that

Mesoamerican metalsmiths carefully controlled the elemental
composition of the two bronzes – copper-arsenic and copper-
tin – in order to achieve two ends. To improve the function-
ality of tools, they added tin or arsenic to copper in low
concentrations (2 to 5 per cent), which provides the necessary
hardness and strength but avoids brittleness. To achieve desired colors in bells and tweezers, artifacts with great symbolic
significance, they added tin or arsenic in high concentrations
(10 to 20 per cent), which alters the colors of the metal to
resemble silver and gold.

Copper and bronze metallurgy was practiced by the Tarascans,
enemies of the Aztecs who lived west of central Mexico. Although the Aztecs of the Valley of Mexico did not adopt the
technology themselves, it had begun to spread through the
Aztec empire in the final century or two before the Spanish
conquest. When the Aztecs conquered territory along the
Tarascan border, they captured towns with metalsmiths and
areas with major copper deposits. An independent metal-
producing area recently has been identified in the Huaxtec
territory in the eastern empire. Our excavations at Capilco,
Cuexcomate, and Yautepec in Morelos yielded surprising numbers of copper and bronze tools. Although these tools were
probably manufactured in west Mexico, metallurgical analyses
by Hosler indicate that some of them were reworked locally to
maintain their shape and hardness. Copper needles, awls, and
chisels were sold in the central Tlatelolco market, probably
imported from the western frontier of the empire. At the time
of the Spanish Conquest, bronze metallurgy was becoming
popular in the Aztec empire, and the people of the Valley of
Mexico may have been on the verge of developing a more
complex metallurgy by adopting copper and bronze smelting
from their Tarascan enemies.

Summary

The makers of the goods described above were not the only
artisans who specialized in utilitarian crafts. In addition to
obsidian knappers, potters, weavers, *maguey* workers and metalsmiths, ethnohistoric sources mention carpenters, mat makers,
sandal makers, broom makers, basket makers, stone cutters,

lime burners, medicine makers, pine resin extractors, pine torch cutters, and many other occupations. Most of these artisans practiced their crafts part-time as a supplement to farming. They sold their goods in the marketplace, which put them at the mercy of economic forces outside of their control. If the demand for their products declined, the families of artisans could devote more effort to farming. Conversely if the demand for craft items increased, or if income from farming decreased, more attention could be given to the household workshop.

At Cuexcomate and Capilco, we found evidence that increasing economic hardship led certain poor peasant households to increase their production of cotton textiles. As standards of living fell in the Late Aztec B period, the houses we identified as the poorest were the ones with the greatest numbers of spindle whorls and spinning bowls. It appears that part-time cloth production was stepped up by the families who lived in these houses to compensate for hardship due to either declines in agricultural production or increases in their tribute burden.

Full-time producers of utilitarian goods may have practiced their crafts in some Aztec cities (such as Otumba; see below), but many utilitarian craft producers lived in rural areas where they could easily combine their craft with agriculture. The craftsmen described above produced the kinds of goods – pottery, clothing, tools – required by consumers in most pre-industrial societies. These petty artisans contrasted greatly with the full-time specialists in luxury goods.

Luxury Crafts

Hernando Cortés and the Spanish conquerors were awed by the exquisite beauty and craftsmanship of Aztec jewelry and ceremonial art. Ornaments of gold and silver, earrings and lip plugs of jade and obsidian, decorative feather art, religious statues of stone, ceremonial knives whose handles were inlaid with shell and turquoise – these and many other luxury goods graced the temples and palaces of the Aztecs. These were not mere baubles, the frivolous playthings of the Aztec nobility. Rather they played a key role in Aztec society, communicating information about status, wealth, etiquette, and belief. Nobles used these goods to show off their position in society. They gave them as gifts to other nobles at important ritual and diplomatic occasions where such gift-giving helped to cement social ties and political alliances (see chapters 6 and 7). Priests also used these objects in rituals, and many of these ended up in the ground as buried offerings (see chapter 9).

Luxury goods had a far more limited demand than cookpots or obsidian blades because many were used almost exclusively by nobles and priests. These items required greater skill and effort to produce. As a result, the organization of production for luxury crafts differed greatly from that for utilitarian crafts. Artisans (or artists) were full-time specialists, and much of their work was done directly for noble patrons. They also sold their goods in the market, where their primary customers were nobles. Some of these items were forbidden to commoners, but others were not. Commoners could purchase these latter goods in the market if they could afford them.

Ethnohistoric documents provide most of the evidence for luxury goods. Archaeologists have uncovered examples of some of these crafts – particularly stone sculptures and items of jewelry – but to date there is archaeological information on the actual production of only one type of item – obsidian jewelry. Most of our knowledge of these crafts comes from the descriptions in Friar Sahagún's *Florentine Codex*. Information on the styles and uses of luxury goods is discussed in chapters 9 and 10.

Featherworking

Feather mosaic was perhaps the art form most unique to the Aztecs. Objects such as fans, shields, warriors' costumes, capes, headdresses, and decorative hangings were made by tying and gluing colorful feathers onto a stiff backing (figure 4.7). These were among the most valuable and esteemed items in Aztec culture. Unfortunately only eight examples survive today. Sahagún's noble informants were very familiar with the featherworkers and their products because many of the craftsmen worked directly for nobles. Most of what we know of featherworking comes from the friar's descriptions.[12]

The great beauty of Aztec feather mosaics derives from the

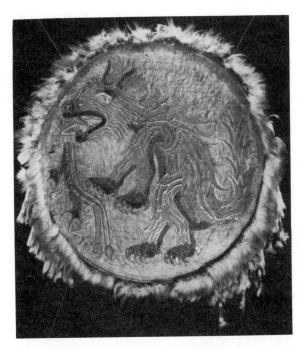

*Figure 4.7   Ceremonial featherwork shield (Courtesy Museum
für Völkerkunde, Vienna, object no. 43.380)*

bright colors of the feathers. Often, the feathers of readily
available local birds such as ducks and turkeys were dyed, but
the most striking colors were provided by the natural feathers
of lowland tropical birds such as parrots, macaws, and the
quetzal. The long tailfeathers of the quetzal in particular were
esteemed for their iridescent green color. Quetzal feathers figured
prominently in the painted and carved art of earlier Mesoamerican civilizations such as the Classic Maya and Teotihuacan.
The name of the Aztec feathered serpent god, Quetzalcoatl
("quetzal-feathered serpent") is a testimony to the importance
of these feathers in ancient Mesoamerica.

Production of a feather mosaic began with the preparation
of a stiff backing panel of cotton cloth and *maguey* fibers, held
together and given strength with several layers of glue. The
design was carefully drawn on a paper and cotton stencil, then
transferred to the backing. The feathers were attached with

maguey twine and glue. Inexpensive local feathers were applied first. These were covered with the more attractive, expensive exotic feathers. Finally, ornaments of gold and other materials often were added as parts of the design.

Sahagún describes a division of labor within the households of featherworkers. The master artisan prepared the stencils and backing, and applied the feathers; women of the household dyed and organized the feathers; and children prepared the glue. Like many Aztec crafts, featherworking was a hereditary occupation. Sons of artisans learned the craft by serving as apprentices. The *Codex Mendoza* shows several master crafts-men, including a featherworker, instructing their sons in their trades (figure 4.8).[13]

Aztec featherworkers lived together in special *calpolli* or neigh-borhoods (see chapter 6) in the major cities such as Tenoch-titlan, Tlatelolco, and Texcoco. The best-known of these *calpolli*, located in Tlatelolco, was called Amantlan, and feather-workers became known as *amanteca*. Within the *calpolli*, the featherworkers had their own temple and school, where they joined together to sponsor and participate in public rituals. The exclusivity of the *calpolli* and the hereditary foundation for apprenticeship in the craft made featherworking a restricted occupation, organized much like medieval European guilds.

Most of the feather mosaics were produced for rulers or other nobles, who provided the raw materials and supported the artisans with food and other necessities. The nobles used featherwork items for a variety of purposes – for clothing, for gifts to other nobles, for palace decorations, and to adorn images of the gods. The artisans were not members of the noble class, however. They could not wear their products, and if they became wealthy, they were prohibited from openly dis-playing their wealth. In addition to their work for the ruler and other high nobles, many amanteca also produced items for sale in the marketplace. This was an independent operation in which the feathers and other raw materials were purchased in the market rather than obtained from a noble patron. Although commoners were permitted to buy feather items in the market, most could not afford to do so. The majority of these items probably were purchased by low-ranking nobles, priests, and wealthy merchants.

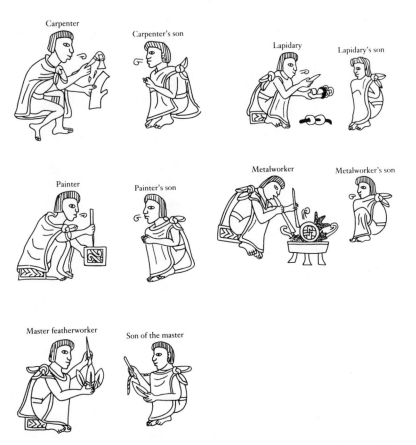

Figure 4.8 Master craftsmen instructing their sons in their crafts (Codex Mendoza 1992:v.4:145; folio 70r)

Goldsmithing

Some of the most beautiful and sophisticated art objects produced by the Aztecs were gold jewelry made with the lost wax process.[14] In contrast to copper and bronze metallurgy, which had not become fully established in the Valley of Mexico, goldworking had developed into an important luxury craft in Tenochtitlan. The technology of goldsmithing entered Mesoamerica from Central America through systems of overland trade during the Classic period. By the Late Aztec period,

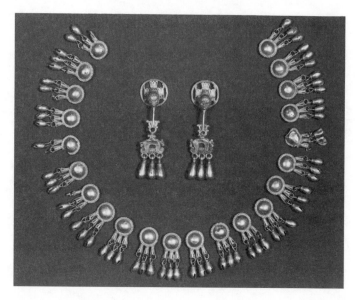

Figure 4.9   Gold necklace and pendants made by lost-wax casting
(Each bead is 3 cm high; photograph courtesy of Dumbarton
Oaks Research Library and Collections, Washington, DC)

the Mixtec peoples of Oaxaca had acquired a reputation as
master goldsmiths. Of the Prehispanic gold objects still in
existence, some of the finest examples come from Mixtec tombs
in the Valley of Oaxaca. We know that a number of Mixtec
artisans came to live in Tenochtitlan, but it is not clear from
the sources whether Aztec gold jewelry was made by resident
Mixtecs, native Aztecs, or both.

Sahagún devotes a chapter to goldsmiths, most of which is
taken up with a detailed description of lost wax casting. This
was the primary technique for manufacturing lip plugs, bells,
pendants and other items of gold jewelry (figure 4.9). A mold
was made of clay, sand, and charcoal. First a solid inner section was fashioned and the outer surface modelled to the desired shape. When it had dried and hardened, a thin layer of
beeswax and resin was placed over the mold and carefully
pressed to cover the contours evenly. The finished gold piece
would be an exact replica of this wax layer. The outer surface
of the wax was modelled into the form desired for the gold

piece, and then it was covered with moist clay to form the outer mold. When this section dried and hardened partially, a tube was inserted for the wax to escape. The completed mold was baked, which caused the clay to harden and the wax to melt and run out. The gold ore was heated over a fire in a ceramic vessel, and the liquid metal was poured into the mold to form the object.

As far as we can tell from the limited evidence in Sahagún and other sources, the goldsmiths were organized in a manner similar to the featherworkers. They lived in their own *calpolli* and participated in common rituals in honor of their patron god, Xipe Totec. Most of their work was done for the king and nobles. The depiction in the *Codex Mendoza* of a goldsmith teaching his apprentice son the trade (figure 4.8) suggests that goldsmithing, like featherworking, was a hereditary occupation. The complexity of the techniques also suggests a hereditary craft with a long period of apprenticeship.

Lapidary Production

Aztec lapidary specialists used a variety of precious stones to make jewelry and other valuable objects. As described by Sahagún:

> Their creations were lip pendants, lip plugs, and ear plugs, ear plugs of obsidian, rock crystal, and amber; white ear plugs; and all manner of necklaces; bracelets.[15]

Obsidian ear spools (also called ear plugs) were among the finest objects made by lapidaries (figure 4.10). Great skill and patience were needed to grind the obsidian into the large thin cylinders favored by Aztec nobles. These ear spools were worn in the earlobes like earrings. Ear spools and lip plugs of obsidian are the only Aztec luxury craft items whose manufacture has been thoroughly documented by archaeologists; this information is discussed in the section on Otumba below. Lapidary producers also worked with jade, turquoise, amethyst, chert, and shell. Jade was the single most valuable material to the Aztecs, partly because of its beauty and rarity (it had to be imported from southern Mesoamerica) and partly because of the symbolism of the color green (which stood for water, fertility,

Figure 4.10 *Obsidian ear spools. These examples of fine jewelry took great craftsmanship to manufacture (Height: 3.5 cm; photograph courtesy the Metropolitan Museum of Art, The Michael C. Rockefeller Memorial Collection, Bequest of Nelson A. Rockefeller, 1979. 1979.206.1088, .1089; all rights reserved, the Metropolitan Museum of Art)*

and value). Necklaces and bracelets of jade beads were among the most common forms of jewelry.

Mosaics were another lapidary product.[16] Small tiles of turquoise were used in abundance with shell and obsidian tiles providing color contrast. The most spectacular Aztec mosaics were human skulls covered partially or entirely with stone and shell tiles. Mosaics and inlays were also applied to jewelry, knife handles, stone sculptures, and a variety of other objects.

Ethnohistoric information on the organization of lapidary production is similar to that for featherworking and goldsmithing. Lapidary craftsmen probably lived in their own *calpolli*, worshipped their own gods, and had a system of apprenticeship and hereditary recruitment (see figure 4.8). Lapidary products were important enough to the noble class that these artisans were able to influence the course of Aztec imperial expansion. Friar Durán states that lapidary workers convinced Motecuhzoma to conquer certain towns in order to provide them with a more secure source of the special sands and abrasives they needed for their craft. According to ethnohistorical sources, Xochimilco in the southern Valley of Mexico was a center of lapidary production. Archaeological fieldwork has recently identified another city with significant number of lapidaries, Otumba.

Otumba: an Aztec Craft Center

The discovery of abundant evidence for specialized craft production at the site of Otumba in the late 1980s took many archaeologists and ethnohistorians by surprise. Prior to the Otumba project, scholars had presumed that most craft specialists lived in Tenochtitlan. Archaeologists who studied smaller cities and towns had found little evidence for craft production beyond the ubiquitous spindle whorls that were discarded or lost in the process of domestic textile production. Some suggested that there had been limited, part-time producers of pottery and stone tools in the rural areas, but most agreed that the existence of large numbers of urban specialists residing in towns outside of the imperial capital was unlikely.[17]

Otumba had been a city-state capital in the Teotihuacan Valley. Unlike most former Aztec towns, the colonial and modern Otumba settlements are adjacent, rather than on top of, the Aztec occupation. The archaeological site is not very impressive today because most of the architecture has been disturbed or destroyed by farming. *Maguey* plants cover the area (figure 4.5). There isn't even a tall pyramid left at Otumba, and from the perspective of monumental archaeology, the site doesn't appear to have much to offer. Yet from the perspective of social archaeology, Otumba has yielded some of the most important evidence to date of Aztec craft production.

The Otumba archaeological project was directed by Thomas H. Charlton, Deborah L. Nichols, and Cynthia Otis Charlton.[18] Thomas Charlton had worked previously on various fieldwork projects in the Otumba area. His observations of certain artifacts on the surface of the Aztec town site (including spindle whorls, obsidian cores, and figurine molds) led him to suspect the existence of numerous specialized craft workshops at Otumba. A fieldwork project was needed to test this hypothesis.

Charlton, Nichols, and Otis Charlton designed a program of systematic surface sampling in which they picked up all artifacts from each of 1,150 five by five meter squares. The entire two square kilometers of the Aztec city was divided into a grid of 50 meter squares. One five by five meter collection was made in each of these squares, with additional collections taken in those areas with abundant craft production artifacts. These intensive surface collections proved to be very successful in documenting craft production activities at Otumba. Most of the town site has been plowed by farmers in recent times, resulting in the churning up of thousands of previously-buried artifacts. The large five by five meter units used for surface collections yielded enough artifacts to reconstruct activities in each area of the site, including both widespread domestic tasks and specialized craft work. By taking at least one surface collection from every 50 meter square of the site, the archaeologists were able to trace the spatial distribution of craft production activities across the entire settlement. The surface collections were augmented by test excavations in specific workshop locations.

The Otumba surface collections contained evidence for the manufacture of seven major types of products: obsidian blades, obsidian bifacial tools, basalt tools, lapidary products, ceramic goods, cotton textiles, and *maguey* textiles. The locations of concentrations of production debris are shown in figure 4.11. Evidence for the manufacture of obsidian prismatic blades consisted of very high concentrations of obsidian in the surface collections coupled with the presence of debitage (the waste byproducts of chipped stone tool making) and exhausted cores (figure 4.1). These remains were concentrated in several discrete areas of the site (figure 4.11), which suggested a series of small household-based workshops. Evidence for the manufacture of obsidian bifacial tools was also recovered by the Otumba project, but not in the urban center; these items were made at outlying rural village sites that had been part of the wider Otumba city-state. Basalt, a porous volcanic rock readily available in the Otumba region, was worked into both domestic implements (such as manos and *metates* for grinding corn) and industrial tools (scrapers for loosening the fibers from *maguey* leaves and polishers for finishing lapidary products). The waste flakes and production tools that indicate basalt working were found at a few scattered locations within the city.

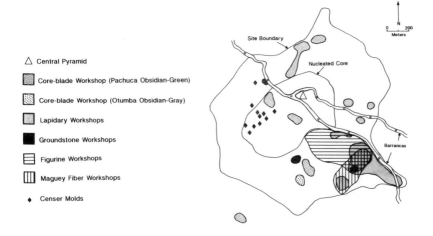

△ Central Pyramid

▨ Core-blade Workshop (Pachuca Obsidian-Green)

▨ Core-blade Workshop (Otumba Obsidian-Gray)

☐ Lapidary Workshops

■ Groundstone Workshops

▤ Figurine Workshops

▥ Maguey Fiber Workshops

◆ Censer Molds

Figure 4.11   Map of the Aztec city of Otumba showing the locations of areas of craft production (After Otis Charlton 1994, figure 8.1; reproduced with permission)

Probably the most spectacular evidence for craft production at Otumba concerned the lapidary industry. From the artifacts recovered in the surface collections and test excavations, Cynthia Otis Charlton reconstructed nearly the entire sequence of steps involved in the manufacture of ear spools, lip plugs, and beads from obsidian and other stones, including chert, and rock crystal (figure 4.12). This is the only case where the complete production process of an Aztec luxury craft has been documented archaeologically.

The lapidary workshops at Otumba were identified by the presence of production tools (perforators and polishers of basalt), pre-manufacture blanks, and partially finished products. Ear spools were made from partially-used prismatic blade cores of obsidian, following the technological steps shown in figure 4.12. Because of the brittleness of the volcanic glass, many items broke in the process of manufacture and were discarded. The Otumba artifacts included broken examples from each step of the sequence shown in figure 4.12. Finished pieces were not recovered in the surface collections, however. Most of these had been traded away in Aztec times, and those that

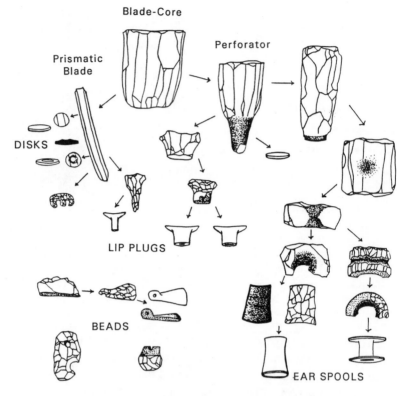

Figure 4.12   Technological sequence for the manufacture of obsidian jewelry (Drawing by Cynthia Otis Charlton; reproduced with permission)

ended up on the surface of the site were broken by plowing or picked up by farmers long before the archaeologists arrived. Most lapidary production was carried out in three zones in the southeast portion of the site (figure 4.11). The artifacts were associated with residences, which implies that artisans worked in their homes or else had workshops close to their houses. It is difficult to determine from archaeological evidence whether the artisans were full-time or part-time specialists.

The Otumba ceramic industries used molds to manufacture several types of objects, including incense burners, figurines, and spindle whorls. Evidence for this production consisted of

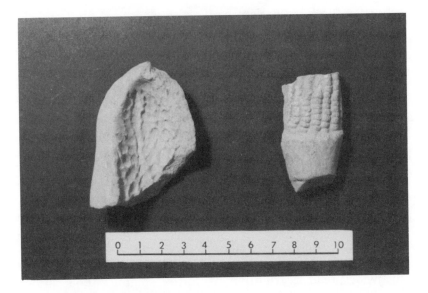

Figure 4.13   Ceramic figurine of a maize ear (right) and a ceramic mold (left) used to form this or other similar figurines. Both artifacts are from Otumba (Photograph by Cynthia Otis Charlton; reproduced with permission)

the ceramic molds, production errors and rejects, and large numbers of the finished products. No kilns or firing areas were located, and the type of extensive excavations required to find such features were beyond the scope of the original Otumba project. Long-handled incense burners, used in both domestic and temple rituals, were manufactured in molds found in the western portion of Otumba. Small ceramic figurines, in the forms of people, animals, and gods, also were produced in large numbers. A large district in the southeast portion of the city contained many molds for figurines (figure 4.13), high concentrations of broken figurine fragments, and instances of duplicate figurines clearly made from the same mold. These workshops also turned out other small mold-made ceramic objects such as clay balls (perhaps used as blowgun pellets), rattle balls, rattles, stamps, and small spindle whorls (see figure 4.2).

Molds for the manufacture of both types of ceramic spindle

whorls – the large variety used to spin *maguey* fiber and the small variety used for cotton – were found at Otumba, but with differing distributions. The small cotton whorls were made in small numbers at the figurine workshops, whereas the large *maguey* whorls were produced in larger numbers in a zone of possible *maguey* fiber workshops. Cotton whorls were recovered from all parts of the site, pointing to widespread domestic cloth production. Used *maguey* whorls, on the other hand, were found primarily in the same southeast zone in which they were produced. This concentration of whorls in one area may indicate the existence of workshop areas dedicated to specialized *maguey* cloth production.

The suggestion that *maguey* fiber (and cloth) may have been produced by specialists in workshops is somewhat controversial. As discussed above, ethnohistoric sources state that spinning and weaving were done by all women in their homes, and the widespread distribution of cotton spinning tools among houses and across sites conforms to this model. *Maguey* cloth workshops are not mentioned in ethnohistoric sources, but if they were limited to smaller cities such as Otumba this is not surprising.

No other Aztec archaeological site has produced this level of evidence for the widespread and concentrated manufacture of so many different craft items. Taken together, the findings of the Otumba project suggest several patterns in the organization of craft production at the city. First, the excavations indicate that production areas or workshops were located within or adjacent to houses rather than in separate workshop buildings. Second, the concentration of several of the industries (particularly the lapidary, figurine, and *maguey* cloth industries) in their own zones or areas points to specialization on the level of the neighborhood or *calpolli*, as Sahagún described for the luxury artisans. Third, the dating of the collections indicates that the major period of occupation and craft production at Otumba was the Late Aztec period, when both production and exchange in central Mexico reached their maximum development.

Just as any successful research project generates as many new questions as it answers, the results of the Otumba project suggest questions for future research. What, for example, was the role of the elite in sponsoring or controlling craft production? This question is difficult to answer at Otumba because plowing of the site has disturbed clear architectural evidence for elite houses or districts.[19] What were the destinations of the goods produced at Otumba? The archaeologists have determined the places of origin for most of the raw materials used in craft production, but tracing the exchange of the finished products is not yet possible. Many of these goods must have been intended for export through the markets since the level of production far exceeded the needs of the 10,000 or so residents of Otumba. But did Otumba craftsmen supply only the Otumba city-state, the wider Teotihuacan Valley, the entire Valley of Mexico, or perhaps an even larger area of the Aztec empire? My excavations at Yautepec in Morelos have yielded fragments of Otumba-style obsidian jewelry (see chapter 8), but it is not yet possible to match the finished artifacts with their places of manufacture.

The Otumba project has contributed greatly to our understanding of the techniques and organization of Aztec craft production, providing the first good evidence for the existence of a center of urban craft specialists outside of Tenochtitlan. How did these products move from producer to consumer? The various utilitarian and luxury crafts were part of an economy with quite sophisticated systems of exchange. The size, organization, and ubiquity of Aztec marketplaces greatly impressed the Spanish conquerors. Anyone – commoners or nobles – could obtain virtually any good or service present in Mesoamerica at these markets. Professional merchants were organized into guilds and both regulated the markets and mounted long trading expeditions to the far corners of Mesoamerica. This was a complex and active economy with several types of currency in circulation, and the Aztec state controlled only a very small part of the overall economy. I now turn from the topic of production to that of exchange.

5

Merchants, Markets, and Money

> On reaching the market-place, . . . we were astounded at the great number of people and the quantities of merchandise, and at the orderliness and good arrangements that prevailed, for we had never seen such a thing before . . . You could see every kind of merchandise to be found anywhere in New Spain.
>
> Bernal Díaz del Castillo[1]

The Aztecs, like many other civilizations, relied on markets and merchants to move goods from producer to consumer. By "market," I mean a physical space – a marketplace – where buyers and sellers congregate to exchange goods and services. Markets of this type are still thriving institutions in modern Mesoamerica, and these marketplaces can provide an idea of what their Aztec predecessors may have been like.[2]

Where they still flourish, markets in the cities tend to be held daily, in permanent buildings. Markets in smaller settlements usually are held only once a week, often in an open public plaza. On market day, otherwise sleepy towns and villages became bustling centers of activity. Vendors set up temporary stalls to sell their wares, and buyers arrive early to take care of their weekly purchases. Some of the vendors are professional merchants who travel from market to market; others are farmers or petty artisans, or members of their families, who sell their products as a part-time activity (figure 5.1). In areas with a high population and a complex economy, individual markets are usually linked together into an integrated market system. Such was the case in the Aztec Valley of Mexico, and in many ways the scale and complexity of the Aztec market system surpassed most modern market systems in Mesoamerica.

Marketplaces

Almost every Aztec settlement, from the imperial capital to the smallest villages, had a marketplace that came alive weekly on

Figure 5.1   A modern Maya woman selling vegetables in the marketplace, Merida, Yucatan (Photograph by Michael E. Smith)

market day (the Aztec week was 5 days long). The sheer volume of goods that moved through Aztec markets was enormous, but the efficiency and success of the market system in distributing goods and services relieved the state of the need to manage exchange activities closely. Unlike in the Inca empire and in some other early civilizations, where the central government maintained heavy control over the economy in general, Aztec markets and trade were largely independent of the state.[3]

The Tlatelolco Market

The biggest marketplace in the ancient New World was located in Tenochtitlan's twin city Tlatelolco. Hernando Cortés, Bernal Díaz del Castillo, and the other Spanish conquerors were astounded by the great size of the market plaza, the tens of thousands of people, the many hundreds of types of goods for sale, and the orderliness and organization of the market. The best description of the market is that of Cortés himself, and it is worth quoting the conqueror in detail to get an idea of the richness of the Tlatelolco market:

> The city has many open squares in which markets are continuously held and the general business of buying and selling proceeds. One square in particular is twice as big as that of Salamanca and completely surrounded by arcades where there are daily more than sixty thousand folk buying and selling. Every kind of merchandise such as may be met with in every land is for sale there, whether of food and victuals, or ornaments of gold and silver, or lead, brass, copper, tin, precious stones, bones, shells, snails and feathers . . .
>
> There is a street of game where they sell . . . rabbits, hares, deer and small dogs which they breed especially for eating. There is a street of herb-sellers where there are all manner of roots and medicinal plants that are found in the land . . . There are barbers' shops where you may have your hair washed and cut. There are other shops where you may obtain food and drink. There are street porters such as we have in Spain to carry packages . . .
>
> All kinds of vegetables may be found there. There are many different sorts of fruits . . . All kinds of cotton thread in various colors may be bought in skeins, very much in the same way as in the great silk exchange of Granada, except that the quantities are far less. They have colors for painting of as good quality as any in Spain, and of as pure shades as may be found anywhere . . .
>
> A great deal of chinaware is sold of very good quality . . . Maize is sold both as grain and in the form of bread . . . Pastries made from game and fish pies may be seen on sale . . .
>
> There is nothing to be found in all the land which is not sold in these markets, for over and above what I have mentioned there are so many and such various other things that on account of their very number and the fact that I do not know their names, I cannot now detail them. Each kind of merchandise is sold in its own particular street and no other kind may be sold there: this rule is very well enforced. All is sold by number and measure, but up till now no weighing by balance has been observed. A very fine building in the great square serves as a kind of audience chamber where ten or a dozen persons are always seated, as judges, who deliberate on all cases arising in the market and pass sentence on evildoers. In the square itself there are officials who continually walk amongst the people inspecting goods exposed for sale and the measures by which they are sold, and on certain occasions I have seen them destroy measures which were false.[4]

The essential features of Cortés's description of the Tlatelolco market – the list of many diverse goods and services, the orderliness of the vendors, and the presence of judges – are repeated in other early accounts. The goods offered for sale included both luxury items and utilitarian goods, plus a wide variety of meat, produce, prepared foods and drink, live animals, and many services. The innumerable tiny stalls selling utilitarian craft goods were operated by the families of artisans. Other stalls were operated by full-time or part-time merchants of various sorts. The well-known, professional *pochteca* merchants (see below) sold their goods in the market, and they also served as the market judges mentioned by Cortés.

The Tlatelolco market was the major marketplace serving both Tenochtitlan and Tlatelolco. It was easily reached from the mainland by either canoe or causeway. Given the limitations on transport in an economy without the wheel or draft animals, the canoe was of paramount importance for moving heavy burdens. Early Spanish observers noted that the lakes around the imperial capital were filled with canoes going and coming from the market. The growth of Tenochtitlan and Tlatelolco from small towns into a single giant metropolis was due in no small part to the success of this market, and the city's island location was an important contributor to that success.

The Valley of Mexico Market System

The Tlatelolco market did not operate in isolation. It formed part of a larger regional system of markets that covered the entire Valley of Mexico. The Nahuatl term *tianquiz* was used to refer to any market, large or small. Nearly all cities and towns had marketplaces, but they were considerably smaller than the Tlatelolco market, and they did not excite much comment. One early writer, Friar Torquemada, stated that there were countless markets in central Mexico, but since he did not have enough space to describe them all, he would limit his description to Tlatelolco.[5] Although markets existed in the Early Aztec period, their size and importance increased greatly in Late Aztec times. All of the eyewitness accounts, of course, pertain to the markets of the Late Aztec B period.

Some clues to the nature of markets outside of Tlatelolco are provided by an early colonial register of the tax paid by vendors in the market of Coyoacan, a city-state capital in the southern Valley of Mexico. The local *tlatoani* (king) collected

*Figure 5.2   An Aztec market. The individuals with wooden
collars are slaves (After Durán 1971:pl.29; drawing by
Ellen Cesarski)*

the market tax in Spanish money; in Prehispanic times the tax
would have been paid in cacao beans or cotton *quachtli,* the
principal forms of money. Most of the Coyoacan vendors sold
utilitarian goods although some luxury items were mentioned.
Vendors included both the artisans who produced the goods
and merchants or sellers whose relationship to the producers
is not known. Among the vendors offering utilitarian wares
were specialized potters (both stewpot makers and griddle
makers), basket makers, obsidian-blade knappers, *maguey-*
garment makers, broom sellers, lime sellers, medicine sellers,
and lake scum sellers. Merchants selling luxury goods included
feather sellers, small bell makers, and metal workers. A drawing of an Aztec market from Friar Durán's account (figure 5.2)
shows four vendors (on the top and left side) selling to three
buyers. Two slaves, with wooden collars, are for sale; the female
one demonstrates her skills at spinning cotton. In the center is
a round altar where images of the market gods were erected.

Some Aztec markets specialized in particular types of goods. For example, markets in the towns of Azcapotzalco and Itzocan were widely known for the sale of slaves. The holy city of Cholula, in the Puebla Valley east of the Valley of Mexico, had a reputation as a center for trade in luxury items such as jewels, precious stones, and fine featherwork. The market in Acolman, a town in the Teotihuacan Valley, was famous for the sale of dogs. Friar Durán described it as follows:

> It was established that the dogs were to be sold in the periodic market at Acolman and that all those desirous of selling or buying were to go there. Most of the produce, then, which went to this *tianguiz* [market] consisted of small- and medium-sized dogs of all types, and everyone in the land went to buy dogs there – as they do today [ca. 1577], because at this time the same trade is carried on. One day I went to observe the market day there, just to be an eyewitness and discover the truth. I found more than four hundred large and small dogs tied up in crates, some already sold, others still for sale. And there were such piles of ordure that I was overwhelmed.[6]

Only a few Aztec markets were specialized in this fashion. The most important distinctions among markets related less to specialized goods than to hierarchical position. The notion of a hierarchy of marketplaces is crucial for understanding the operation of the Valley of Mexico market system, an example of what economic anthropologists call a complex interlocking market system.[7] In the Valley of Mexico, there were four hierarchical levels of markets or central places. The huge Tlatelolco marketplace was the sole example of the top level. The second level consisted of a few cities whose markets were larger or more important than most. Texcoco, the second-largest city, was a second-level market center, as was Xochimilco. The third level comprised markets in city-state centers like Otumba, Coyoacan, and Acolman. Finally, the lowest hierarchical level was filled by the markets of the smaller towns and villages. The levels were distinguished by the numbers of people buying and selling (with greater numbers attending the higher-level markets), the quantity and variety of goods and services offered (with more offered at higher-level markets), and by frequency. The highest-level markets met daily, the city-state markets met once a week (every five days), and the smallest markets met even less frequently.

The periodic schedule of the markets suited the needs of both merchants and consumers.[8] Itinerant merchants travelled from town to town, setting up at each marketplace on market day. This circuit allowed them to cover a wider area, thereby satisfying a larger demand for their goods, than if they were limited to a single marketplace. Most consumers did not need to attend the market every day, so the periodic schedule was convenient for them, also.

Aztec markets were not just economic institutions; they also served an important social function. Friar Durán described the social attraction of Aztec markets as follows:

> The markets were so inviting, pleasurable, appealing, and gratifying to these people that great crowds attended, and still attend, them, especially during the big fairs, as is well known to all. I suspect that if I said to a market woman accustomed to going from market to market: "Look, today is market day in such and such a town. What would you rather do, go from here right to Heaven or to that market?" I believe this would be her answer: "Allow me to go the market first, and then I will go to Heaven." She would be happier to lose those minutes of glory to visit the marketplace and walk about hither and thither without any gain or profit, to satisfy her hunger and whim to see the *tianguiz*.[9]

The excursion into town on market day was a social event that provided one of the few opportunities for people who lived in different towns or villages to meet one another. On market day one could learn the latest news or gossip, talk with friends and colleagues, meet potential spouses, and generally keep up with the social life of the community, while also taking care of purchases and seeing the latest goods and styles. Most marketplaces had one or more shrines whose gods watched over the proceedings (figure 5.2), and market day also had its religious functions to complement its economic and social aspects.

Merchants

The occupation of merchant was an important one among the Aztecs. From written sources we know of at least two types of professional merchant: the *pochteca* or guild-merchants of the Valley of Mexico who traded on an international scale, and regional merchants whose activities were confined to smaller areas. In the *Florentine Codex*, Friar Sahagún devoted all of book 9 to the *pochteca*, and as a result we have considerable information on their activities and lifestyle; in contrast, there are only scattered references to Aztec regional merchants.

The *pochteca* were full-time professionals who occupied a special status within Aztec society that was lower than the nobility but higher than most commoners. Their activities included trade expeditions both within and outside of the empire, oversight of marketplaces in the Valley of Mexico, and foreign service for the emperor in the form of spying and fighting with enemy states. Although some of the *pochteca* trade was carried out directly for the state, the bulk of their transactions were privately motivated and financed. Most of the abundant luxury goods that Aztec nobles used to display their wealth and status – items such as jewelry, stone carvings, and fancy clothing – were either purchased from *pochteca* or made from materials brought by *pochteca*, who had obtained them from foreign or local sources.

Some *pochteca* became quite wealthy to the point where their riches surpassed those of many nobles. Since merchants were not part of the noble class, however, they could not display their wealth openly in public. Much of their trade was carried out in secret to hide the extent of their success. When a group of *pochteca* returned home from a lengthy expedition, they arranged to enter the city under the cover of darkness:

> Not by day but by night they swiftly entered by boat. And as to their goods, no one could see how much there was; perhaps they carefully hid – covered up – all the boats ... And when he had quickly come to unload what he had acquired, then swiftly he took away his boat. When it dawned, nothing remained.[10]

The *pochteca* were organized into guilds with closely-controlled, hereditary membership. These guilds existed in only twelve cities: Tenochtitlan, Tlatelolco, Azcapotzalco, Cuauhtitlan, Huitzilopochco, Chalco, Coatlinchan, Huexotla, Mixcoac, Otumba, Texcoco, and Xochimilco. These cities, all located in the Valley of Mexico, included the major political capitals (Tenochtitlan and Texcoco), the most active economic centers (Tlatelolco, Otumba, and Xochimilco), and other important

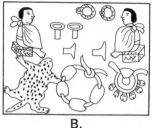

A.   B.

Figure 5.3   Pochteca *merchants. A: merchants following a trail*
with loads of merchandise on their backs (After Sahagún
1950–82:bk.9:fig.13); B: merchants in a market with some of
their wares: gold finger rings, gold lip plugs, obsidian lip plugs,
a jaguar skin, a necklace of jade and turquoise, and a pendant
of gold (After Sahagún 1950–82:bk.9:fig.3; drawings by
Ellen Cesarski)

city-state capitals. Merchants were hierarchically ranked; among
the categories were "principal merchants" at the top, followed
by slave dealers, disguised and spying merchants, and ordinary
pochteca who were called *oztomeca*. At the bottom of the order
were apprentice merchants who were in the process of learning
the trade. The *pochteca* guilds had their own laws of conduct,
which they enforced in their own courts, distinct from the
regular legal system.

The *pochteca* organized large expeditions lasting many
months to conduct their trade with distant areas. Each expedition would involve several merchants and apprentices as well
as a crew of professional carriers or *tlamama* to bear the loads
of goods in large backpacks (figure 5.3A). Friar Sahagún noted
that the merchants were trained soldiers and carried weapons
for protection:

> As they traveled the road, they went girt for war. They bore their
> shields, their obsidian-bladed swords, [and] their devices, because
> they passed through the enemy's land, where they might die [and]
> where they took captives.[11]

The merchants would plan their itinerary carefully with stops at
a succession of marketplaces in order to obtain the best bargains
possible. In Mesoamerica, these merchants were permitted to

cross foreign borders, even those between hostile enemies. When *pochteca* traded in markets outside of the empire, they often served as spies for the Mexica, gathering information on resources, armies, and defenses. A portion of their trade was conducted directly for the emperor. For example, the emperor Ahuitzotl (r. 1486–1502) gave the *pochteca* 1,600 cotton cloths, which they traded for such luxury items as jade, shell, and feathers for the ruler. He also provided an armed guard for the expedition, which passed through or near enemy territory.

Most of the goods traded by the *pochteca* were luxury items of high value but low bulk that could be transported easily by human carrier.[12] As described by Friar Durán, the profession of merchant involved:

> buying and selling, going forth to all the markets of the land, bartering cloth for jewels, jewels for feathers, feathers for stones, and stones for slaves, always dealing in things of importance, of renown, and of high value. These [men] strengthened their social position with their wealth.[13]

Among the trade goods of the *pochteca*, listed by Sahagún, were elaborately-decorated capes and skirts, colorful tropical bird feathers, numerous objects of gold, necklaces, spinning bowls, earspools, obsidian blades and knives, shells, coral, needles, animal fur and skins, various herbs and dyes, slaves, and jewelry of jade, jadeite and turquoise (figure 5.3B).

Far less information exists about the regional merchants, called *tlanecuilo,* who were not part of *pochteca* guilds. We do know that these middlemen were common participants in Aztec markets. They tended to trade in a smaller range of goods than the *pochteca*, and most of their goods were foodstuffs and utilitarian items, not luxuries. These included cacao, maize, amaranth, chia, chili, tortillas, turkeys, fish, salt, sandals, cotton, gourd bowls, baskets, and wood.[14] Many of the *tlanecuilo* specialized in a particular type of good, for example salt was a common specialty. The division of labor among merchants, with *pochteca* trading primarily in luxuries and *tlanecuilo* in food and utilitarian goods, ensured that markets throughout the empire were well supplied with all types of goods. How did consumers buy these goods?

Figure 5.4 Cacao pods. Cacao beans, which grow inside these pods, were used as currency (Photograph by Dean Lambert; reproduced with permission)

Money

Some marketplace exchanges may have been carried out by bartering one good for another, but the Aztecs also used at least two forms of money: cacao beans and cotton textiles.[15] Cacao beans grow in large pods on trees in the southern tropics of Mesoamerica (figure 5.4) and are the main ingredient in chocolate. Cacao was costly because it had to be brought to central Mexico from distant lowland areas, of which the southernmost imperial province of Xoconochco was the primary source. Although the Aztecs made a form of hot chocolate beverage, only nobles could afford to drink it. Most people used cacao as currency.

Cacao beans were used for small purchases. For example, one obsidian blade was worth 5 cacao beans. An early colonial list of market prices from 1545 gives an idea of the worth of various goods as expressed in cacao beans, assuming that prices had not changed too radically in the 25 years following the Spanish conquest:

- One good turkey hen is worth 100 full cacao beans, or 120 shrunken cacao beans . . .
- A hare or forest rabbit is worth 100 cacao beans each.
- A small rabbit is worth 30.
- One turkey egg is worth 3 cacao beans.
- An avocado newly picked is worth 3 cacao beans . . .
- One large tomato will be equivalent to a cacao bean . . .
- A long narrow green chile, 5 (for a cacao bean) . . .
- A newly picked prickly pear cactus fruit is equivalent to one cacao bean, when fully ripe two cactus fruit (for a cacao bean) . . .
- Chopped firewood [a bundle or log] is equivalent to 1 cacao bean . . .
- A tamale is exchanged for a cacao bean . . .
- Fish wrapped in maize husks is worth 3 cacao beans.[16]

The use of cacao for currency was so widespread and economically important that counterfeiting and deceptions were serious problems. Unscrupulous vendors would remove the outer skin from a bean and stuff it with dirt or sawdust. The doctored "beans" were then mixed with a batch of real beans to be passed off on naive customers. That this practice was commonplace is implied by a Nahuatl-language Christian confessional manual recorded by Friar Alonso de Molina in 1569. The priests would ask merchants:

And when you sold cacao beans, perhaps you mixed your bad cacao beans with the good ones to merchandise them all together, whereby you deceive the people? . . . And perhaps you toast the small, the shrunken cacao beans, whereby you enlarge them so they will appear plump?[17]

There were even specific laws to punish cacao counterfeiters.

For larger purchases, the Aztecs used *quachtli*, cotton capes of standardized sizes. Any family, noble or commoner, could weave *quachtli* as part of their normal domestic cloth production (see chapter 4). Nobles, city-states, and temples also received them through tribute payments. There were different sizes and grades of *quachtli* with corresponding levels of value. Three common grades were worth 65, 80, and 100 cacao beans each, and some highly valuable examples were worth up to 300 cacao beans. It was said that 20 *quachtli* could support a commoner for a year in Tenochtitlan. Among the expensive items that could be purchased with this money were gold lip plugs (25 *quachtli* each) and necklaces of fine jade beads (600 *quachtli*).

Material Evidence for Aztec Commerce

The ethnohistoric accounts of markets and merchants reviewed above provide a good overview of the forms and organization of Aztec commerce, but they are short on concrete information about the movements of the specific goods that were exchanged. Archaeology has begun to fill in this missing information. In some cases, the mere presence of distinctive foreign goods at a site provides evidence for trade. For example, when Aztec III Black-on-Orange ceramics, manufactured in the Valley of Mexico, turn up at distant sites, we know that some sort of exchange must have taken place. In other cases, the origins of artifacts cannot be determined easily, but sophisticated techniques of chemical analysis can reveal the place of origin for some of the raw materials used in their manufacture. These techniques, which have been applied primarily to obsidian and pottery, allow archaeologists to trace exchange routes and trade connections with great precision.

Obsidian Exchange

Obsidian, because of its superior cutting abilities and the large numbers of finished blades that could be produced from a single core, was one of the most widely-traded goods in ancient Mesoamerica. The volcanic glass occurs in a limited number of natural deposits (all in highland areas), and obsidian from each geological source has a slightly different chemical composition. When an obsidian artifact is analyzed by one of several chemical techniques, its composition can be compared to samples taken from the various source areas to determine the geological location from which the obsidian originated.[18] Unfortunately we cannot determine the places where the material may have been worked between the quarry and the final location of the artifact at a site.

Fortunately for archaeologists, obsidian from the Pachuca source area has a distinctive green tint that easily distinguishes it from most other Mesoamerican obsidians without the need for expensive chemical analyses. Pachuca was the major source of obsidian for the Aztecs, and artifacts made of the distinctive green material are common at virtually every known Aztec site. Even at Otumba, whose city-state territory included the Otumba obsidian source, obsidian from Pachuca was imported for its superior qualities of prismatic blade manufacture. Sites like Cuexcomate and Yautepec in Morelos have yielded large quantities of obsidian, which was much preferred for tools over chert, an abundant, locally-available stone. Of the thousands of obsidian artifacts that we collected from these sites, over 90 per cent are of the green Pachuca variety.

Friar Sahagún lists obsidian blades among the goods traded by the *pochteca*, and Pachuca obsidian has been found at Late Aztec sites throughout much of Mesoamerica, including Yucatan and other Maya-speaking areas far beyond the borders of the Aztec empire. Pachuca obsidian even found its way to sites in the enemy Tarascan empire, and obsidian from Tarascan-controlled sources has been found at Aztec sites in Morelos. Native historical accounts give the impression that the Aztecs and Tarascans had little to do with each other beyond their battles and imperial activities (see chapter 7), but they pertain primarily to the activities of states and kings and are full of propaganda and elite ideology. The archaeological record, on the other hand, provides direct evidence for the concrete actions of people. Whatever Aztec and Tarascan nobles may have said about each other, merchants crossed imperial borders, and commoners bought and used obsidian tools that originated in enemy territory.

Ceramic Exchange

The use of chemical analysis to study exchange is much more difficult for ceramic artifacts than for those of obsidian, partly because the raw material – clay – is far more widely distributed.

In most cases, the fired clay cannot be traced to a specific point of origin. Nevertheless, from patterns in the chemical composition of potsherds, the archaeologist often can infer the number of different ceramic production centers represented in a collection of artifacts. Plotting the results on a map may point to the general areas where the production centers were located. A recent study of the chemical composition of the most abundant type of Aztec decorated ceramic (Aztec III Black-on-Orange) by Mary Hodge, Leah Minc, Hector Neff and James Blackman has overturned prior models of Aztec ceramic exchange and revealed that the system of production and exchange was more complex than previously thought.[19]

Fine-paste, orange ceramic bowls and plates painted with black designs were in use throughout the time of Aztec occupation of the Valley of Mexico. During the Early Aztec period, there were several distinct painting styles, each with limited spatial distributions (these styles are variants of the types Aztec I and Aztec II Black-on-Orange). This suggested to scholars that three to five regional production-exchange systems had operated in the valley. Chemical analyses of sherds from the different styles confirmed this interpretation and revealed the operation of several different local market systems with little exchange of ceramics between them.

In the Late Aztec period, a single style of painted ceramic, Aztec III Black-on-Orange, came to dominate the inventories of households in the Valley of Mexico. The painted designs on these ceramics are simple and busy, with many thin parallel lines combined with other motifs (figure 5.5). These ceramics give the impression of being mass produced. In comparison with the Early Aztec types, Aztec III ceramics show a high degree of stylistic uniformity throughout the Valley of Mexico and in the foreign areas to which they were traded (the plate shown in figure 5.5 was an import excavated from the provincial town of Cuexcomate in Morelos). Most archaeologists had assumed that this uniformity of style resulted from the operation of a single workshop or cluster of workshops, which supplied the entire Valley of Mexico with these pots through the market system.

The chemical analyses indicated a different situation, however. There were in fact at least four production zones for

Figure 5.5   Imported Aztec III Black-on-Orange ceramic plate excavated at Cuexcomate (Photograph by Michael E. Smith)

Aztec III ceramics, located in or near the cities of Tenochtitlan, Texcoco, Chalco, and Ixtapalapa. The workshops in each zone used local clays from around the lakes, shaped the clay into the same forms, and painted the vessels using a single, Valley-wide style. Although Mary Hodge and Leah Minc have been able to identify a few painted motifs whose use was largely limited to a single production area, most of the painted decorations are virtually identical in the four zones. These findings show that ceramic production was more decentralized than previously thought, and they imply a high level of exchange and stylistic interaction within the Valley of Mexico that led to a single popular style being produced in several different areas. This study also illustrates the pitfalls of studying ancient artifact exchange and interaction on the basis of style alone, without the benefit of chemical analysis.

During the Early and Late Aztec periods, the potters of each region of central Mexico developed their own distinctive ware of painted ceramics. Various styles of polychrome painting, with red, black, and orange designs on a white background,

Figure 5.6   Cholula Polychrome ceramic tripod plate
(Diameter: 23 cm; Photograph courtesy of the Saint Louis Art
Museum, no. 85–1950)

were applied to serving vessels in the valleys to the east, south, and west of the Valley of Mexico. These painted bowls were widely traded among regions, and many Aztec families, commoners and nobles alike, owned and used vessels from several different areas. The most elaborate polychrome ceramics were produced in Cholula (figure 5.6) and were among the most widely-traded wares in central Mexico. It was said that Motecuhzoma II would only eat off plates and dishes from Cholula, the finest in the empire.[20]

The simpler Aztec III Black-on-Orange pottery was also popular outside of its zone of origin in the Valley of Mexico. Examples imported from the valley are found at Late Aztec

Figure 5.7 Imported Valley of Mexico ceramic sherds from Cuexcomate and Capilco in Morelos. Upper left: Aztec III Black-on-Orange; upper right: Texcoco Fabric-Marked salt vessels; lower row: Xochimilco Polychrome (Photograph by Michael E. Smith)

archaeological sites throughout central Mexico. But it was not the only pottery from the Valley of Mexico that was exported to other areas. Excavations in Morelos typically uncover several decorated types imported from the Valley of Mexico (figure 5.7). One of these ceramic imports, called Texcoco Fabric Marked, was a basin for salt transport.

The Aztecs produced salt by boiling and evaporating the salt water from the Valley of Mexico lakes in large crude ceramic basins. The salt was packed into the same basins for transport.[21] Broken sherds from these salt vessels are easy to identify because their surfaces bear the impressions of coarse, burlap-like, *maguey* cloth that was applied to the vessels before firing to give them texture (figure 5.7). Salt vessels are found in large quantities at most Aztec archaeological sites in central Mexico. Every Aztec-period house I have excavated in Morelos yielded numerous sherds of this type, further evidence for extensive trading relations between the Valley of Mexico and surrounding areas. Major salt works were present in several of the outer provinces of the Aztec empire, but within 100 kilometers or so of the Valley, most households obtained their salt through trade with producers from around the Valley of Mexico lakes.

A Complex Economy

The various economic institutions and practices described in chapters 3, 4, and 5 all worked together in a dynamic and complex economy that bound the various parts of the Aztec empire into a single economic, social, and cultural unit. The growing populations required increased production of food and tools; the craftsmen who manufactured obsidian tools or ceramic vessels required merchants to sell their goods and to obtain raw materials; the merchants required money to facilitate their transactions; the use of money required additional production (for cloth) and trade (for lowland cacao); and the overall dynamism and prosperity of the economy encouraged further population growth. These trends are evident in the results of archaeological studies that have focused on the transition from the Early Aztec to the Late Aztec periods. Late Aztec occupations yield more imported artifacts, have more evidence for craft production activities, and show signs of heavier reliance on intensive farming methods.[22]

The market system was the institution that linked together the various sectors and regions within this dynamic economy. Marketing was also the one activity that allowed the average person to get ahead economically. As might be expected, some people tried to profit through cheating and deception. This concerned the first Spanish priests in central Mexico, and Friar Molina's confessional manual contains the following entries for petty traders:

> And when you sell chilis, perhaps you mix the small ones, the damaged ones with the large ones, whereby you deceive the people?

> And when you bought good capes, perhaps you inserted them among the poor ones? And when you filled in the holes of the

holey capes, perhaps you did not show your customer that the capes were holey, damaged, whereby you made sport of him?[23]

The fact that such practices were singled out by Friar Molina shows how important marketing was and how far some people would go to gain from their commercial dealings.

Clearly the Aztec economy was highly commercialized and dynamic, but it was not a capitalist economy. There was no wage labor, land was not a commodity to be bought and sold (except under certain limited circumstances), and opportunities for investment were limited to *pochteca* expeditions. Marketplace trade gave the Aztec commoners and merchants a chance to advance themselves, but only up to a point. The markets and the economy were embedded in a rigid system of social classes, and no amount of economic success would enable one to cross class barriers.

6

Family and Social Class

Here is the home of some people none of whom is baptized. The householder is named Tematl. His wife is named Teicuh. He has two children. The first is named Yaotl, now ten years old. The second is named Iconhui, now five years old. Here is his field: 10 matl [long], 7 matl wide that he works. Here is his tribute: every 80 days he delivers one quarter-length of a tribute cloak, one narrow cloak, and one turkey hen. That is all; no cacao, nothing else whatever. That is all. Here there are four included in his home.

Entry for a commoner household in a Nahuatl-language census from the town of Quauchichinollan, Morelos, ca. 1540[1]

The family or household was the basic social unit in Aztec society, but only in the past two decades have we begun to learn much about Aztec families. Thanks to translations of Nahuatl documents, such as the one quoted above, and archaeological excavations of houses, we are now gaining an appreciation for patterns of family life, household organization, and gender roles. One of the important new findings is the great influence that social classes played in structuring Aztec life and society. There were two social classes, nobles and commoners, separated by a wide and unpassable chasm.[2]

Nobles or lords ran the government, owned the land, commanded the army, and lived a more luxurious lifestyle than commoners. Although commoners greatly outnumbered nobles, they were obliged to serve these lords and pay them tribute. These great inequities might suggest that Aztec commoners were oppressed serfs leading bleak lives of servitude. This was not the case, however. Commoners had considerable control over their own destinies, and most managed to meet their basic needs and even provide themselves with some level of economic comfort in spite of their duties to lords and kings. Much of the evidence for this observation comes from recent excavations of houses and villages, where the hidden lives of anonymous peasants and artisans are being revealed for the first time.

Growing Up Aztec

In spite of the importance of social classes, there were many similarities in the way noble and commoner children were raised. The *Codex Mendoza* provides the most vivid and complete description of the Aztec life cycle.[3]

Birth and Childhood

As in all cultures, childbirth was an important event among the Aztecs. Women were aided by a midwife, whose duties went beyond simply helping with the birth process. Midwives also supervised the rituals that accompanied birth and named the newborn child. The *Codex Mendoza* describes the midwife's duties after birth as follows (see figure 6.1):

> At the end of four days after the infant's birth, the midwife carried the infant, naked, and took it to the courtyard of the house of the one who has given birth. And in the courtyard they had placed a small earthen tub of water on rushes or reeds [as a mat] called *tule*, where the said midwife bathed the said infant . . . And after the said bath, the said midwife ordered [three] boys to call out loudly the new name of the infant . . . And the name they gave it was that which the midwife wished. And at the beginning, when the infant was taken to be bathed, if it was a boy, they carried him with his symbol in his hand, and the symbol was the tool used by the boy's father, whether of the military or professions like metalworker, woodcarrier, or whatever other profession [figure 6.1, top right] . . . And if the infant was a girl, the symbol they gave her for bathing was a distaff with its spindle and its basket and a broom, which were the things she would use when she grew up [figure 6.1, bottom right]. And they offered the male infant's umbilical cord, along with the little shield and arrows symbolized in bathing, in the place where they warred with their enemies, where they buried it under the ground. And likewise for the girl, they buried her umbilical cord under the *metate*, a stone for grinding tortillas.[4]

The midwife

The symbols

The three boys who call out the name of the recently-born infant

The rushes with their little earthen pan of water

The broom, distaff and spindle, and little basket

Figure 6.1 Aztec childbirth customs. The midwife is about to bathe the newborn (Codex Mendoza 1992:v.4:119; folio 57r)

This presentation of symbols to the newborn established the child's gender identity early in life. Boys were expected to grow up to be warriors and to have an occupation like their father's, and girls were expected to grow up to manage the household, where cooking, weaving, cleaning, domestic offerings, and child rearing were their major activities. The descriptions of Aztec childhood in the Codex Mendoza show the differential training of boys and girls. By five years of age, boys were already,

> toting light loads of firewood and carrying light bundles to the *tiangues*, or market place. And they [mothers] taught the girls of this age how they had to hold the spindle and distaff in order to spin.[5]

By the age of seven, boys had learned to use nets to catch fish, and girls were spinning cotton (see figure 4.3).

The young were kept in line by a combination of threats of

corporal punishment and speeches that stressed correct behavior. Parents "gave them good advice so they would always apply themselves and spend their time in something to avoid all idleness."[6] Aztec punishments were severe, as these examples from the Codex Mendoza show:

> An 8-year old boy is being warned by his father not to be deceitful, or he will be punished by being pierced in the body with maguey spikes.

> Likewise they punished them [10-year olds] for being rebellious, beating them with sticks and offering other threats.

> They punished the eleven-year-old boy or girl who disregarded verbal correction by making them inhale chile smoke, which was a serious and even cruel torment.[7]

Until the age of fifteen, nearly all training was carried out in the home by the parents. The *Codex Mendoza* shows women teaching their daughters to spin, to weave, to sweep, and to cook and prepare food (see figures 3.2, 4.3). Fathers are depicted instructing their sons in a variety of tasks including fishing, carrying, and marketing. In another part of the *Codex*, skilled craftsmen instruct their sons in their work (see figure 4.8).

School

All boys and girls attended school at some point between ten and twenty years of age. There were two types of school: the *telpochcalli* ("youth's house") for commoners and the *calmecac* for nobles and exceptional commoners.[8] A *telpochcalli* was located in every town, and large cities had many, one in every *calpolli* (neighborhood). All commoner boys attended these schools, where they lived under spartan conditions. Girls also attended, but we do not know whether they lived on the premises. Instruction was carried out separately for boys and girls. All of the students received training in singing, dancing, and musical instruments, mostly for rituals.

Young men worked on civic projects, from carrying firewood for the temples to repairing temples, roads, and bridges. The major focus of male education in the *telpochcalli*, however, was military training. Seasoned warriors instructed the youths in martial arts, and then the students went off to war for practical training. At first they assisted by carrying baggage and arms for soldiers; later the novices carried their own arms. Eventually, they were allowed to participate fully in battle and to attempt to capture enemy prisoners for sacrifice.

The *calmecac*, a more exclusive school, was attended by nobles and the most promising commoner youths. These schools, each associated with a major temple, provided training for future leaders in government, the priesthood, and the military. Self-control, discipline, and obedience were stressed in the live-in *calmecac*. According to Friar Durán, instruction covered a wide variety of subjects:

> all the arts: military, religious, mechanical, and astrological, which gave them knowledge of the stars. For this they possessed large, beautiful books, painted in hieroglyphics, dealing with all these arts [and these books] were used for teaching.[9]

Military and religious arts were the most important subjects at the *calmecac*. The younger students trained as novice priests, and their duties included sweeping, gathering decorative boughs and sacrificial *maguey* thorns, and helping the head priests with offerings of incense, sacrifices, musical performances, and astronomical observations. As students advanced, they also trained for battle, much like the students in the *telpochcalli*, and they eventually advanced to the level of full warriors.

Adult Life and Social Roles

Marriage

Young men married in the late teens or early twenties, but young women married much younger – often as early as 10 or 12 years old. When a young man's parents decided that he was ready to marry, they consulted with his teachers and with relatives to select an appropriate bride.[10] An elderly female matchmaker approached the young woman's parents. If the negotiations were successful, the groom's family consulted soothsayers to determine an appropriate day for the ceremony. It was thought that a marriage celebrated on an unlucky day would not succeed.

Wedding ceremonies took place in two parts, beginning with an elaborate all-day feast at the bride's house. Her mother and female relatives worked for days to prepare tamales to feed the many people who would attend. The guests were served in a particular order, and each was given food, flowers, tobacco, and drink (cacao and *pulque*). At sunset the bride was bathed and clothed in a special outfit. She then received a lecture from the elders of the groom's family:

> Forever now leave childishness, girlishness; no longer art thou to be like a child . . . Be most considerate of one; regard one with respect, speak well, greet one well. By night look to, take care of the sweeping, the laying of fire. Arise in the deep of night [to begin domestic tasks].[11]

Following the speeches, the bride was carried by the groom's relatives to his house. Relatives of the couple accompanied the bride in a procession with torches. The second part of the wedding ceremony, at the groom's house, is described in the *Codex Mendoza* (see figure 6.2) as follows:

> And when they arrived at the groom's house, the groom's parents led her to the patio of the house to receive her, and they put her in a room or house where the groom was waiting. And the bride and bridegroom sat on a mat with its seats, next to a burning hearth, and they tied their clothes together, and offered copal incense to their gods. And then two old men an two old women, who were present as witnesses gave food to the bride and bridegroom, and then the elders ate.[12]

The elders then gave advice to the newlyweds; this is shown by the speech scrolls in figure 6.2. After four days, another feast was held with food and drink, dancing, and exchanges of gifts between the new in-laws.

Once married, young people assumed adult roles and responsibilities, and these varied tremendously depending upon one's social class, occupation, place of residence, and gender.

Gender Roles

In daily life most men worked outside the home, whereas the house was the domain of women. Most men were farmers who spent the day in their fields during the agricultural season (May

Figure 6.2 Aztec wedding ceremony. The bride and groom have tied their capes together to signal their union. Below them a feast is waiting, and on the sides older relatives are giving the young couple advice (Codex Mendoza 1992:v.4:127; folio 61r)

through November, the central Mexican rainy season). During the rest of the year men were typically away from home, fulfilling their service obligations, either as warriors (chapter 7) or as laborers. Artisans worked closer to home, in their house, yard, or a nearby workshop, often assisted by their families. Women spent most of their time in and around the home. Their major activities were childrearing, cooking, housekeeping, domestic ritual, weaving, and marketing.[13] A woman's contributions to the household economy were considerable. Her textiles were needed to pay tribute, and any extra cloth a women made could be exchanged for other goods. She did the marketing for the family, buying the weekly necessities and selling the family's surplus food or craft products. Even noble-women, who did not have to produce tribute cloth or worry about bargains in the marketplace, spent much of their time spinning and weaving, for this was an important part of gender identity regardless of social class.

Commoner women spent much of their work time cooking and preparing food. Grinding corn for tortillas and tamales was the single biggest task. Before the advent of mechanical mills, modern Mesoamerican peasant women would spend five or six hours each day grinding corn for the family's meals. Aztec women must have spent a similar amount of time at the *metate*. A woman's cooking duties often went beyond the needs of her immediate family. Her tamales and sauces were left as offerings at the temples (where they were eaten by the priests). She sometimes was required to provide food for the local lord, and she could be called upon to make tortillas and other provisions when her city-state's armies marched off to war.

Women had a more important role in domestic ritual than men. When a woman swept her house and yard with a broom every morning, she was doing more than simply cleaning her home. She was setting the world straight by purifying the domestic realm. Sweeping was also a crucial part of the rituals that priests carried out at the temples and the *calmecac*. The power of brooms thus linked women and priests in a common battle against the forces of disorder and darkness. Women also carried out other domestic rituals such as burning incense and maintaining the household altar.

Death and Burial

The Aztecs believed in several afterworlds and one's fate depended upon the manner of one's death.[14] Soldiers who died in battle and sacrificial victims went to an eastern solar realm to accompany the sun during its rise to zenith. Women who died in childbirth went to a western solar realm where they accompanied the sun during its setting. People who died by drowning or other causes related to the rain god (such as lightning or certain diseases) went to the earthly paradise of Tlalocan. Most people, however went to one of the nine levels of *Mictlan*, the underground realm of death.

Friar Durán gives information on Aztec funerals and burial:

> Some people were buried in the fields; others, in the courtyards of their own homes; others were taken to shrines in the wood; others were cremated and their ashes buried in the temples. No one was interred without being dressed in his mantles, loincloths, and fine stones. In sum, none of his possessions were left behind; and if he was cremated, the jar which received his ashes was filled with his jewelry and stones, no matter how costly. Dirges similar to our responses were chanted, and [the dead] were mourned, great ceremonies taking place in their honor. At these funerals [people] ate and drank; and if [the deceased] had been a person of quality, lengths of cloth were presented to those who had attended the funeral. [The dead man] was laid out in a room for four days until [mourners] arrived from the places where he had friends. Gifts were brought to the dead man; and if the deceased was a king of chieftain of a town, slaves were killed in his honor to serve him in the afterlife . . . The funeral rites lasted for ten days filled with sorrowful, tearful chants.[15]

Some of these practices are evident in a group of fourteen burials excavated at Cuexcomate and Capilco. All of the skeletons at these sites were children or infants. They were buried under the house-floor or in the yard next to the house. Most were placed in an upright sitting position, which coincides with images of mummy bundles in Aztec pictorial sources. Some individuals were buried with ceramic bowls as offerings whereas others were buried without any goods (figure 6.3). The placement of burials in and around the house gives clues to Aztec attitudes toward death. Deceased children were still considered part of the family, and they took their place within the domestic compound. It is likely that families conducted rituals or made offerings to their deceased members, much as modern Mesoamerican peoples do in the Day of the Dead ceremonies on November 2.

An intriguing issue about these burials is the absence of adults. Burials in general are rare at Aztec sites, and some archaeologists think this is due to the prevalence of cremation. I disagree, because cremated remains were buried in ceramic jars or urns, and few such urn burials have been excavated outside

Figure 6.3 Remains of a commoner child buried next to his family's house at Capilco (Photograph by Michael E. Smith)

of palaces and temples.[16] Another explanation for the lack of adult burials is that they were located in cemeteries outside of settlements, and archaeologists simply have not found the cemeteries. One possible Aztec cemetery was found in the ruins of Xochicalco, very close to Capilco and Cuexcomate. Xochicalco was a large powerful urban center in the Epiclassic period between AD 700 and 900, but by Aztec times the city was in ruins. Excavations at Xochicalco by Kenneth G. Hirth uncovered an area with several adult burials accompanied by Early and Late Aztec offerings in an area without Aztec architecture. Perhaps the ruins of Xochicalco still had symbolic importance several centuries after the city collapsed, and local people selected the area as a special place to bury their adult dead.[17]

Social Classes

Nobles or lords composed only five to ten percent of the total Aztec population, but they were firmly in control of society.[18]

Unlike elites in more open societies, the position and privileges of the Aztec nobility were rigidly specified by law (an example is the reforms of Motecuhzoma II, p. 52). Such laws limited the use or consumption of key goods, such as decorated capes, fancy jewelry, or two-story houses, to the nobility. Lords were further distinguished from commoners by birth, for membership in the nobility was strictly hereditary.

In practical terms, the power and wealth of the Aztec nobility rested on their control of land, labor, and tribute. All of the land in a city-state belonged ultimately to the *tlatoani*, but he granted estates to high lords called *tetecuhtin* (singular: *tecuhtli*) and to important temples. These estates were passed on to the descendants of the *tecuhtli*, or maintained in perpetuity by the temples. Below the rank of *tecuhtli* were the regular nobles, or *pipiltin* (singular: *pilli*). Most *pipiltin* served a *tecuhtli* or *tlatoani*, often residing in or around his palace.

To Aztec nobles, peasants and other commoners existed to serve them. *Macehualli* (plural: *macehualtin*), the term for commoner, means "subject," but commoners varied in their degree of subjugation, from the heavy burdens of slaves to the relative freedom of the *pochteca* merchants. Most commoners, however, had a number of typical obligations to their lord, first and foremost of which was to provide him with regular payments of tribute in goods. These payments were assessed by family and consisted of cotton *quachtli*, food items, or specific goods produced by the family. Commoners also provided their lord with regular labor service. Men cultivated the lord's land, women spun and wove for him, and both sexes worked as domestic servants. Such duties typically rotated among the lord's subjects, with each family contributing several weeks of work each year. These payments of goods and labor, called *tequitl*, were the basic duties of nearly all commoners.

In addition to *tequitl*, commoners were called upon to serve nobles for various special activities. The Aztecs did not have a standing army, and troops were conscripted for each campaign. When a large project was carried out, such as the construction of a temple or canal system, commoners were called up in a labor draft for the occasion. Just how heavy were the obligations of commoners? The paucity of numerical data in documentary sources makes this a difficult question. We don't know how many days of labor were required each year, how many *quachtli* were owed, or how much time it took to produce them.[19] Archaeological studies, however, do suggest some answers.

Commoners

Peasants and the Calpolli

Peasants, like most other commoners, were organized in wards and *calpolli* groups. A *calpolli* was a group of families who lived near one another, were subject to a single lord, controlled a block of land, and often shared a common occupation.[20] In urban settings, *calpolli* comprised neighborhoods, and many economic specialists such as merchants and artisans lived together in their own *calpolli*. In rural areas, Nahuatl-language written records used the term to describe two different sizes of settlement. A small *calpolli*, or ward, comprised a cluster of ten to twenty houses, the families who lived in them, and their assigned agricultural land. The village of Capilco in Morelos, with its 21 simple houses (figure 3.8), was probably such a ward. The term *calpolli* was also used to denote a much larger grouping composed of several wards under a common *tecuhtli* lord. In some rural *calpolli*, the wards were spread widely over the landscape; in others they were clustered together to form a rural town. These settlements typically had a *telpochcalli* school for their youth, and many also had a temple, a market, and perhaps a ballcourt. Many *calpolli* included wards in both urban and rural settings. The urban wards typically included the residences of the leading nobles and other *calpolli* officials, while the rural wards consisted primarily of peasants.

Calpolli lands were farmed by the member households. In theory the governing council of the *calpolli* divided the land among the constituent families. In practice, however, individual plots were inherited informally from one generation to the next. If new land opened up, or if an existing plot was left abandoned, the *calpolli* council would reallocate the land. Rights of use for an individual plot could be sold, but the land remained under the general jurisdiction of the *calpolli* and *altepetl* (city-state). Ethnohistorian James Lockhart describes the situation as follows:

> A land sale, then, was openly brought before the authorities, and a feast-like ritual accompanied the transfer like any other. Indeed, one way of looking at a transaction of this type is that the seller for a consideration relinquished his allocation from the altepetl/calpolli and permitted the authorities to reallocate it in the usual way to the buyer.[21]

One feature of rural life that is not completely clear is the relationship between rural *calpolli* and nobles. Nobles often lived in rural *calpolli* towns (see discussion of Cuexcomate below). Many or most *calpolli* were under the jurisdiction of a noble, who held ultimate control of the *calpolli* land. Nobles also held lands apart from *calpolli*, and peasants who worked these lands may not have belonged to a *calpolli*. These commoners were considered dependent upon their lord, perhaps in a fashion analogous to medievel European serfs. These dependent workers may not have had the same degree of control over their farm plots as *calpolli* members, although the situation is far from clear in the sources.

Rural Life

The site of Cuexcomate, with 135 simple houses, was probably a rural *calpolli* town.[22] In addition to the peasant houses, Cuexcomate also had a small palace, a temple, a public plaza, and a special civil building that may have been a *telpochcalli* (figure 3.8). The Cuexcomate *calpolli* comprised three or four wards. Families at Cuexcomate and the nearby single-ward village of Capilco lived in small one-room houses with sun-dried mud brick (adobe) walls and thatched roofs. All that remains of their houses today are the wall foundations and floors that were constructed of stone (figure 6.4). When in use, these houses probably looked much like modern adobe peasant houses (figure 6.5).

Nahuatl census records tell us that small houses such as these were home to either nuclear families (as in the quotation at the start of the chapter) or joint families that consisted of more than one married couple.[23] In many areas, the average

Figure 6.4 Wall foundations and floor of a peasant house excavated at Capilco (Photograph by Michael E. Smith)

household size was five to six members although, in some communities, the average size exceeded eight persons per household. Sometimes servants or other unrelated persons lived with a family. Many houses were arranged in small patio groups with two to five houses built around a common open courtyard (figure 3.8). Although the residents of a patio group often were related, perhaps as a multi-generation extended family, in other cases, unrelated families lived together. The Nahuatl term for these units is *cemithualtin*, meaning "those in one yard."

The houses at Capilco and Cuexcomate were so small that most domestic activity probably took place in the patio outside, which was kept clear of debris. People threw their trash to the sides and rear of the house, and the study of artifacts from these locations provides information about the activities and social conditions of the families who lived in each house. Broken potsherds from ceramic cooking pots, storage jars, serving bowls, and tortilla griddles give abundant evidence for the preparation of meals by the women of Capilco and

*Figure 6.5   Modern adobe peasant house in the village of
Tetlama, not far from Capilco (Photograph by Michael E. Smith)*

Cuexcomate. When pots broke, sherds accumulated around
the house and yard. Friar Sahagún noted that Aztec babies,
"spend their time piling up earth and potsherds, those on the
ground."[24] In addition to the tens of thousands of such sherds
excavated from each house, obsidian blades and basalt grinding tools, such as the *metate* for maize, provide additional
evidence for kitchen activities (obsidian and basalt tools were
also used for other domestic activities, and in some cases they
were used for craft production). Every house excavated at these
sites also yielded ceramic spindle whorls and spinning bowls,
and many had bronze sewing needles. Several types of ritual
artifacts were found at all houses, including figurines and incense burners.

Whereas women's activities – food preparation, textile manufacture, and domestic offerings – left abundant material evidence for archaeologists to find, men's work is almost invisible at
these sites. Most of the men were probably farmers, but farm
tools or other evidence of farming are not found in domestic

contexts. Family members in some houses worked part-time making paper from tree bark (see chapter 10). This paper, used for both writing and rituals, was a major tribute good paid by the inhabitants of Morelos to the Aztec empire.

To judge from the nature of the artifacts found around each house, the peasants of Capilco and Cuexcomate were quite well-off economically. They were able to obtain trade goods from all over central Mexico, including obsidian from Pachuca and Otumba, salt from the Valley of Mexico, bronze goods from western Mexico, and ceramic serving bowls from the Valley of Mexico, Cholula, Toluca, Cuernavaca, and Yautepec (figure 5.7). These imported bowls, many of them with elaborate polychrome decoration, were found in nearly all houses. The large number of imported goods suggests that the inhabitants of Capilco and Cuexcomate were able to produce sufficient crops, textiles, paper, and other goods beyond their domestic needs and tribute quotas to enter the markets as active participants.

The presence of a noble's palace at Cuexcomate does not appear to have had much effect on the economic conditions of peasants since the artifacts from commoner houses at Cuexcomate were almost identical to those from houses at Capilco, where there were no nobles. If peasants had been severely exploited to the point where they spent all of their time meeting household and tribute needs, we would not have recovered such a rich and varied domestic artifact inventory at every house. Nevertheless, there were signs of social and economic stress just before the Spanish conquest. In the Late Aztec B period (AD 1430–1520) the standard of living of both commoners and nobles at these sites declined. Demographic, economic, and political expansion had apparently reached the point of diminishing returns. An increasing burden of tribute (both local and imperial) and declining agricultural yields probably combined to lower the standards of living of most families.[25]

Urban Commoners

In many ways the lives of urban commoners were not very different from the lives of rural peasants. Both were *macehualtin*

Figure 6.6   Wall foundations of urban commoner houses excavated at Yautepec (Photograph by Michael E. Smith)

subject to nobles, and both lived as members of *calpolli*. Most Aztec cities were small settlements, and many urban residents were farmers or part-time craftspersons whose domestic conditions resembled those of peasant families in rural villages. On the other hand, cities were the place of residence and seat of government for the *tlatoani*, and urban commoners were more likely than their rural cousins to be subject directly to the royal palace. Also, because cities were the locations of major markets and concentrations of nobles, urbanites were more likely to be craft specialists. Specialists in the luxury crafts, in particular, would have benefitted by living and working near the king and other noble patrons.

In our excavations at the urban center of Yautepec in Morelos we found that the houses of commoners were only slightly larger and fancier than those at Capilco and Cuexcomate (figure 6.6).[26] They were far more similar to rural peasant houses than to noble residences. Their domestic artifacts were nearly identical

Figure 6.7 Remains of commoner adults buried next to a house at Yautepec (Photograph by Lisa M. Cascio)

to those excavated at the rural sites with one major difference. Evidence for part-time domestic craft production was much more abundant and widespread among Yautepec houses than at their rural counterparts. Some Yautepec households were involved in producing blades and other tools of obsidian, and the manufacture of ceramic figurines was also a common domestic activity (as evidenced by molds similar to those found at Otumba). We also found adult burials at Yautepec (figure 6.7).

Slaves

At the bottom of the social scale were the slaves, *tlacotin* (singular, *tlacotli*). People became slaves through debt or punishment, but not through birth; slavery was not hereditary. Slaves could marry, have children (who were free), and even own property. Anyone could own a slave, but most slave-owners were nobles. The owner of was responsible for feeding and housing the slave and had control over the slave's labor.

People sold themselves into slavery when they could not support themselves. During the great famine of the 1450s, for example, many Aztecs sold themselves to people of the Gulf Coast where economic conditions were better. Slaves used the purchase amount (said to be 20 *quachtli* in Tenochtitlan) to support themselves for a year or so, after which time they would begin their servitude. Some people incurred such large debts through gambling on the game *patolli* or the ballgame that selling themselves as slaves was the only way out. Failure to pay tribute was another way to become a slave, with the purchase price going to cover the tribute debt. Some other crimes were also punishable in this way.

The change in status from free citizen to slave was an official act that had to be witnessed formally by four officials. Slaves then either began work for their master or were sold in the market. Some *pochteca* merchants specialized in trading slaves, and several markets were known as centers for the slave trade. Slaves for sale were identified by large wooden collars (figure 5.2). Although slaves could in theory be used for any type of work, in practice most worked as servants in the palaces of lords. Female slaves were particularly valued for their spinning and weaving skills and were put to work making *quachtli* for their owners (the slave for sale in figure 5.2 shows off her spinning abilities for prospective buyers). The Aztecs did not use large gangs of slaves to perform heavy labor for farming or public works projects, and the overall economic contribution of slaves was quite modest.

Social Mobility

Two avenues by which commoners could raise their position were success at warfare and the priesthood. Warriors were ranked by the number of enemy soldiers they had captured, and a highly successful commoner soldier could reach a status far above his compatriots. In the middle years of the Aztec empire, Motecuhzoma I created a special title, *quauhpilli*, for the most accomplished warriors. They were given some of the privileges and responsibilities of nobles. This category of "nobles by achievement" was later abolished by Motecuhzoma II, who insisted that only true, hereditary nobles could enjoy the privileges of the elite stratum. Successful warriors still gained prestige, but they remained firmly within the commoner class. Success in the ranks of the priesthood (chapter 9) could also elevate the status of a commoner, but again they could not cross the threshold into the nobility.

The great wealth of the *pochteca* merchants and luxury artisans suggests that they may have formed an emerging Aztec middle class. Nobles had gained their wealth and position through control of land and the labor of commoners, the traditional bases of power in ancient Mesoamerica. One of the changes of the Late Postclassic period was an explosion of commerce throughout Mesoamerica, not just within the Aztec empire. Long-distance trade and local marketplaces thrived, which gave merchants and artisans new opportunities to gain wealth and influence. By tapping this new source of wealth that was outside of the nobility's traditional power base, many merchants and artists rose above the mass of commoners. Not being nobles, however, they had to hide their wealth and present a modest appearance.

Nobles and Their Palaces

Nobles lived and worked in large sumptuous compounds or palaces. These served as residences and as administrative buildings where the lord attended to the affairs of whatever social or political institution (such as *calpolli* or city-state) was under his direction. There was enormous variation in the size and elegance of palaces, which expressed a noble's position within society. In this section I examine the palaces of four nobles to illustrate that variation and to give an idea of the activities that took place in the residences of lords. These four nobles range from a lowly provincial *pilli* to one of the imperial kings of the Aztec empire.

A Rural Pilli at Cuexcomate

The town of Cuexcomate was laid out around a central public plaza. On the east side was a small temple-pyramid probably dedicated to the town's patron deity. The north and west sides

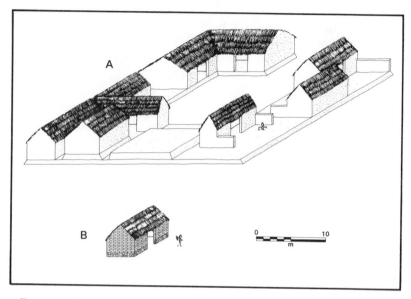

*Figure 6.8   Artist's reconstruction of the Cuexcomate palace (A)
in comparison with a commoner house (B) (Drawing by
Rachel Sader)*

of the plaza were occupied by compounds consisting of inter-
connected mounds. We excavated several mounds and patios
in these compounds and came to the conclusion that they were
elite residences. Group 6 on the west was occupied during the
Late Aztec A period and was the larger and better preserved of
the two compounds. Group 7 on the north was occupied only
during the following Late Aztec B period. Here, I focus attention on group 6 as an example of the palace of a low-ranking
provincial noble.[27]

Group 6 at Cuexcomate was not a very imposing sight prior to
excavation, appearing as several low mounds arranged around
a patio. These mounds turned out to be the ruins of a noble's
palace, whose size and architectural quality set it far above the
predominant commoner houses at the site. Our crew cleared
off the top layers of rubble on these mounds to uncover the
architectural plan of the final construction stage. We also excavated into the mounds and located the remains of three earlier
construction stages. Figure 6.8A is an artist's reconstruction of

how group 6 may have looked in the early 1400s, shortly before its abandonment. At that time, it consisted of a series of connected low platforms around a patio with rooms, passages, and shrines built on top of the platforms. The platforms were built of stone and covered with a layer of red painted lime plaster.

Our hypothesis that group 6 was the palace of a noble is based upon both the architecture and the artifacts. With a surface area of 540 sq meters, this compound is much larger than the typical commoner house at the site (commoner houses averaged around 20 sq meters). The manner of its construction and the materials used were far superior to those of the commoner houses. The elevation of rooms on platforms also set group 6 apart from commoner houses, most of which were built at ground level. The artifacts found in the trash deposits adjacent to the compound were typical domestic wares (cookpots, serving bowls, obsidian blades, and the like), but with a greater proportion of fancy imported items than in deposits from commoner houses.

This arrangement of rooms elevated on platforms that surround a central patio is consistent with ethnohistoric descriptions and maps of Aztec palaces in the Valley of Mexico. This compound was probably the residence of a low-ranking provincial *pilli* to whom the 250 or so inhabitants of the Late Aztec A *calpolli* of Cuexcomate paid tribute. Nobles often were polygamous, and the individual room blocks may have been separate apartments for the lord's wives. Servants or artisans in the service of the lord probably lived in neighboring commoner houses. For example, houses in a nearby commoner patio group had very high frequencies of paint pigments and bark beaters, which suggests that their residents were artisans who made paper and paints. These items would have been used by the nobles of group 6 or their scribes to produce historical and religious painted books. Group 6 was abandoned in the 1430s or 1440s, at which time a second and far more modest elite compound, group 7, was built on the empty north side of the plaza. We don't know why group 6 was abandoned, but conquest by outsiders may have had something to do with it. From historic documents, we know the area was conquered twice at about that time: once in the 1420s

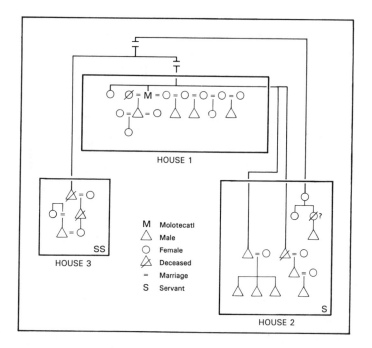

*Figure 6.9   Genealogy of the inhabitants of the palace of
Molotecatl tecuhtli showing the residents of the three structures
(Based upon Carrasco 1972; drawing by Ellen Cesarski)*

by the expanding Cuauhnahuac state and again around 1440
by the Aztec empire under Itzcoatl.

Molotecatl, a Tecuhtli *Lord in Molotlan*

Molotlan was a *calpolli* that comprised an urban neighborhood,
probably in the city of Yautepec. Molotecatl, a *tecuhtli* lord in
charge of Molotlan, was almost certainly of higher rank than
the *pilli* who lived in group 6 at Cuexcomate. We know
Molotecatl's name and something about his social position from
a Nahuatl-language census compiled very shortly after the
Spanish conquest.[28] The document called him "Molotecatl
tecuhtli" and listed the inhabitants of his palace, along with
the other members of the Molotlan *calpolli*. Figure 6.9 shows
the genealogy of Molotecatl's extended family, who inhabited

three structures that probably were raised on platforms and arranged around a patio. Molotecatl lived in house 1 with his five wives and children, the children and grandchild of a deceased wife, and a sister. House 2 contained three family units, headed by a great aunt and two of Molotecatl's brothers, and a kitchen servant (perhaps originally a slave). House 3 was inhabited by the extended family of Molotecatl's deceased uncle as well as two servants, one of whom was a messenger and the other a woman who spun and wove. These three houses and the patio constituted Molotecatl's palace, which was probably a larger version of the Cuexcomate palace pictured in figure 6.8.

Molotecatl was in charge of the *calpolli* of Molotlan, a large neighborhood that comprised 128 households, divided into nine wards ranging from one to 32 households in each. Molotecatl owned the land of the entire *calpolli*, much of it valuable irrigated farmland. The commoner members paid him tribute in order to farm individual plots. The tribute of the *calpolli* members consisted of cotton cloth, farm produce, and labor service. To fulfill their labor service, commoner women came to the palace to spin and weave, which furnished Molotecatl with a large supply of cloth that contributed greatly to his wealth. *Tecuhtli* lords such as Molotecatl used part of their cloth income to pay their own tribute to their king.[29] In the case of Molotecatl, archaeologists have excavated the palace where his king lived.

The Tlatoani *of Yautepec*

For many years archaeologists were aware of a large Aztec-period mound at the edge of the modern town of Yautepec in Morelos, but none of us had any idea of the importance of this structure. When the mound was threatened by urban expansion in the 1980s, a local citizen's group organized to help save it. A team of Mexican government archaeologists began excavations at the mound in 1989, under the direction of Hortensia de Vega Nova, and fieldwork has continued through 1996. The excavators discovered an enormous stone platform some 6,000 sq meters in area (0.6 hectares, or about 1.5 acres) that had been the royal palace of the *tlatoani* of Yautepec. This is the first Aztec royal palace to be excavated by archaeologists.[30]

Figure 6.10 Rooms and passages in the palace of the tlatoani
of Yautepec (Photograph by Michael E. Smith)

Yautepec was a powerful polity whose *tlatoani* ruled over
four or five lesser city-states in the Yautepec river valley. The
Aztec city of Yautepec, located under and adjacent to modern
Yautepec, was the largest city in the area, and the sumptuous
royal palace was of a size befitting the power of the city's king.
The outer walls of the structure were sloping panels of stone
four meters high that presented an imposing image to the people
of Yautepec. Entrance was by a single stairway up the west
side of the building, which led to a passageway into the heart
of the palace. Excavations on top of the platform have uncovered numerous courtyards, rooms, and passages, all constructed
of stone covered with layers of lime plaster (figure 6.10). Unlike
the Cuexcomate palace, whose walls were painted with a simple coat of red, the Yautepec palace walls were covered with
elaborate polychrome murals. There is evidence for several
stages of construction at this structure. To date, archaeologists
have cleared only about one-quarter of the palace. If there was
a large central patio or courtyard, it has not been found yet.

Some idea of the nature of activities at royal palaces can be learned from ethnohistoric description of one of the largest and most sumptuous palaces in the entire Aztec empire, that of Nezahualcoyotl, king of Texcoco.

Nezahualcoyotl, Imperial Ruler of Texcoco

Nezahualcoyotl became ruler of Texcoco and the Acolhua peoples during the final years of Tepanec dominance. He helped the Mexica king Itzcoatl defeat the Tepanecs in 1428 and was one of the founding kings of the Triple Alliance empire. He went on to become one of the most respected and renowned of the Aztec rulers with a reputation as a statesman, soldier, builder, poet, and lawgiver. The story of Nezahualcoyotl's life was recorded in the early 1600s by the chronicler Fernando de Alva Ixtlilxochitl, a direct descendant of the Acolhua king. Alva Ixtlilxochitl devoted two chapters of his work to a description of Nezahualcoyotl's palace.[31] His information came from an earlier drawing of the palace, oral histories, and his own observations of the ruins of the palace.

Nezahualcoyotl's compound in Texcoco measured 1,032 by 817 meters, an area of 84.3 hectares (over 200 acres). It consisted of numerous buildings, gardens, temples, a ballcourt, a zoo, and a market, all surrounded by massive adobe brick walls. The many sections of the palace building described by Alva Ixtlilxochitl included living quarters for the king; living quarters for the queen and attendants; servant's quarters; a throne room; many chambers and halls for judges, councilors, officials, and ambassadors; a hall for warriors; a science and music hall; a section for poets, philosophers, and historians; an archive room; storehouses for weapons; and storehouses for tribute from subject kings. Although we do not know the size of the palace building itself, it may have been comparable to that of Motecuhzoma II in Tenochtitlan, which measured 2.4 hectares.[32]

Part of the palace compound was a religious sector with over 40 temples and other structures, among them a tall twin-temple pyramid dedicated to the deities Tlaloc and Huitzilopochtli, a round pyramid for Quetzalcoatl, sacrificial stones, priests' residences, and a special *calmecac* for the education of royal youth. In all there were over 300 rooms in the palace compound. This was the central administrative center of the Acolhua domain where much of the business of state was carried out. The city of Texcoco covered about 4.5 square km, and the palace compound occupied much of the city center.

Apart from his achievements as king of the second most powerful state in the Aztec empire, Nezahualcoyotl was famous as an intellectual, poet, and philosopher. He was an expert architect and builder, who designed the dikes that regulated the waters of Lake Texcoco and kept Tenochtitlan from flooding. Nezahualcoyotl had a number of smaller palaces scattered around his kingdom, the best known of which was Texcotzinco. Here, on a hilltop above Texcoco, he built a center for ritual and relaxation which included a residence, a bath complex, and a botanical garden.[33] The canals, aqueducts, and pools at Texcotzinco have delighted visitors from Aztec times to the present day.

Relations among Nobles

All nobles regardless of rank, from lowly *pipiltin* to the high kings, shared an interest in maintaining and protecting their privileged positions and lifestyles. They developed an extensive network of interaction that promoted a strong sense of group solidarity and accentuated their separation from commoners. Nobles could only marry other nobles, and they used marriage alliances to link separate families and dynasties into a single, interlocking kinship network.[34] The practice of a low-ranking ruler or noble marrying the daughter of a more powerful ruler was widespread in Mesoamerica and the Aztec kings used it extensively (see the discussion of the third Mexica *tlatoani*, Huitzilihuitl, in chapter 2).

The exchange of luxury goods among nobles reinforced their interaction network. Nobles presented their peers with gifts of cloth, feathers, jewelry, and the like on many occasions. A major setting for such gift-giving was the state ceremony. These occasions were held for coronations, funerals, temple dedications, and victory celebrations. Typically the host city invited nobles from all over, including foreign and enemy lords. Large-scale theatrical presentations were staged for commoners and nobles alike, and then the nobles withdrew for more exclusive festivities. They ate and drank together, exchanged gifts, listened to speeches, participated in dances, and generally enjoyed themselves away from the eyes of the commoners. The bonds forged and maintained among the nobles were so strong that they crossed political borders and even bound enemy nobles together. Tlacaelel, advisor to the Mexica kings, articulated this principle in a speech reported by Friar Durán:

> It seems to me that it would not be unreasonable to invite them again [nobles and rulers of the enemy states of Tlaxcalla and Metztitlan] to this solemn occasion because, even though we are enemies in the wars that we wage, in our festivities we should rejoice together. There is no reason why they should be excluded since we are all one, and in these times it is reasonable that there be a truce and sociable communication among the rulers.[35]

This "truce and sociable communication among the rulers" was a primary form of diplomacy between politically-independent city-states, and it reveals the close connections between social class and the state.

7

City-State and Empire

The conquered people gave themselves as vassals, as servants, to the Aztecs and they paid tribute in all things created under the sky . . .

There were such vast quantities of all these things that came to the city of Mexico that not a day passed without the arrival of people from other regions who brought large amounts of everything, from foodstuffs to luxury items, for the king and the lords.

Friar Diego Durán[1]

The Aztec empire generated large amounts of tribute that greatly enriched Tenochtitlan and the two other capital cities, Texcoco and Tlacopan. The Mexica of Tenochtitlan were proud of their position as lords of a great empire, and they glorified the power and exploits of their kings. The Mexica viewpoint became enshrined in the works of chroniclers such as Sahagún and Durán, who after the Spanish conquest recorded the native history of the Mexica. Influenced by the accounts of the chroniclers, some writers have concluded that the empire was the single most dominating institution in the daily lives of the Aztecs. But recent research, relying more upon administrative documents, has led many scholars to a different conclusion. The empire was certainly a rich and mighty institution, but the city-state was more influential in Aztec life and politics. Aztec city-states were independent polities ruled by kings who controlled modest hinterland areas from their capital towns. Most people gave political allegiance to their local city-state, not to the empire, and the city-state formed the social and economic universe within which they lived out their lives. The Aztec empire was built on a foundation of city-states, and these units maintained their identity and many social and political functions even under imperial control.

City-States

Altepetl

Altepetl is the Nahuatl term usually translated as city-state or kingdom.[2] For the Aztecs, an *altepetl* was a community with laws, boundaries, a central town with surrounding farmland, and a *tlatoani* or king. There were about 50 of these city-states in the Valley of Mexico in 1519, and the Aztec empire ruled over an additional 450 subject city-states. Native histories often describe city-states as founded by immigrant peoples, the early Nahuatl migrants from Aztlan or later migrating groups.

The founding of a new *altepetl* was heralded by the construction of a royal palace, a temple-pyramid, and a market. These three structures both practically and symbolically established the city-state as the pre-eminent political, religious, and economic unit in the lives of its inhabitants. The royal palace was the heart of the city-state. It served not only as the residence of the *tlatoani*, but also as the center of administrative and social activity. The temple housed the image of a patron god who watched over the citizens of the *altepetl*. The size and luxury of the central temple communicated the importance and success of the city-state. When a city-state was conquered in warfare, its defeat was symbolized by a burning temple (see figure 1.6). The market provided an economic focus for exchanges that helped bind the city-state together.

The royal palace, temple, and market were normally located near one another and formed the nucleus for a town or small city. This urban center contained wards of the more important *calpolli* in the city-state. Labor obligations in the city-state, such as service at the palace or public works projects, rotated among the constituent *calpolli*. In some respects, the *altepetl* can be considered a *calpolli* writ large. Sometimes the *calpolli* were composed of peoples from different ethnic groups, including both Nahuatl speakers (such as Mexica, Acolhua, Chalca, or Tlahuica) and others (such as Otomi, Matlatzinca, or Mixtec). As a result, Aztec city-states were often multiethnic, with political boundaries cutting across ethnic divisions.

The Tlatoani *(King)*

Friar Sahagún provides us with the Aztec nobles' view of a good *tlatoani*:

> The good ruler (is) a protector; one who carries (his subjects) in his arms, who unites them, who brings them together. He rules, takes responsibilities, assumes burdens. He carries (his subjects) in his cape; he bears them in his arms. He governs; he is obeyed. (To him) as shelter, as refuge, there is recourse.[3]

Tlatoque were selected by a high council of *tetecuhtin* nobles, male kin of the deceased ruler. Usually a brother or a son succeeded to the office, but sometimes a nephew or grandson of the previous ruler was chosen (see the genealogy of the Mexica *tlatoque* in figure 2.6). The council deliberated to find the appropriate successor, who was viewed as the god Tezcatlipoca's selection to the post. Tezcatlipoca, sometimes known as "We his slaves," was the most powerful Aztec deity. Among the Mexica many *tlatoque* had been successful war leaders under earlier rulers.

The installation of a new Mexica *tlatoani* involved a series of elaborate ceremonies and activities – a rite of passage through which the chosen noble was transformed into a being worthy of speaking in the voice of Tezcatlipoca. First, the candidate stood naked before the image of the god Huitzilopochtli to present offerings. He then went into retreat with his *tetecuhtin* for four days of fasting and penance. Upon emergence, he was required to lead a brief military excursion to gather captives for sacrifice at his installation ceremony. An all night prayer vigil to Tezcatlipoca preceded the formal installation ceremony. The entire kingdom and *tlatoque* and nobles from other city-states were invited to witness the pageants, theatrical presentations, dance, music, and human sacrifices that accompanied the ruler's installation. These ceremonies were intended to impress upon the citizens the link between the new king and the god Tezcatlipoca, the supernatural basis for political authority.

Tlatoque were also concerned with the dynastic basis of their authority. Political legitimacy for the Aztec kings was derived from their genealogical connections with the earlier Toltec dynasty of Tula. The Aztec concept for legitimate rulership, *tlatocayotl*, depended upon this apparent lineage. Each local Aztec city-state dynasty could trace its ancestry back to Tula, although in many cases the genealogies were fictional. When the Mexica, newly settled at Tenochtitlan, wished to establish a *tlatocayotl* for the first time, their ruler, not yet a *tlatoani*, married a princess from Culhuacan whose pedigree provided a direct link to the Toltec kings that the subsequent Mexica dynasty would follow.

The *tlatoani* owned or controlled the land within his city-state, and he received the tribute of both his direct commoner subjects and his subordinate lords. He served as the military leader of the polity by organizing campaigns, overseeing the defense of the city-state, and sometimes leading his troops into battle. In addition to being the voice of Tezcatlipoca, the *tlatoani* sponsored religious celebrations and led many of the state rituals. Finally, as protector of his people, he settled disputes that could not be resolved through the normal process of judicial hearings.

The power and exalted position of the *tlatoani* led to a luxurious lifestyle. He wore the costliest clothing, ate the most exotic delicacies, had access to the greatest number of servants, aides, and entertainers, and lived in the most sumptuous palace in the kingdom. Many nobles and commoners served in the royal court. In painted manuscripts a king was depicted wearing a pointed crown and seated on an elevated platform (figure 1.6). This platform or throne was covered with one or both of the ancient Mesoamerican symbols of royalty: a reed mat or a jaguar pelt.

The *tlatoani* was assisted by a council of nobles and a series of lower-ranking bureaucrats. Other lords served as judges to hear suits, and in some city-states, there was a group of superior or appeals judges. An early Spanish governor of New Spain, Alonso de Zorita, described Aztec judges as follows:

> The Indian judges of whom I spoke would seat themselves at daybreak on their mat dais, and immediately begin to hear pleas. The judges' meals were brought to them at an early hour from the royal palace. After eating, they rested for a while, then returned to hear the remaining suitors, staying until two hours before sundown. Appeals from these judges were heard by twelve superior judges, who passed sentence in consultation with the ruler.[4]

Mapping City-States

Recently, ethnohistorians and archaeologists have joined forces to reconstruct the Aztec political landscape for the first time.[5] This effort to map the boundaries and settlements of Aztec city-states has been facilitated by the new focus on administrative documents as a major source of data. The first step in this procedure is to determine which cities or towns in an area had a *tlatoani* and to locate these on a map. The second step is to reconstruct the territories of these capitals, and the third step involves correlating the city-state territories with known Late Aztec archaeological sites.

Native histories contain information on the *tlatoque* of various towns, but the best sources of data are the *Relaciones Geográficas*[6] and other similar reports on sixteenth-century towns. These often mention whether particular towns had a "universal lord" or a "natural lord" prior to 1519, the Spanish terms for *tlatoani*. Such documents also typically list the smaller towns and villages that were subject to the head town, and they may also include a list of towns in neighboring city-states. Where this kind of detailed document is lacking, which unfortunately is the case for much of the Aztec area, records of the early Spanish *encomiendas* may be helpful. *Encomiendas* were land grants given by the Spanish crown to individual Spaniards. They were assigned on the basis of pre-existing political units; in the Valley of Mexico, for example, the territories of many Aztec city-states became separate Spanish *encomiendas*. The colonial towns that served as the centers of *encomiendas* almost always had been *tlatoani* centers before the Spanish conquest.

Once the *tlatoani* centers and their subjects have been identified, it is usually a simple matter to locate them on a map. Aztec Texcoco, Chalco, Otumba, Yautepec, or Toluca were located precisely where the modern cities of these names are located today. Some names were changed. For example, the Spaniards had trouble pronouncing Cuauhnahuac and the city's name became Cuernavaca ("cow horn"). In other cases, towns were moved forcibly by the Spaniards, and some Aztec towns were abandoned completely, which makes it difficult to impossible to locate the original Aztec *tlatoani* center.

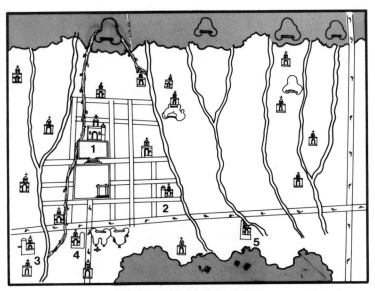

Figure 7.1 Map of the city-state of Coatepec from the Relación
Geográfica *of 1579. East is at the top. The central town
(no. 1) is shown with a church and plaza; nos. 2–5 indicate
dependent villages (After Acuña 1984–87:vol.6:150.
Drawing from Hodge 1994:48; reproduced with permission)*

Mary G. Hodge's research on political geography in the Valley
of Mexico illustrates these methods.[7] The 1579 *Relación
Geográfica* from Coatepec not only lists subjects of the town
but also provides a map (figure 7.1). Using this document and
other sixteenth century reports and lawsuits, Hodge was able
to map the extent of Coatepec and nearby city-states as they
existed in 1519. She then compared her ethnohistoric map of
this area with the results of the Valley of Mexico Archaeological Survey Project and was able to assign the many small- and
medium-sized sites to their appropriate city-state (figure 7.2).
Hodge has produced the most accurate and complete political
map of the Aztec Valley of Mexico to date, and the application
of her procedures to other areas promises to yield additional
insights.

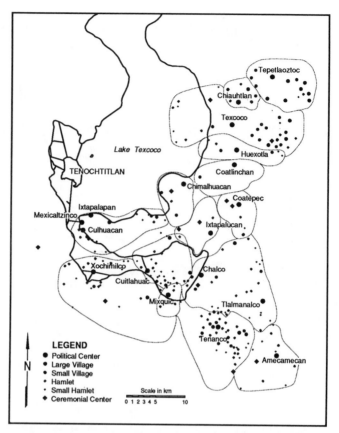

Figure 7.2   Map of city-state territories in the southeastern Valley of Mexico (not all of the Aztec sites in this region are depicted on the map) (From Hodge 1994:56; reproduced with permission)

Relations among City-States

Aztec city-states did not exist in isolation. They formed large, regional groups whose member states were in constant communication and interaction with one another. Somewhat paradoxically, nearby city-states engaged simultaneously in both peaceful interactions – trade, political alliances, and visits among lords – and relations of warfare and domination. These regional groups or systems of city-states were quite volatile, and they alternated between periods of stability and episodes of unrest and rapid change. In this sense, the Aztec political landscape resembled other historically-known city-state systems such as those of Archaic and Classical Greece, Early Dynastic Sumeria, Medieval Italy, and nineteenth-century west Africa. In all of these cases, nearby city-states were linked by a similar language and culture but maintained their political autonomy and distinctiveness.[8] Competition among sister city-states is endemic in these settings. In the Aztec case, this competition frequently led to conquest and political domination, culminating in the formation and expansion of the Triple Alliance empire.

Peaceful Relations

Nearby city-states maintained three main types of peaceful relations: trade, elite networks, and political alliances. Aztec city-states were small in size, and very few could afford to be economically self-sufficient. Political borders did not stop either merchants or consumers from travelling to markets in foreign city-states. Specialized markets attracted customers from large areas. For example, people from city-states all over the northeast Valley of Mexico traveled to Acolman to shop at its famous dog market. When people needed a costly or specialized item not available at their local city-state market, they could travel to the nearest large market to make their purchase. Nobles from Acolman, for example, might go to Texcoco or Tenochtitlan to buy jewelry and feathers.

As discussed in chapter 6, royal families and other nobles were heavily involved in many activities that transcended the borders of individual city-states. Nobles often married across city-state lines, partly to forge political alliances and partly for the simple reason that in many small city-states there were not enough potential spouses who were nobles. Lords commonly visited their peers in other city-states to participate in ceremonies, festivals, and political summits. Friar Durán describes many of these events. When Nezahualpilli, king of Texcoco, died in 1515, nobles from all over central Mexico attended his funeral:

> Then the other leading men of Tenochtitlan, one after another, made sorrowful speeches to the body of the Texcoco king, expressing condolences for his death but speaking to him as if he were still alive. Each one presented jewels and other gifts, according to his

possibilities. The king of Tacuba also sent slaves and gifts of royal mantles and jewels, as did the ruler of Chalco and the lords of Xochimilco and of the Marquesado [i.e., Cuauhnahuac]. Noblemen of all the land came with quantities of jewels and gifts and with many slaves.[9]

The economic and social ties among city-states did not prevent them from fighting one another in an attempt to achieve political domination, however.

Warfare and Domination

The goal of warfare among the Aztecs was to conquer other city-states in order to force them to pay tribute.[10] Warfare was not used to expand the territory of a state since the losing city-state typically maintained its *tlatoani*, government, and lands intact. The losing king simply had to acknowledge the dominance of the victorious king and agree to pay him a specified amount of tribute each year. A secondary goal of warfare was to capture enemy soldiers for sacrifice. Human sacrifice was a fundamental part of Aztec religion, and most victims were soldiers captured in battle.

War and battle were dominant themes running throughout Aztec culture. There were no permanent standing armies, and military service was required of all males. Success in warfare was an important part of male identity (figure 6.1). Birth was compared to combat, and women who died in childbirth were likened to warriors. All boys were taught military skills and values at the *telpochcalli* and *calpolli* schools.

The public status of a young man was determined by the number of enemy captives he had taken in battle. Various ranks of warriors were proclaimed publicly by dress and jewelry. New soldiers with no captives could wear only plain capes and not jewelry. Upon taking his first captive, a soldier became a "leading youth" and was allowed to wear special face paint and a decorated cape in public; he also became eligible for marriage. With each additional captive, a man gained new privileges. For example, a four-captive warrior could dance at important public ceremonies and wear fine lip-plugs and a headband with eagle feather tassels. The most successful warriors joined elite military orders known as eagle warriors, jaguar warriors, Otomi warriors, and shorn warriors. These exalted soldiers were the commanders and leaders in battle, and they enjoyed many privileges back home. Eagle and jaguar warriors, for example, could dine at the royal palace, drink *pulque*, and keep concubines. The advancement of a young man up the military ladder was a source of great pride for his family and *calpolli*.

Aztec warfare was ritualized and followed a distinct protocol, although actual battles were fierce and serious. The ruler of a city-state bent upon expansion first sent ambassadors to request the surrender of the targeted town. Gifts were offered to the local lord and the consequences of refusal were described. These threats included military conquest, the possible destruction of the town, and the imposition of a heavy burden of tribute. Sometimes a local *tlatoani* submitted willingly, assuming a lower rate of tribute; in other cases, he sent the ambassadors home with scorn, and war soon followed. The king of the aggressor state could raise an army quickly from among the eligible youths and experienced soldiers, and the women provided food and supplies for the campaign. Although these procedures did not lead to surprise attacks, they did not prevent the use of ambush and trickery on the battlefield.

Forces were led into battle by the most experienced warriors, with the sounds of drums and trumpets urging on the attack. Once battle was joined, soldiers fought with determination and vigor. The primary offensive weapons were thrusting spears and swords. The Aztec sword (*maquahuitl*) consisted of a long, flat wooden handle into which were fitted rows of obsidian blades (figure 7.3). The extreme sharpness of the obsidian blades made these swords very effective weapons. The Spaniards described several instances in which Aztec soldiers cut off the heads of horses with a single blow. The bow and arrow was used as an offensive weapon also, and some groups made use of clubs and slings.

Soldiers normally carried shields into battle. These were made of wood covered with elaborate decorations, often of feathers (see figure 7.5). The Spaniards described Aztec shields as quite good at stopping arrows and swords. Soldiers wore body armor of thick, quilted cotton cloth that could stop arrows and darts. War leaders adorned themselves with feather tunics, headdresses, armbands, and other decorative clothing.

Figure 7.3   Soldiers carrying maquahuitl *swords into battle
(After Sahagún 1950–82:bk.8:fig.78; drawing by Ellen Cesarski)*

The need to capture enemies for sacrifice greatly influenced
the nature of fighting in Aztec wars. At one level, armies sought
to kill numerous opponents to gain victory. On another level,
however, soldiers tried to injure or cripple enemy fighters
in order to capture them alive. Captures made by a group of
soldiers brought far less status than solo seizures, so most
soldiers fought individually, one-on-one, each opponent seeking to subdue the other for capture.

Victory on the battlefield came when one army succeeded in
killing and capturing enough enemy soldiers to subdue and
demoralize its opponent. Sometimes victory required the conquest and partial destruction of a city, as indicated in the burning
temple glyph for a conquered city (figure 1.6). Each army returned to its capital, one with rejoicing and celebration, the
other with tears and sorrow. The victorious king set the tribute
quota for the conquered city-state, and the losing monarch was
forced to pay tribute while acknowledging the superiority of
his conqueror. In most cases, the victor did not depose the
conquered king nor attempt to administer directly the territory
of his new domain. So long as the tribute continued to flow to
the victors he and his successors usually avoided meddling in

the internal affairs of subject states. This form of indirect rule was put to use when the Triple Alliance began its program of imperial expansion after 1428, and explains many characteristics of that empire as the Spaniards encountered it in 1519.

The Empire of the Triple Alliance

What Kind of Empire?

The principles of warfare, tribute payment, and indirect rule outlined above were worked out among the Aztec city-states during the twelfth through fourteenth centuries. When the Triple Alliance of Tenochtitlan, Texcoco, and Tlacopan was formed in 1428, the rulers put these practices to work to build their empire. Together, these states easily achieved military and political control of the Valley of Mexico. Once they had consolidated the economic and demographic power of the Valley of Mexico, they set out to dominate an ever-increasing area. By 1519, the alliance controlled an area greater than any previous Mesoamerican realm. But was this loosely organized group of city-states an empire? Some scholars state that because of major deficiencies, "this was not an empire at all."[11] The Aztecs had no standing armies, they left conquered kings in office instead of sending governors or administrators to the provinces, they did not build an infrastructure of roads, cities, or warehouses throughout their realm, and fortresses and garrisons were few and far between. Ethnohistorian Ross Hassig counters this argument by analyzing the Aztec empire from a comparative perspective. He shows that the Triple Alliance was in fact typical of a certain kind of ancient empire.

Historians and political scientists divide empires into two basic types: territorial or direct, and hegemonic or indirect.[12] The popular image of an ancient empire is represented by large territorial domains such as the Roman, Assyrian, or Inca empires. All of these had standing armies, direct political control of the provinces, and major construction programs. Their rulers attempted to incorporate subject peoples into the culture of the dominant power. Hegemonic empires, by contrast, rule through indirect control, using a combination of force and persuasion to gain compliance by client kings. Far less effort is devoted to managing the affairs of subject peoples. Examples of ancient hegemonic empires include Athens during the Classical period, certain portions of the Roman empire, and the Aztec Triple Alliance. The alliance's Mexica rulers, however, did not lack deliberate strategies and plans for imperial expansion and administration; in fact they employed several distinct strategies to create and exploit the empire for their own ends.

Imperial Control in the Valley of Mexico

The first goal of the newly-formed Triple Alliance was to gain control over the city-states of the Valley of Mexico.[13] Once these had been conquered or otherwise incorporated into the empire, the imperial rulers initiated a series of political reforms designed to tighten their control and to prevent nearby city-states from rebelling or resisting. These reforms went beyond the heretofore accepted pattern of city-state expansion that I discussed above and signalled the beginnings of a new, higher level of political and social control and integration. Unfriendly *tlatoque* were removed from office and replaced by nobles sympathetic to the empire. A system of tributary provinces was established that was separate from the pre-existing city-state governments. Tribute was collected directly by imperial tribute-collectors, thereby keeping it out of the hands of local city-state rulers. Under this system the imperial kings could deal with subject rulers as allies and colleagues, not tribute payers, at the same time that they were assessing heavy tribute payments from their colleagues' commoner subjects.

As the empire expanded outside the Valley of Mexico, two factors shaped the continuing development of city-states within the Valley. First, the final conquest of Chalco in 1465 brought an end to the warfare that had been endemic among the Valley of Mexico city-states. Under the resulting *pax azteca* of the Late Aztec B period, the market system flourished, and the entire valley became more tightly integrated economically and socially. Second, the growth of the empire in the outer provinces produced a great influx of riches into the valley in the forms of tribute and trade goods. The imperial rulers strengthened their bonds with other dynasties by sharing some of this wealth as gifts to nobles at increasingly frequent and sumptuous gatherings and ceremonies. Marriage alliances among the Valley of Mexico nobility also strengthened regional ties.

Tribute and Warfare in the Outer Provinces

Aztec imperial expansion was motivated by economic interests: the Triple Alliance wanted access to a regular supply of wealth and riches from foreign lands.[14] The growing numbers of commoners in Tenochtitlan and the other imperial capitals required ever increasing amounts of food, cloth, and other necessities, and the nobles required exotic luxury goods to maintain their lifestyles and social positions. To obtain these goods, the Mexica kings and their Acolhua allies devised two fundamental strategies. The economic strategy involved the conquest of rich areas and the establishment of a program of regular tribute payments as well as the encouragement of trade and markets throughout the empire. The Aztecs were not the only imperialists in Late Postclassic Mesoamerica, however. When their expansion brought them into conflict with other powerful enemies, the Triple Alliance devised a second strategy. This frontier strategy involved the creation of client states along enemy frontiers to shoulder much of the burden of protecting the empire so that tribute and trade could flourish in the inner provinces.

These two strategies led to the creation of two distinct types of imperial provinces in the outer empire. Tributary provinces included city-states well under imperial control that could provide the regular tribute and trade required by the economic strategy. These provinces tended to comprise the city-states with the longest history of imperial control and those distant from major Aztec enemies such as the Tarascan empire or Tlaxcalla. Strategic provinces on the other hand were established to help maintain the imperial borders and frontiers without massive investment by the Triple Alliance. A recently compiled map of the empire (figure 7.4) shows the locations of the tributary and strategic provinces as they existed in 1519. These fifty-five provinces contained some 450 city-states, all subject to the Triple Alliance in some manner (table 7.1).

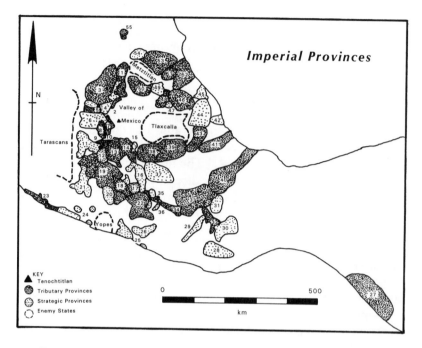

Figure 7.4 Map of the provinces of the Aztec empire. See table 7.1 for the names of the provinces (After Berdan et al. 1996; drawing by Kori Kaufman)

The Economic Strategy

Groups of adjacent conquered city-states were organized into tributary provinces. A prominent town was selected to head each province, and those towns gave the provinces their names. In some cases the head town was the capital of the most powerful city-state in the province, while in others a less prominent town was selected. The Triple Alliance assessed each province an annual tribute quota. This information was recorded in manuscripts stored in the imperial capitals. The second part of the *Codex Mendoza* is an early colonial copy of one such imperial tribute roll. Each province was allotted one or two pages in the *Codex*. The province of Coayxtlahuacan, located in the modern state of Oaxaca and inhabited by Mixtec speakers, provides an example (figure 7.5, no. 33).

Table 7.1   Provinces of the Triple Alliance Empire

No.	Province	Type
1	Axocopan	Tributary
2	Atotonilco (de Pedraza)	Tributary
3	Xilotepec	Tributary
4	Chiapan	Strategic
5	Xocotitlan	Tributary
6	Ixtlahuaca	Strategic
7	Cuahuacan	Tributary
8	Tollocan	Tributary
9	Ocuilan	Tributary
10	Malinalco	Tributary
11	Temazcaltepec	Strategic
12	Tlachco	Tributary
13	Cuauhnahuac	Tributary
14	Huaxtepec	Tributary
15	Ocuituco	Strategic
16	Chiauhtlan	Strategic
17	Quiauhteopan	Tributary
18	Tlacozauhtitlan	Tributary
19	Tepequacuilco	Tributary
20	Zompanco	Strategic
21	Tetellan	Strategic
22	Tlapan	Tributary
23	Cihuatlan	Tributary
24	Tecpantepec	Strategic
25	Ayotlan	Strategic
26	Ometepec	Strategic
27	Xoconochco	Tributary
28	Miahuatlan	Strategic
29	Teozacualco	Strategic
30	Teozapotlan	Strategic
31	Ixtepexi	Strategic
32	Coyolapan	Tributary
33	Coayxtlahuacan	Tributary
34	Tlachquiauhco	Tributary
35	Yoaltepec	Tributary
36	Tecomaixtlahuacan	Strategic
37	Acatlan	Strategic
38	Ahuatlan	Strategic
39	Tepeacac	Tributary

Table 7.1   (Cont.)

No.	Province	Type
40	Tochtepec	Tributary
41	Cuetlaxtlan	Tributary
42	Cempoallan	Strategic
43	Quauhtochco	Tributary
44	Xalapa	Strategic
45	Misantla	Strategic
46	Tlatlauhquitepec	Tributary
47	Tetela	Strategic
48	Tlapacoyan	Tributary
49	Cuauhchinanco	Strategic
50	Atotonilco (el Grande)	Tributary
51	Atlan	Tributary
52	Tochpan	Tributary
53	Tzicoac	Tributary
54	Huexotla	Strategic
55	Oxitipan	Tributary

See Figure 7.4 for the locations of provinces by number.
Source: Berdan et al. (1996)

Coayxtlahuacan was the head town of the province, so its glyph was painted at the top of the page.[15] Other towns in the province, most of them capitals of city-states, are listed under the head town. The remainder of the page lists the imperial tribute goods and the quantities to be paid. A feather attached to the top of an item indicates the quantity 400; a flag stands for 20. The five symbols along the top of the page represent capes and other textiles, totalling 2,000 items. Another page of the codex states that these textiles were delivered semiannually, so the province of Coayxtlahuacan paid a total of 4,000 textiles each year. Other tribute items paid annually were two feathered warrior costumes with shields; two strings of jade beads; 800 quetzal feathers; 40 bags of cochineal dye; 20 gourd bowls of gold dust, and one royal feather headpiece. These goods were assembled and sent to Tenochtitlan by an imperial tribute collector called a *calpixqui*. Unfortunately we know almost nothing about the actual collection of tribute in the

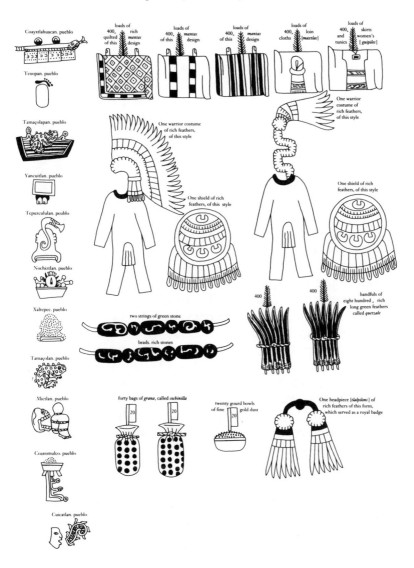

Figure 7.5 The tribute of the imperial province of
Coayxtlahuacan as depicted in the Codex Mendoza
(1992:v.4:91; folio 43r)

outer provinces. Did each town contribute a small portion of the whole range of a province's tribute, or did towns specialize in the type of tribute they paid? Did a province's tribute collector have underlings in each town? To what extent did imperial tribute collectors rely upon local kings and officials to help gather the goods? This is one of the major gaps in our knowledge of the operation of the Aztec empire.

When all of the imperial tribute in the *Codex Mendoza* is added up, the quantity and diversity of goods are impressive (table 7.2). The most common items, paid by almost every province, were capes of cotton or *maguey*. As easily transportable items of money and wealth, it is not surprising that textiles were the principal tribute goods of the empire. Nearly all provinces also provided warrior costumes and shields, tribute that symbolized the military domination of the empire over the provinces. Luxury goods, particularly tropical feathers, were also major tribute items, as were many specialized goods such as copal incense, paper, and liquidambar. Foodstuffs, animal products, and building materials were minor items of imperial tribute.

In many cases, the empire used the tribute system to obtain local specialties from the provinces. For example, cochineal dye, produced from an insect that lives on the prickly pear cactus, was produced in many towns in the Coayxtlahuacan region (figure 7.5); bark paper was a major item of tribute from towns in Morelos, where it was produced in quantity; and the Pacific coastal province of Cihuatlan paid in seashells, cacao, and other local products. On the other hand, many tribute goods were not native to the provinces that had to pay them. Of the tribute demanded of Coayxtlahuacan, the tropical feathers were not available in highland Oaxaca, nor were the jade beads or gold dust. In order to obtain these exotic goods, the people of Coayxtlahuacan had to engage in commerce with other areas. At first glance, it may seem that the Aztecs demanded this nonlocal tribute merely to save themselves the trouble of obtaining distant goods, such as feathers, gold, or jade, directly. But Aztec merchants also supplied these and other exotic goods to Tenochtitlan independently of the tribute system. Another explanation for the prevalence of nonlocal tribute is that it was part of a deliberate effort to stimulate trade and commerce throughout the empire.

Table 7.2   Imperial tribute as recorded in the Codex Mendoza

Category	Item	Total Annual Amount[a]
Textiles and clothing	Quachtli and other capes	128,000 items
	Garments	19,200 items
	Raw cotton	4,400 loads
	Cochineal dye	65 bags
Military supplies	Warrior costumes with shields	665 sets
	Canes for arrows	32,000 items
Jewelry and luxuries	Colorful feathers	29,680 items
	Feather products	7 items
	Feather down	20 bags
	Lip plugs	82 items
	Amber	2 large pieces
	Turquoise masks	10 items
	Other turquoise items	5 items
	Jade beads and stones	22 strings
	Gold objects	65 items
	Gold dust	60 bowls
	Gold bars	10 items
	Copper/bronze bells	80 items
	Copper/bronze axes	560 items
Foodstuffs	Maize and other staples	88 large bins
	Chiles	1,600 loads
	Honey	3,800 jars
	Salt	4,000 loaves
	Ground grain	320 baskets
	Cacao beans	680 loads
Animal products	Live eagles	2 or more
	Deer skins	3,200 items
	Jaguar skins	40 items
	Bird skins	160 items
	Seashells	1,600 items
Building materials	Lime for construction	4,400 loads
	Wood beams and planks	14,400 pieces

Table 7.2 (Cont.)

Category	Item	Total Annual Amount[a]
Miscellaneous products	Copal incense	64,000 balls
	"	3,200 baskets
	Balls of rubber	16,000 items
	Paper	32,000 sheets
	Reed mats and seats	16,000 items
	Canes	48,000 items
	Gourd bowls	17,600 items
	Pottery bowls	2,400 items
	Yellow ocher	40 pans
	Liquidambar	16,000 cakes
	"	100 jars
	Carrying frames	800 items
	Firewood	4,800 loads

[a] I use Frances Berdan's calculations of the annual quantities of tribute (Berdan and Anawalt 1992:v.1:154–156). The organization by category is my own.
Source: Codex Mendoza (1992:f.18v–55r)

This forcing of provincial peoples to engage in long-distance trade to obtain tribute goods was part of the economic strategy of the Triple Alliance. In addition to demanding tribute payments, imperial rulers took a number of steps to promote and encourage trade and markets. For example, the *pochteca* and other merchants were encouraged and backed by the empire, and key market towns in the provinces were protected from foreign interference. The empire thus employed two tactics to implement its economic strategy: direct state control through regular tribute payments, and indirect promotion of commerce, whose benefits were felt throughout Mesoamerica.

The Frontier Strategy

The expanding Aztec empire soon ran up against powerful enemy states who could not be subdued. Its two most intractable enemies were Tlaxcalla and the Tarascan empire.[16] Tlaxcalla included several Aztec city-states who banded together to successfully resist conquest by the Triple Alliance. Although surrounded by the empire and under siege, the Tlaxcallans were still holding out when the Spaniards arrived in 1519. The Tarascan polity was a powerful, non-Aztec empire whose size and influence matched that of the Triple Alliance. When direct warfare failed to subdue these states, the Aztec rulers devised a frontier strategy to keep them at bay. City-states located along the enemy frontiers were brought into the empire through conquest or threat, but they were treated more as allies than as subjects. In lieu of regular tribute payments, these client states were asked to maintain the borders and to give occasional "gifts" to the empire; they were not listed in the *Codex Mendoza* or other imperial tribute rolls. This situation was described in the *Relación Geográfica* from the town of Totoltepec, a client state on the Tarascan border:

> The Mexican king Axayacatl made war [on the people of Totoltepec] until he subjugated them. They did not bring him tribute because they were on the Tarascan frontier; they supplied the Mexica soldiers that were stationed there and at the fortress of Oztoma. A few times each year they sent presents to Mexico consisting of capes, green stones, and copper.[17]

Some of these client states engaged in low-intensity warfare with the enemies, others manned fortresses, and some supplied garrisons (as in the case of Totoltepec above). The direct economic benefit of these city-states to the empire was minimal, although most did engage in some form of trade with Aztec merchants. Rather, their role in the empire was strategic: they helped to protect the borders so that imperial tribute and trade activities in the inner tributary provinces could proceed unimpeded in a safe, peaceful climate.

These client states were so successful that the empire only needed a small number of fortresses and garrisons along the borders, although many of the border states maintained their own local fortresses or defenses. The Aztec fortress at Oztoma was located at a particularly strategic location along the Tarascan border, in an area rich in minerals (including copper and gold) that was an active target of Tarascan expansion in the late fifteenth century. Oztoma also guarded the town of

Alahuistlan, a major regional market and the leading producer of salt in the western provinces of the Aztec empire.[18]

Mexica Propaganda and The Limits of Empire

Ethnohistoric sources that derive from statements of the Mexica nobility do not always mesh with the view of the Aztec empire I have presented above. The Mexica were reluctant to admit their failed efforts to conquer Tlaxcalla, the Tarascans, and some other states. Their own accounts of the empire in the chronicles gloss over these shortcomings. For example, Friar Durán gives the following description of a state ceremony in Tenochtitlan that involved the display and exchange of lavish gifts among Mexica nobles and their guests from other states:

> They saw that [the Mexica] were masters of the world, their empire so wide and abundant that they had conquered all the nations and that all were their vassals. The guests, seeing such wealth and opulence and such authority and power, were filled with terror.[19]

This account is clearly a statement of propaganda, not fact, since the Mexica had not by any means "conquered all the nations." In their public statements the Mexica conveniently forgot Axayacatl's devastating defeat at the hands of the Tarascans.

Tlaxcalla, the independent eastern Aztec states surrounded by the empire, is another case in point. When some Spanish soldiers asked Motecuhzoma and his generals why they did not complete their conquest of this renegade area, they received the following excuse:

> We could easily do so; but then there would remain nowhere for the young men to train [militarily], except far from here; and, also, we wanted there to always be [nearby] people to sacrifice to our gods.[20]

In other words, they claimed that the Triple Alliance was not really trying to conquer Tlaxcalla but preferred to engage in "practice" wars. The Mexica called these battles "flowery wars" (*xochiyaoyotl*) to distinguish them from wars of conquest. The Tlaxcallan rulers, however, responded to this question quite differently. They told the Spaniards that the Aztecs had them surrounded, had cut off their foreign trade in luxuries and salt, and were trying hard to defeat them, but had yet to succeed. Again, the Mexica words ring more of propaganda than of truth.[21] The Tlaxcallans were formidable foes indeed and the Triple Alliance simply was not powerful enough to defeat them. The Tlaxcallans later delivered a fatal blow to their enemy when they allied themselves with Hernando Cortés and participated in the conquest of Tenochtitlan in 1521.

The Triple Alliance may not have managed to "conquer all the nations," but the "wealth and opulence" that so impressed visitors to Tenochtitlan were real enough. When one considers the imperial tribute pouring into the capital two to four times a year together with the trade goods imported by Aztec merchants, the volume of incoming wealth was immense. This imperial wealth was instrumental in the growth of Tenochtitlan, and the size and grandeur of the capital city were concrete manifestations of the economic success of the empire.

8

Cities and Urban Planning

As long as the world will endure, the fame and glory of Mexico-Tenochtitlan will never perish.

Chimalpahin[1]

Tenochtitlan, the Aztec imperial capital, was the largest city ever built in the ancient New World. Founded in AD 1325, Tenochtitlan grew into an island metropolis of 200,000 inhabitants. Until recently, almost all surviving information on Aztec urbanism concerned this great metropolis, and next to nothing was known about other Aztec cities. Most had been destroyed or buried under Spanish and, later, modern communities. Once Spain took control over Mesoamerica in 1521, Spanish colonists moved into many Aztec cities and immediately began to refashion them into European-style urban centers. These settlers rarely left descriptions of the earlier communities. Yet other cities and towns were abandoned soon after the Spanish conquest.

Today, the few surviving Aztec urban settlements have become rather unassuming archaeological sites. Because they lack the huge pyramids and other grandiose architecture that for so long attracted archaeologists, these sites were ignored by early investigators. Many modern writers have assumed that other Aztec cities were simply small versions of Tenochtitlan, but recent archaeological work has shown this to be false. When fieldworkers following the "social archaeology" approach turned their attention to urban centers such as Otumba, Huexotla, Xaltocan, and Yautepec, they discovered a very different type of settlement from the imperial capital.

Outside of Tenochtitlan, urban settlements were small in size and today would be considered quite rural in appearance. Houses were small and widely spaced, with orchards and gardens filling the area in between them. Yet these towns and cities functioned as urban centers. People from the entire polity depended upon the city-state's central settlement. It contained markets, temples, and administrative buildings that served a wider hinterland, and these institutions, not size or population density, made a community urban.[2] In this chapter I review the new evidence concerning smaller Aztec cities and then discuss the more traditional information on the imperial capital.

City-State Capitals

Fictional Visit to Amecameca, an Aztec City

The following fictional vignette gives an idea of how a typical Aztec city-state capital in the Valley of Mexico might have appeared to a visitor.[3]

Opan, whose name means "On the road," is an itinerant merchant approaching the city-state capital of Amecameca in the southeast Valley of Mexico. He is a *pochteca* merchant from the Acolhua capital Texcoco, and his small party of five *tlamamah* (carriers) are bringing obsidian tools and jade jewelry from Otumba to exchange for various local and imported goods at the Amecameca market. Situated near the major pass between the Valley of Mexico and Morelos, Amecameca lies along an ancient trade route, and its markets offer imported goods from lowland areas to the south.

The edge of the city is demarcated by low, stone field walls which separate the surrounding cornfields from urban houselots. The walled houselots are fairly large, and include gardens, turkey pens, trash heaps, and open yard areas in addition to the adobe-walled houses and storehouses. Opan notices that houses in Amecameca are somewhat smaller than those in his native Texcoco but their construction and form are quite similar. In some cases, two or three houses are arranged around a small patio (much like the rural town of Cuexcomate described in chapters 3 and 6); in other cases, a single house occupies a lot. Although most houses are within shouting distance of one or more neighbors, privacy is maintained by the large size of the houselots and the dense foliage of the many fruit trees and other garden crops tended by each family.

After a short walk past the green gardens of the outer city, the travellers pass a small market plaza next to a modest temple-pyramid. There are a few other unassuming stone buildings nearby. A number of people look with interest on the merchant's party. This plaza must be the center of one of the *calpolli* of Amecameca, he thinks. Opan wonders how many of these neighborhoods make up the city of Amecameca, certainly far fewer than in Texcoco. Nevertheless, Amecameca is a good-sized city for one so far from the central lakes of the Valley. A vendor beckons from under her awning, but her wares hold no alure for Opan. What a change from Otumba, he muses. There, many of the neighborhoods specialize in one or more crafts, and good bargains can be found in the small *calpolli* markets; in fact several bundles of the obsidian blades Opan carries were purchased at such a neighborhood market in Otumba. But this *calpolli* market in Amecameca offers only some corn, beans, and ceramic cookpots. Opan becomes anxious. Will the central market have the cotton, paper, feathers, and other goods he is seeking?

The group moves on toward the city's center, and Opan continues to silently compare Amecameca to other settlements they have just passed through. The residential areas of this urban center, an important city-state capital with more than one *tlatoani*, so far look identical to the small villages along the Chalco-Amecameca road. The large houselots and gardens with ample greenery make all of these hinterland cities and towns appear rural to an urbanite from Texcoco, the second-largest Aztec city. How do these provincials react when they visit a real city like the imposing imperial capital Tenochtitlan, which dwarfs even the great ancient city of Texcoco? Opan's thoughts are interrupted when the group at last reaches the center of town and the features that distinguish Amecameca from a village appear.

Their first glimpse of the city's center is the temple-pyramid, which towers over all other structures. The road they have followed ends at the back of the royal palace; a complex of stone buildings built on a large, low platform. It is still early, and several peasants from the countryside wait listlessly in the shade for a palace official to assign them tasks for the day. The palace and temple, the largest buildings in the city-state, both face onto an open plaza, where many people mill around, perhaps waiting for a ceremony to begin. The market is on the opposite, southern side of the plaza, so the group must go around the central area. Opan turns right to pass along the west side to avoid the crowd gathering near the pyramid. Here, on the west side of the plaza, a game is in progress in the ballcourt and the bearers slow down to catch a glimpse of the action. Opan hurries them on, however, since his destination is now in view.

It is market day in Amecameca, and the market plaza is filled with throngs of buyers amid the many stalls and booths. Opan notes with satisfaction that only a few vendors offer obsidian blades or jewelry. A local associate of Opan's guild has already paid the market tax and saved a choice stall, so after a brief conversation with the market judge, Opan unpacks his wares. These are what separate cities from villages, he thinks, the market, the pyramid, the palace, the plaza, and the throngs of people who gather around them to take care of their personal and professional needs. What would a merchant do without cities and towns?

Urban Planning and Layout

Most Aztec cities and towns were founded by Aztlan immigrants in the twelfth and thirteenth centuries. The layout of the capital cities followed a plan with a long heritage in Mesoamerica. In this tradition, cities were arranged around a sacred central zone which comprised a rectangular public plaza bordered by the important civic and religious buildings. The orientation and placement of the central buildings were carefully planned, often following the dictates of astronomical principles. Outside of the central precinct, however, formal planning was abandoned. Houses, workshops, markets, schools, and neighborhood temples were dispersed throughout the city, separated by gardens and open lots. This ancient pattern of urban layout was used by most Mesoamerican civilizations of the Classic and Postclassic epochs, including the lowland Classic Maya and the Zapotecs of the Valley of Oaxaca, and it was natural for the early Aztecs to draw on this tradition when they designed their first cities.[4]

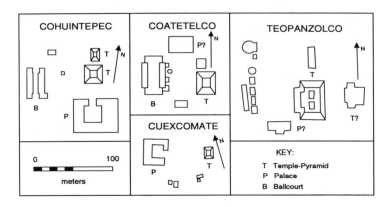

Figure 8.1   Plans of the central precincts of four Aztec urban centers in Morelos (Drawing by Michael E. Smith)

Aztec city-state capitals, such as Amecameca, Otumba, and Yautepec, played a more important role in the daily lives of most people than did the distant imperial metropolis. Peasants came to town to attend the market, to participate in religious ceremonies, to pay their tribute, and to take care of innumerable other social and administrative obligations. A large, open public plaza formed the heart of the city, with the *tlatoani's* palace, a temple, and other civic structures arranged along its four sides (figure 8.1). The temple-pyramid always occupied the east side. A single or double stairway led up the west or front side of the pyramid to the platform on top. Roofed temple rooms that housed the idols of the city-state's patron gods crowned the pyramid. This structure was the central focus of supernatural power in the city and polity. Many cities had a ballcourt along the plaza, where the Mesoamerican ballgame was played (see chapter 9). Other civic buildings that faced the plaza could include a *telpochcalli* school or various smaller temples or shrines.

These stone buildings and the plaza itself were laid out with a common orientation, usually close to the cardinal directions. The consistency of this pattern among surviving city centers suggests that urban central zones were carefully planned in accordance with basic principles of political and religious cosmology. The close proximity of the palace and temple would have reinforced the link between the earthly realm of the *tlatoani* and the sacred realm of the gods. The king ruled for the gods, and his political power had supernatural backing. The layout and orientation of these central precincts is consistent with the Aztecs" preoccupation with the east–west passage of the sun and a four-directional cosmology.

Outside of the sacred central zone, Aztec cities showed little evidence for planning or controlled growth. Houses and house groups were scattered here and there, buildings did not follow a common orientation, and formal streets or avenues were absent. Nobles and commoners lived in wards and *calpolli*. At least some of these urban *calpolli* were specialized economically.[5] Houses in most Aztec cities were small, simple structures built of adobe bricks. Cuexcomate, a rural town, not a city-state capital, is the only center whose housing pattern has been mapped completely (figure 3.8). The houses and patio groups of its 800 residents were distributed across an area of 14.6 hectares with considerable open area within the town that was probably devoted to farming. Most Aztec cities were larger than Cuexcomate; the average city-state capital in the Valley of Mexico had 9,000 inhabitants in an area of 200 hectares (2 square km). The population densities of the larger urban settlements, however, were similar to that of Cuexcomate (the city-state capitals averaged 45 persons per hectare, whereas the density at Cuexcomate was 55 persons per hectare). This suggests that Cuexcomate's pattern of scattered houses separated by large open lots may also have characterized other Aztec urban centers.

Only a few cities managed to grow beyond the modest size of their contemporaries, usually when a polity experienced great political and economic success as capital of a large domain or empire. Apart from the obvious case of Tenochtitlan, examples include Azcapotzalco (the Tepanec capital before 1428) and Texcoco (Tenochtitlan's partner in the Triple Alliance) in the Valley of Mexico, and Cuauhnahuac in Morelos. Little survives of these cities archaeologically, and only Texcoco has any useful ethnohistoric descriptions.[6] These cities all had more than 20,000 inhabitants, and their central precincts were probably larger and more impressive than most cities.

Urban Archaeology at Yautepec

Yautepec was an important capital city in Morelos with several nearby city-states subject to its *tlatoani*. As discussed in chapter 6, Yautepec has the only surviving Aztec royal palace. After the success of the initial seasons of Hortensia de Vega Nova's excavations at the palace, my wife and I were invited by the Mexican government to work at Yautepec. The palace was on the edge of the modern town with Aztec residential areas extending into agricultural fields to the west and south. This left major areas of Aztec Yautepec open for fieldwork. De Vega Nova continued her work at the palace and we concentrated on excavating houses and other features in other parts of the site. Although fieldwork at the palace is still not completed, and our analyses of artifacts are still in progress, the two complementary projects have already uncovered much new information on Aztec urban life.[7]

In our first season of fieldwork, we used surface concentrations of artifacts to trace the size and shape of the Aztec city. This was easy in the plowed fields, but required patience and perseverance within town. Our field crews spent a lot of time knocking on doors and explaining our purpose to the people of Yautepec so that they would let us root around in their yards for potsherds, obsidian, and other traces of Aztec occupation. I was surprised at how well we were able to find artifacts in and around modern Yautepec, and the goodwill of the citizens contributed greatly to our success. We made several hundred collections of artifacts from two by two meter squares (figure 1.7) and used computer-generated maps of artifact density to help draw the borders of Aztec Yautepec. The city reached its maximum extent, 210 hectares (2.1 square km), in the Late Aztec B period, just prior to the Spanish conquest. Although there were some earlier villages at the site, the major occupation began in the Early Aztec period, which suggests that Yautepec, like other Aztec cities, was founded by Aztlan immigrants.

Our second season was devoted to excavations of houses, garbage middens, and other key areas in and around Aztec Yautepec.[8] We placed excavations in various parts of the modern

Figure 8.2 Excavation of an urban commoner house in Yautepec. This house was first discovered by a public works crew while grading the street (Photograph by Michael E. Smith)

town, including schoolyards, vacant lots, residential neighborhoods, churchyards, plowed fields, and even a street. In all we placed excavations in 17 different areas of Yautepec. Twelve of these 17 excavations were undertaken specifically to find buried houses. We located and excavated seven Aztec houses (figure 8.2; see also figure 6.6 and accompanying discussion) as well as numerous other domestic deposits.

The locations of the excavations and houses are shown superimposed on our map of Yautepec in figure 8.3. We dug one elite residence (structure 6), five commoner dwellings (structures 1–4 and 7), and one intermediate structure (no. 5). This is the first set of urban Aztec houses excavated anywhere in central Mexico. We were somewhat surprised that the urban houses (see chapter 6) were quite similar in size and construction to the rural houses we had excavated previously at Cuexcomate and Capilco (chapter 3). The population density of Yautepec was not much higher than the rural sites,[9] and this

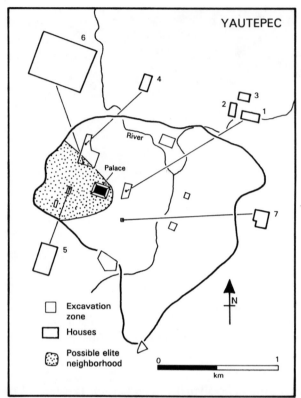

*Figure 8.3 Map of Aztec Yautepec showing the locations of our
excavation zones and the houses that were excavated in 1993.
The houses are drawn to a common scale; the largest, structure 6,
measures 23 by 18.5 meters (Drawing by Ellen Cesarski)*

implies that this city had considerable open space for gardens
and fields within its borders.

Preliminary results indicate that there may have been a zone
of wealthy residents to the west of the royal palace, perhaps a
calpolli with primarily nobles and/or wealthy commoners.
Although the houses we excavated in other parts of the city
were smaller than those in this one neighborhood, we think
that most Yautepec residents were fairly prosperous. The artifact assemblages from all of the excavated houses included
many imported goods (such as obsidian from Pachuca, salt
from the Valley of Mexico lakes, pottery from many parts of

central Mexico, and copper and bronze from the Tarascan territory) in addition to local items. In domestic contexts throughout Yautepec, we uncovered considerable evidence for the production of goods such as obsidian tools and jewelry, ceramic figurines, bark paper, and cotton textiles. None of these artifact deposits, however, were heavy enough to suggest that they were the remains of workshops. Unfortunately, we cannot tell from our scattered excavations whether Yautepec had economically specialized *calpolli* similar to those at Otumba.

The locations of the colonial and modern Yautepec settlements, just to the north of Aztec Yautepec, contributed enormously to the success of our fieldwork. In most central Mexican towns, the Spanish settlement was constructed directly on top of the Aztec settlement. The Spaniards typically tore down the Aztec pyramid to make a base for construction of a Catholic church. We tested this notion by excavating in and around Yautepec's sixteenth-century church and convent but found no evidence for a temple or other Aztec structure beneath. We do not know why the early Spanish settlers of Yautepec founded their town to the north of the Aztec city, but as archaeologists we are grateful for this turn of events.

Rural and Urban

Rural and urban contexts were not as sharply differentiated as they are in modern societies. Most Aztec cities were quite "rural" in appearance, owing to their unplanned residential districts, farming within the urban site, the presence of large houselots, and an overall low population density. Outside of the downtown area, cities did not look much different from towns and villages. A similar comparison can be made in the opposite direction: there was much of the "urban" in the countryside. Nobles lived in rural areas as well as in the city. Many crafts were produced in the countryside, and peasant families were remarkably well connected to central Mexican market networks. Aztec peasants were not impoverished, isolated serfs but rather prosperous and sophisticated producers and consumers.

The explanation for this similarity between the rural and the urban lies in the nature of Aztec economic and political organization. Economic and demographic expansion in the Early

Aztec period set the scene for prosperity in both urban and rural areas. In Late Aztec times, the growth of stable city-states made the countryside a safe place to live and work. The ensuing expansion of merchant activity and marketplace trade linked all parts of central Mexico – rural and urban – together into a single economic network. Peasants did not have to move to the city to prosper, and urbanites did not have to give up the farming life or differentiate themselves socially from their country cousins. Tenochtitlan, however, did not fit this pattern of rural-looking cities. The Mexica capital was a settlement of a different order than other Aztec cities.

Tenochtitlan

> Proud of itself
> is the city of Mexico-Tenochtitlan.
> Here no one fears to die in war.
> This is our glory.
> This is Your Command,
> oh Giver of Life!
> Have this in mind, oh princes,
> do not forget it.
> Who could conquer Tenochtitlan?
> Who could shake the foundation of heaven?
> Aztec poem[10]

Tenochtitlan was a city built to impress visitors, both human and divine. Just as the city awed the first Spaniards who saw it Tenochtitlan also overwhelmed Aztecs visiting from the provinces (figure 8.4).[11] Part of Tenochtitlan's grandeur derived from its sheer size (200,000 inhabitants on an island of 13.5 square km) and part reflected the deliberate planning and layout of the city. This was not just a political capital and market center. Tenochtitlan was forged into a sacred imperial city whose size and layout proclaimed the Mexica view of their destiny as rulers of the empire.

Urban Planning and Layout

Tenochtitlan was the last of the city-state centers to be founded by the Aztlan migrants.[12] The Mexica began by constructing a

Figure 8.4 Reconstruction of the city of Tenochtitlan (looking east) on the eve of Spanish conquest (Detail from a painting by Miguel Covarrubias in the Museo Nacional de Antropología e Historia, Mexico City. Photo: Robert Frerck, Odyssey Productions, Chicago)

shrine to their god Huitzilopochtli at the place where they had seen the omen of the eagle perched on a cactus. The name Tenochtitlan means "Among the Stone-Cactus Fruit;" its glyph is a fruited nopal cactus growing out of a stone (figure 1.6). The town was laid out around the shrine, which was soon enlarged into a stone pyramid. This structure, with twin stairways leading to two temples, was the earliest stage of the Templo Mayor. In its early days, Tenochtitlan probably resembled the city-state capitals described above, with a formally-planned city center surrounded by unplanned residential quarters.

The Mexica's growth in power and influence during the Late Aztec A period (AD 1350–1430) was mirrored by explosive growth in the size and prosperity of Tenochtitlan. In the Late Aztec B period, following the Tepanec war of 1428, Tenochtitlan became capital of the empire and the Mexica set out to redesign the city to differentiate it from other Aztec cities and towns.

The Mexica saw themselves as heirs to the powerful ancient empires of Teotihuacan and Tula, and they deliberately appropriated principles and concepts from the ruins of those abandoned capitals in order to refashion Tenochtitlan in their image. First, they used a grid layout, similar to that at Teotihuacan, to establish a common alignment for all buildings. Second, they effected a radical change in the layout of the downtown area by walling off a sacred religious precinct from the rest of the city. Third, they deliberately copied architectural and sculptural styles from Teotihuacan and Tula in their rebuilt downtown area.[13]

Unlike the haphazard layouts of most towns and cities, the entire urban area of Tenochtitlan was carefully planned and rebuilt according to fundamental political, religious, and practical principles. The regular grid pattern demonstrated the power of the Mexica rulers. In ancient civilizations around the world, only strong kings were capable of impressing their will on a city by designing the whole settlement sufficiently in advance to produce a grid layout. The application of the grid plan to Tenochtitlan was a public statement about the grandeur and power of the island city and its links to ancient Teotihuacan.

The influence of religion was also felt in the planning and layout of Tenochtitlan. The city's grid was established close to the cardinal directions (the orientation of streets and buildings was 6.5 degrees east of true north). In Mesoamerican cosmology, the four cardinal directions had important symbolic significance, each with its own gods, rituals, and colors. This religious cosmology, which normally found expression only in the central precincts of city-state capitals, was extended to the entire city of Tenochtitlan. Major avenues extended out from the sacred precinct along the cardinal directions, dividing the city into four major quarters (figure 8.5). Because it monitored the path of the sun, the east–west axis was the more important one, and this was reflected in the placement and orientation of the Templo Mayor and other shrines in the sacred precinct.

In addition to these political and religious influences, practical considerations also contributed to the adoption of a grid plan at Tenochtitlan. A rectilinear grid is the easiest layout to use in a rapidly expanding city. As rocks and fill were brought from the shore to reclaim land for *chinampas* and houses, it

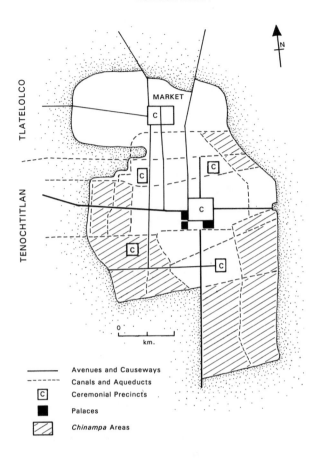

*Figure 8.5   Map of Tenochtitlan and Tlatelolco
(After Calnek 1972:108; drawing by Ellen Cesarski)*

was convenient to lay out canals and roads at right angles, following a single orientation for the entire city.

The Mexica drew upon their knowledge of the central ceremonial zone at Tula (figure 2.3) to redesign their downtown area. In place of the open public plaza bordered by religious and civic buildings that was standard at other Aztec cities, the Mexica created a walled sacred precinct whose buildings were arranged in a pattern similar to that used at Tula. Limiting public access to the precinct was part of a Mexica plan to elevate their religion to a mystical state cult (see chapter 9). In a further break with prior Aztec practice, each Mexica king constructed his own palace rather than reusing a single palace as at smaller Aztec cities. These palaces were built next to, but outside of, the sacred precinct. The Mexica kings further emphasized their associations with Teotihuacan and Tula by erecting buildings in the styles of these ancient capitals; archaeologists have excavated at least one structure in each style near the central Templo Mayor in the sacred precinct. The kings also had sculptures carved in the ancient Teotihuacan and Toltec styles and displayed these in and around the precinct. By the late 1400s, the architectural transformation of Tenochtitlan was complete, and the city was one of the largest and most impressive urban centers in the whole world. What did it look like to visitors?

Fictional Visit to the Imperial Capital

This fictional vignette describes Tenochtitlan from the perspective of a visitor from the provinces.

The young provincial lord Mihua ("Possessor of arrows") has been invited to attend his first state ceremony at the imperial capital. He is the eldest son of the *tlatoani* of Yautepec, who cannot attend because of other committments. Mihua crosses the mountains on foot with his personal servant, and they pass through several settlements on their way to one of the causeways that lead to Tenochtitlan. These cities and towns are larger and busier than those of his valley at home, he notes. As they start across the western causeway toward the capital, the young noble is greatly impressed at the huge city spread out before him (see figures 8.4 and 8.5). He has never seen a road as wide or straight as this causeway, nor an aqueduct as large and well-made as the one that runs along the road carrying fresh water to the city from springs at Chapultepec on the shore.[14]

While on the causeway, Mihua marvels at the drawbridges that can be raised to let canoes pass through. He realizes that these could also be pulled up for defense in case of attack. But then who would ever attack this enormous and powerful city? The lake surrounding Tenochtitlan seems full of boats, particularly in the northern area around Tlatelolco, home of the central market. There are the small canoes of individual farmers or craftsmen bringing their goods to market, and the larger vessels with shaded seats carrying fancily-dressed lords on their way to the capital.

At the outskirts of the island city, Mihua sees miles and miles of greenery from the maize and vegetables that grow year-round in the *chinampa* plots. His servant comments that these densely-planted fields make the farms back in Yautepec look pretty scraggly. The Yautepec countryside is known far and wide in the provinces for its highly fertile irrigated croplands, but even the most productive plot cannot match the exuberant maize, beans, and amaranth of the *chinampas*. Long straight canals run everywhere, including both thoroughfares for large boats carrying people and goods, and small canals for farmers moving among their fields. The visitors notice the small, flat-roofed houses of farmers built on solid land in the midst of their family plot.

The provincial lord marvels at a high and mighty Mexica noble, who, dressed in incredible finery, rides in a flat-bottomed barge with a decorated awning for shade. Mihua complains to his servant about the luxurious treatment afforded the Mexica lord while nobles visiting from important cities like Yautepec have to fight their way along the causeway through crowds of merchants, servants, and other commoners.

The visitors come to the end of the *chinampa* area and the causeway widens into a road traversing the main residential zone of the city. Like the canals and *chinampas*, the roads and houses are all aligned along the same north–south and east–west grid that covers the city. Nonfarming commoners live in small houses similar to their farming cousins, but the houses are packed much closer together than anything back in Yautepec. Several generations of an extended family emerge from a modest house along the avenue, and Mihua is secretly pleased that even in the great Tenochtitlan commoners live crowded together in small houses, just like back home. The travellers come upon a sumptuous two-story house surrounded by well-tended gardens, obviously the palace of a noble. These luxurious buildings become more common along the avenue as the two proceed toward the city center, but smaller commoners' houses can be seen back behind the palaces, off the central thoroughfare.

At the intersection with another wide straight avenue, Mihua glances down to the left and sees towering pyramids and crowds of people. The ceremonial precinct dwarfs any that he has seen before, but he remembers his father's instruction not to be fooled by the district precincts in Tenochtitlan. This is only the center of one of the four great quarters of the city, not the heart of the city that is his destination. Crossing the street, servant and master enter what appears to be a new *calpolli*. Mihua had noticed professional carriers hauling heavy loads of copper and gold to workshops in the last neighborhood. A glimpse of the end of a procession in honor of the god Xipe Totec, patron of metalworkers, confirms his opinion that they had just passed a metalworker's *calpolli*. In this new neighborhood, yards are surrounded by high walls. Some men emerge from a doorway, and Mihua looks in and sees a large, well-built house of a single story. The men are well dressed and prosperous-looking, but they wear the clothing of commoners, not nobles. These must be the famous *pochteca*. Mihua has heard that the city also contains neighborhoods composed entirely of foreigners where people speak strange languages and dress oddly, but he has yet to see any of these people along the main west avenue.

The approach to the center of Tenochtitlan is signalled by larger crowds of people in the streets and plazas and by the increasingly grandiose architecture of nobles' palaces, temple-pyramids, and other government buildings. The huge Templo Mayor looms over the center of the city, the blood on its stairs visible from a great distance. The travellers have arrived at the wall of the sacred precinct and the end of the avenue. Just outside the precinct are several palaces of the Mexica *tlatoque*. Mihua is awed not only at the size and luxury of these compounds (far larger than his father's royal palace back home), but also at their number. Each Mexica *tlatoani* has built his own palace, leaving the homes of his predecessors as monuments to the greatness of the dynasty. Mihua has heard rumors of this practice, which is contrary to the usual Aztec custom of using the same palace for successive kings. He locates the correct palace from his father's instructions and enters the outer courtyard, where he asks directions of an important-looking official. Just then his second cousin, a low-ranking member of the Mexica royal family, arrives and the two young lords head for the sacred precinct to witness a gladiator sacrifice. Mihua's servant stays at the palace to help at various tasks until his lord returns.

The sacred precinct of Tenochtitlan, larger than some provincial towns, greatly impresses Mihua. The walled compound measures about 500 meters on a side.[15] Inside he can see numerous temples, altars, shrines, schools, and assembly halls, dominated by the towering twin-stair Templo Mayor pyramid (figure 1.1). He knows that at any time of day, some ceremony is taking place, either a public spectacle such as a sacrifice or procession, or a private ritual by priests, warriors, or other important persons. The size and grandeur of this inner sacred city overwhelms the provincial visitor, who stops to stare. His cousin is amused at this typical newcomer's reaction to the sacred precinct. In Yautepec and other city-state capitals, the state religion is served by a single, modest temple-pyramid located on the central public plaza; here in Tenochtitlan religion occupies its own inner city, closed off from public view and even separated by a wall from the palace of the emperor. These Mexica gods must be powerful indeed, Mihua thinks.

9

Creation, Sacrifice, and the Gods

How the gods had their beginning and where they began is not
well known. But this is plain, [that] there at Teotihuacan . . .
when yet there was darkness, there all the gods gathered themselves together, and they debated who would bear the burden,
who would carry on his back – would become – the sun. And
when the sun came to arise, then all [the gods] died that the sun
might come unto being . . . And thus the ancient ones thought
it to be.

Friar Bernardino de Sahagún[1]

A fundamental idea of Aztec religion was that the gods sacrificed themselves in order to benefit humankind. In one myth,
the gods threw themselves into a huge fire to create the sun; in
another they spilled their own blood in order to create people.
These myths established a debtor relationship between humankind and the gods – a debt that could be repaid only through
offerings of human blood and life. Human sacrifice and bloodletting, also known as autosacrifice, were primary forms of
ritual in Aztec society.

The earliest Mesoamerican religions focused on agricultural
fertility and worship of the sun. The great Classic-period civilizations of the Maya and Teotihuacan harnessed these themes
to the goals of the state through selective use of human sacrifice and bloodletting. The Aztecs borrowed much of their religion from their predecessors at Teotihuacan and Tula, but the
Aztlan migrants also brought their own gods and rituals with
them. Aztec religion was a complex blend of these two traditions, unified by emphases on blood, sacrifice, and debt payment. With their rise to power following the Tepanec war, the
Mexica rulers and priests began a deliberate transformation of
their religion to link the gods, myths, and ceremonies even
more strongly to the interests of the state and empire.

Myths of creation provide a gateway into the complexities

of Aztec religion. The Aztecs had numerous diverse, even contradictory myths describing the creation of the world, the gods, people, and things. Four of these myths are presented here to illustrate some of the fundamental concepts of Aztec ritual and belief.[2]

Myths of Creation

The Four Suns

At the beginning of creation there was an original high god, Ometeotl ("Two-Deity"), who existed in both a male form, Ometecuhtli ("Two-Lord"), and a female form, Omecihuatl ("Two-Lady").[3] This couple produced four sons: Tezcatlipoca, Xipe Totec, Quetzalcoatl, and Huitzilopochtli. The latter two were given the task of creating the earth, other gods, and people. With the births of these four gods, a cycle of creation and destruction began that continues to the present day.

There have been four previous ages or "suns," each controlled by a different god and peopled by a distinctive race. Each sun was destroyed by a different cataclysm. The god Tezcatlipoca presided over the first sun, when a race of giants roamed the earth. This sun was destroyed by jaguars who ate the giants and destroyed the earth. During the second sun, presided over by Quetzalcoatl, humans who lived on acorns populated the earth. This sun was destroyed by hurricanes, and the people were transformed into monkeys. People of the third sun, under the god Tlaloc, ate aquatic seeds. The world was destroyed by a fiery rain and humans were turned into dogs, turkeys, and butterflies. The fourth sun, presided over by Clalchiuhtlicue, was a time of gatherers who ate wild seeds. They were turned into fish in a great flood.

The fifth sun is the age we still live in today. Its presiding deity is Tonatiuh, the sun god, and its people are maize-eaters. According to Aztec myth, this world too will be destroyed, by earthquakes, and its people will be devoured by sky monsters. The destruction of a world age or sun can only come at the end of a 52-year cycle known as the calendar round (see chapter 10), but the number of cycles that will pass before the cataclysm is unknown. Therefore, when a cycle was completed, and the sun began to rise on the first day of a new calendar round, the Aztecs celebrated a ritual known as the New Fire ceremony to give thanks for another cycle of existence. The last New Fire ceremony was conducted in 1507. If the Aztec calendar is projected forward, nine cycles have been completed since that date, and our current cycle will end in AD 2027.

Quetzalcoatl and the Bones of the Ancestors

The creation of the fifth sun, the current age, fell to Quetzalcoatl and Tezcatlipoca. In one version of this myth, the two gods found the earth completely covered with water from the flood that ended the fourth sun. The giant earth monster Tlaltecuhtli ("Earth Lord"), a crocodile-like creature, swam in the sea searching for flesh to eat. The gods turned themselves into serpents, entered the sea, and tore Tlaltecuhtli in half. The upper part of her body became the land, and the lower part was thrown into the sky to become the stars and heavens. Plants and animals grow from the back of Tlaltecuhtli and rivers pour from her body.

With the land and sky in place, the gods were ready to create people. They sent Quetzalcoatl to the underworld, Mictlan ("Place of the dead"), to retrieve the bones of the people from the fourth sun:

> And then Quetzalcoatl went to Mictlan. He approached Mictlan-tecuhtli and Mictlancihuatl [Lord and Lady of the underworld]; at once he spoke to them:
>
> "I come in search of the precious bones in your possession. I have come for them."
>
> And Mictlantecuhtli asked of him, "What shall you do with them, Quetzalcoatl?"
>
> And once again Quetzalcoatl said, "The gods are anxious that someone should inhabit the earth."
>
> And Mictlantecuhtli replied, "Very well, sound my shell horn and go around my circular realm four times."
>
> But his shell horn had no holes.[4]

The false conch horn was the first of several tricks that Mictlan-tecuhtli used to block Quetzalcoatl's mission. Quetzalcoatl called upon worms to drill a hole in the shell, and bees to make the horn play. When Mictlantecuhtli heard the horn, he at first allowed Quetzalcoatl to gather the bones, but later changed his mind. His helper spirits dug a hole, and a quail appeared and startled Quetzalcoatl, who tripped and lost consciousness. The bones were scattered and broken, and the quail chewed on them. Quetzalcoatl finally rose, gathered up the bones, and escaped from Mictlan.

Quetzalcoatl carried the bones to Tamoanchan, a place of paradise. The old goddess Cihuacoatl ("Woman Serpent") ground them on the metate and placed the powder in a jade bowl. Quetzalcoatl and the other gods gathered around and shed their blood upon the ground bones, and the first people of the fifth sun were made.

The Birth of the Sun at Teotihuacan

Once the earth, people, and maize had been created, the gods gathered in the darkness at Teotihuacan to bring forth the sun. Two gods were chosen for the task: Tecciztecatl, a rich, power-ful, and haughty lord, and Nanahuatzin, a weak, poor, scab-covered god. A huge pyre was built for a fire sacrifice. The gods called upon Tecciztecatl to throw himself into the fire. Four times he attempted to do their bidding, only to stop short. Then Nanahuatzin gathered his resolve, ran, and leaped into the flames, where his body was quickly burned up. Shamed at his earlier timidity, Tecciztecatl also jumped into the fire, followed by an eagle and a jaguar. For their bravery, these two animals became warriors, patrons of the two great Aztec mili-tary orders.

A great light appeared as Nanahuatzin rose in the east as Tonatiuh, the sun god. Then Tecciztecatl also rose as a second sun. The gods worried that the world would be too bright, so they threw a rabbit at Tecciztecatl to dim his light. He became the moon, on whose surface a rabbit can still be seen today. But the sun did not move in the sky. The gods sent a falcon to ask Tonatiuh why he did not move. He replied, "Why? Be-cause I'm asking for their blood, their color, their precious substance."[5] The gods realized they must sacrifice themselves to make the sun move across the sky. Quetzalcoatl performed the deed, cutting open the chests of the gods and removing their hearts to offer up to Tonatiuh. And so the sun assumed its correct path across the sky. The Aztecs believed that just as these gods sacrificed themselves for the sun, so too people had to provide blood and hearts to keep the sun going.

The Heroic Birth of Huitzilopochtli

The goddess Coatlicue ("Serpent Skirt") was doing penance and sweeping at Coatepec ("Serpent Hill") when she saw a ball of feathers float down from the sky. She took the feathers and placed them inside her shirt. When she finished sweeping, Coatlicue went to remove the feathers, but they were gone. In fact, they had impregnated the goddess. Her children, the Centzon Huitznahua ("The Four Hundred Southerners") became aware of her pregnancy:

> And when the Centzon Huitznahua saw that their mother was already with child, they were very wrathful. They said, "Who brought this about? Who hath made her heavy with child? She hath dishonored and shamed us!"

> And their elder sister, Coyolxauhqui, said to them, "My elder brothers, she hath affronted us; we must slay our mother, the wicked one who is already with child . . ."

> And when Coatlicue learned of this, she was sorely afraid and deeply saddened. And her child, who was in her womb, comforted her. He spoke and said to her: "Have no fear; already I know [what I must do]."[6]

Coyolxauhqui and her siblings dressed for war and climbed the hill of Coatepec toward Coatlicue. Just as they reached the summit, Coatlicue gave birth to Huitzilopochtli. The newborn god was fully mature and ready for battle with his shield, darts, war paint, and Xiuhcoatl (fire serpent weapon).

> Then with it [the Xiuhcoatl] he pierced Coyolxauhqui, and then he quickly struck off her head. It came to rest there on the slope of Coatepec. And her body went falling below; it went crashing in pieces; in various places her arms, her legs, and her body kept falling.[7]

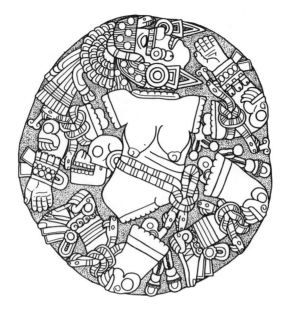

Figure 9.1   Drawing of large stone disk showing Coyolxauhqui's dismembered body (Diameter: 3.25 m. Drawing by Emily Umberger; reproduced with permission)

Huitzilopochtli then chased the Centzon Huitznahua and killed most of them.

This mythological event was commemorated on a large carved stone, which depicts Coyolxauhqui's dismembered body (figure 9.1). The Coyolxauhqui stone was part of a buried offering placed in front of the stairway to Huitzilopochtli's shrine on the Templo Mayor. The pyramid itself was referred to as Coatepec, and the human sacrifices that occurred on its summit reenacted Huitzilopochtli's victory over Coyolxauhqui.

Gods and Priests

Historical Background

There is a disparity between two of the myths recounted above: in the first myth, Huitzilopochtli is said to have been created

Figure 9.2   Classic-period antecedents of the Aztec gods Tlaloc and Quetzalcoatl from the Pyramid of the Feathered Serpent at Teotihuacan (Photograph by Michael E. Smith)

by Ometecuhtli and Omecihuatl; in the last, he was born from the womb of Coatlicue. Was Huitzilopochtli a high creator god, or just another patron deity? This is only one example out of many inconsistencies and contradictions found in the corpus of Aztec myths and religious accounts. The Aztecs had a dynamic, evolving religion, forged from the mixture of several diverse traditions. These elements had yet to be fully synthesized and integrated when the Spaniards arrived in 1519.[8] The major inspirations for the development of the Aztec gods, myths, and rituals were the traditions of earlier central Mexican civilizations (particularly Teotihuacan), the Aztlan migrants from northern Mexico, and the peoples conquered by the expanding Aztec empire.

A number of Aztec gods can be traced back to Classic-period Teotihuacan. Carvings on the Pyramid of the Feathered Serpent, for example, depict two of these deities (figure 9.2). The feathered serpent was either Quetzalcoatl or an earlier form of this god, and the goggle-eyed figure, known as the Storm God at Teotihuacan, may have been an early form of the Aztec rain god Tlaloc, or perhaps Xiuhcoatl.[9]

Other gods were brought to central Mexico by the Aztlan migrants. Huitzilopochtli, whose primary associations were with blood and warfare, had been the patron deity of the Mexica from the time of their migration from Aztlan. The ascension of the Mexica to power was accompanied by the elevation of Huitzilopochtli from a simple patron god to a powerful high god. Tlacaelel, advisor to the Mexica kings, "went about persuading the people that their supreme god was Huitzilopochtli."[10] The two temples atop the Templo Mayor pyramid were dedicated to Tlaloc and Huitzilopochtli. These central temples of the Aztec empire symbolized the social and cultural blend that made up the Aztec world: Tlaloc, the ancient central Mexican god of rain and fertility, sat next to Huitzilopochtli, the newly-arrived Mexica god of warfare and sacrifice. Some gods also were adopted from conquered peoples and integrated into the imperial pantheon of Tenochtitlan. The idols of these gods were removed from their home temples and set up in the Coacalco, a special temple that was a kind of prison for foreign gods.

The Teotl Concept

The Nahuatl term *teotl* means deity or sacred power. This is a complex and multi-faceted concept that does not fit well with modern preconceptions of ancient polytheistic religion. We tend to think of ancient gods in terms of the Greek pantheon. Zeus, Athena, Poseidon, and the other Greek gods were very human-like with their own unique personalities, powers, and domains. They often took human form and entered society undetected. Aztec gods, on the other hand, are better viewed as invisible spirits or forces whose roles, natures, and forms blended together. Each deity had certain characteristic attributes or insignia. Many of these, such as hats, pendants, clothing, and jewelry, were shared by more than one god. As a result scholars often disagree over the correct identification of gods in the codices or sculptures. Gods were sometimes depicted in human form, and on ritual occasions, people impersonated deities by dressing in their insignia. One would never have mistaken a god for a person, however.

Many gods had special roles as patrons of particular social or ethnic groups. Just as Huitzilopochtli was the patron of the Mexica people, many cities and *calpolli* had their own patron gods. Occupational groups also had their own gods: Tezcatlipoca was the patron of kings; Quetzalcoatl of priests; Teteoinnan of midwives; and Xipe Totec of goldsmiths.

Written sources contain names for as many as two hundred distinct gods and goddesses, several of whom were closely related to one another, sometimes as transformations of a single deity. One such common transformation involved the concept of duality. Ometeotl (god of duality, literally "Two-Deity"), for example, contained male and female transformations, Ometecuhtli ("Two-Lord") and Omecihuatl ("Two-Lady"). Sometimes Quetzalcoatl was a priestly creator god, but at other times he donned special insignia to become Ehecatl, god of wind.

It is difficult to keep track of Aztec deities with all of their transformations and blending. Ethnohistorian H.B. Nicholson has superimposed an order upon this pantheon by classifying the gods into 14 complexes of closely-related deities. He groups these complexes into three overarching themes: celestial creativity and divine paternalism; rain, moisture, and agricultural fertility; and war, sacrifice, blood, and death (table 9.1). Each of the deities in the table is at the head of a complex or group of gods and goddesses who are related in their themes and roles. These 14 complexes encompass 129 deities as listed by Nicholson. An example of a deity complex, the Tezcatlipoca complex, is shown in table 9.2. Tezcatlipoca ("Smoking Mirror"), was the most powerful god in terms of influence on people's lives. Four gods in this complex – Moyocoyani, Telpochtli, Titlacahuan, and Yaotl – are versions of Tezcatlipoca himself, and the others are deities closely related to the smoking mirror. I have used Nicholson's system to structure the following descriptions of the gods.[11]

Deities of Celestial Creativity and Divine Paternalism

Nicholson's first theme, celestial creativity and divine paternalism, covers the original creation of the world and the ultimate source of life.

Table 9.1   The principal Aztec deities

Deity	Meaning	Themes and Roles
Deities of celestial creativity and divine paternalism		
Ometeotl	Two-god	Original creator of the gods
Tezcatlipoca	Smoking mirror	Omnipotent power, patron of kings
Xiuhtecuhtli	Turquoise lord	Hearth and fire
Deities of rain, moisture, and agricultural fertility		
Tlaloc	(uncertain)	Rain, water, agricultural fertility
Centeotl	Maize god	Maize
Ometochtli	Two rabbit	Pulque, maguey, fertility
Teteoinnan	Mother of gods	Earth and fertility; patroness of curers and midwives
Xipe Totec	Our lord with the flayed skin	Agricultural fertility; patron of goldsmiths
Deities of war, sacrifice, blood and death		
Tonatiuh	He goes forth shining	Sun
Huitzilopochtli	Hummingbird of the left or south	War, sacrifice, sun; patron of the Mexica
Mixcoatl	Cloud-serpent	War, sacrifice, hunting
Mictlantecuhtli	Lord of the place of death	Death, underworld, darkness
Other deities		
Quetzalcoatl	Quetzal-feathered serpent	Creation, fertility, Venus, wind; patron of priesthood
Yacatecuhtli	Nose-lord	Commerce; patron of merchants

Each of these deities heads a deity complex of closely-related gods and goddesses.
Source: Nicholson (1971:Table 3)

Creation, Sacrifice, and the Gods

Table 9.2   Gods of the Tezcatlipoca complex

Deity	Meaning	Themes and Roles
Tezcatlipoca	Smoking mirror	Omnipotent universal power
Chalchiuhtotolin	Jade turkey	Penitence
Itztli	Obsidian blade	Justice, punishment
Ixquimilli	Eye-bundle	Justice, punishment
Metztli	Moon	Moon
Moyocoyani	Maker of himself	Universal power
Omacatl	Two reed	Feasting, revelry
Tecciztecatl	Person from the place of conch-shells	Moon
Telpochtli	Male youth	Patron of *telpochcalli* school
Tepeyollotl	Heart of the hill	Caves, darkness, jaguars
Titlacahuan	We his slaves	Universal power
Yaotl	Enemy	Universal power

It is not clear whether all of these were separate deities or alternative names for Tezcatlipoca.
Source: Nicholson (1971:Table 3)

Ometeotl   In his guise as the couple *Ometecuhtli* and *Omecihuatl*, Ometeotl was the original creator of the gods and the world. These abstract celestial deities were invoked in sacred poetry and philosophical works, but had no formal cult dedicated to their worship.

Tezcatlipoca   Tezcatlipoca is often described as the Aztec high god (figure 9.3). In his obsidian mirror, "Tezcatlipoca could see all that took place in the world,"[12] and he carried arrows to inflict punishment on wrongdoers. People were filled with fear and dread before the awesome power of Tezcatlipoca:

> Thus I fall before thee, I throw myself before thee; I cast myself into the place whence none rise, whence none leave, the place of terror, of fear. May I not have aroused thy annoyance; may I not have walked upon thy fury. O master, O precious nobleman, O our lord, perform thy office, do thy work![13]

It is fitting that this most powerful god was the patron of kings.

Xiuhtecuhtli   Xiuhtecuhtli was associated with fire and life. Fire figured prominently in many rituals and a sacred fire was always kept burning at the temples. In his manifestations as *Huehueteotl* ("Old God"), this god presided over the domestic hearth fire, where household rituals were performed. Two goddesses in this complex were *Chantico* ("In the House") and *Coyolxauhqui* ("Painted with Bells"), the unlucky rebellious sister of Huitzilopochtli (figure 9.1).

Deities of Rain, Moisture, and Agricultural Fertility

The gods of rain, moisture, and agricultural fertility were among the most actively worshipped of Aztec deities, by both priests and lay persons. Nicholson groups the many fertility gods into five complexes.

Tlaloc   The ancient Storm God of Teotihuacan (figure 9.2) is a possible ancestor of Tlaloc, the principal rain god among the Aztecs. Tlaloc's main purpose was to send rain to nourish maize and other crops. In figure 9.3, he is shown using a digging stick to cultivate maize in an irrigated field. Tlaloc had four or five versions or transformations, the *Tlaloque*, who assisted him. They brewed the rain in huge vats in caves on mountaintops, from whence they also sent out thunder and lightening.

Centeotl   The cult of the maize god Centeotl overlapped the cult of the Tlaloc complex. The cult included various deities of solar warmth, flowers, feasting, and pleasure, such as *Xochipilli* ("Flower Prince") and *Macuilxochitl* ("Five Flower"), the patron of the game patolli.

Ometochtli   Ometochtli was one of a group of 400 rabbits, the Centzon totochtin, who were deities of the alcoholic beverage *pulque*. The goddess *Mayahuel* was a fertility figure who personified the maguey plant itself.

Teteoinnan   Teteoinnan represented a complex of many female earth deities that were associated with agricultural and

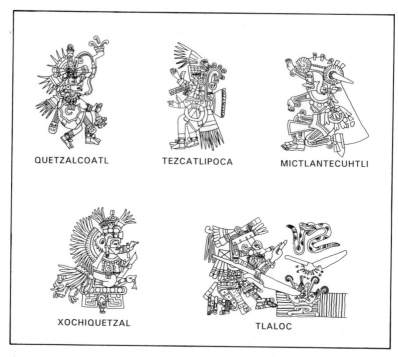

*Figure 9.3   Five Aztec gods. Quetzalcoatl and Tezcatlipoca
(Codex Borbonicus 1974:22); Mictlantecuhtli (Codex Borbonicus
1974:10); Xochiquetzal (Codex Telleriano-Remensis; Quiñones
Keber 1995:f.22v); Tlaloc (Codex Borgia 1976:pl.20)
(Drawing by Ellen Cesarski)*

sexual fertility. An important member of this group was
Xochiquetzal ("Flower-Quetzal Feather;" see figure 9.3), a
young and attractive goddess of sexual desire, flowers, feasting, and pleasure. She was the female counterpart of Xochipilli
and Macuilxochitl and had jurisdiction over pregnancy and
childbirth. Xochiquetzal was also the patroness of spinning
and weaving. *Tlazolteotl* ("Filth Goddess"), another earth
mother figure, was associated with sexual excess and childbirth (figure 9.4). Just as the earth was the place of birth, it
was also the place of death. Several goddesses in this complex
have affiliations with death, among them Cihuacoatl ("Serpent
Woman") and Coatlicue ("Serpent Skirt"), the mother of
Huitzilopochtli.

Figure 9.4   The goddess Tlazolteotl giving birth
(Height: 20 cm; photograph courtesy of Dumbarton Oaks
Research Library and Collections, Washington, DC)

Xipe Totec   Xipe Totec was a powerful fertility god and the object of a gruesome ritual of sacrifice. After the victim was killed, his skin was removed to be worn by a priest or by a deity impersonator who symbolically became the god. Carved and painted images of Xipe Totec can be identified by the flayed skin that covers the wearer inside; the sculpture in figure 9.5 is a particularly graphic example.

Deities of War, Sacrifice, Blood, and Death

Deities of war, sacrifice, blood, and death required human blood in order to maintain the earth, the sun, and life itself. This

*Figure 9.5 The god Xipe Totec. The deity wears the flayed skin
of a sacrificial victim, tied across his back (Height: 77 cm;
photograph courtesy of the National Museum of the American
Indian, Smithsonian Institution, 16/3261)*

blood was provided through either autosacrifice – personal
bloodletting as a form of worship – or human sacrifice. Because most sacrificial victims were obtained in battle, these
deities encouraged warfare and, hence, imperial expansion.

Tonatiuh   Tonatiuh, the sun god, overlapped considerably with
Ometeotl and, as such, represented a kind of high creator god.
Whereas the benign, fertility-related aspects of the sun were
represented in the Centeotl complex, Tonatiuh was more involved in the militaristic and sacrificial aspects of the sun. He
was the patron god of warriors, who fulfilled their duty to the
sun by capturing prisoners to sacrifice on the pyramid.

Huitzilopochtli With strong solar associations, the powerful war god Huitzilopochtli required a constant supply of sacrificial victims.

Mixcoatl Mixcoatl and the closely-related *Camaxtli* were gods of warfare and hunting. Originally associated with northern Chichimec groups, these deities became patrons of the Tlaxcalteca, Huexotzinca, and other enemy Aztec groups east of the Valley of Mexico. Another god in this complex was *Tlahuizcalpantecuhtli*, a god of stars and the sky closely connected to the planet Venus.

Mictlantecuhtli There were many gods and goddesses of death and the underworld, of whom Mictlantecuhtli (figure 9.3) was the most prominent. *Tlaltecuhtli* ("Earth Lord"), who was torn in half to form the earth and the sky, also belonged to this complex.

Other Deities

Two deities do not fit easily into the three themes described above: Quetzalcoatl and Yacatecuhtli.

Quetzalcoatl Quetzalcoatl, the feathered serpent (figure 9.3), was one of the most important gods of ancient Mesoamerica. His attributes cut across all of the above themes. As a prime creator, he was associated with Ometeotl and Tezcatlipoca, and in his guise as Ehecatl, god of the wind, he belonged with Tlaloc. The patron of the *calmecac* school and of the priesthood, Quetzalcoatl was a god of learning and knowledge. The high priests of Tenochtitlan were given the title "Quetzalcoatl."

Yacatecuhtli Yacatecuhtli was the patron god of the *pochteca* merchants.

Priests

Each of the gods had one or more temples where its idol was kept, and each had a group of full-time priests dedicated to its worship.[14] Most priests were men who had begun their training early, in the *calmecac*. Noble youths who showed ability and inclination were joined by promising commoner boys whose parents had dedicated them to the priesthood. These young men carried the title *tlamacazton* ("Little priest") and spent about a year learning the rudiments of priestly lore and duties. The most accomplished of them were chosen to become full priests, or *tlamacazqui* ("Giver of things"). Female priests, *cihuatlamacazqui* or "Female giver of things," were less common than males. Also trained at the *calmecac*, most of these women served for only a short while and then left the priesthood to marry.

Priests had three main types of duties. Most important was the performance of rituals. Priests kept the sacred fires burning in large braziers, played music at ceremonies, and made numerous offerings to the gods. They left food for idols, offered their own blood by autosacrifice, and burned incense. Incense made from the sap of the *copal* tree was offered at nearly all ritual occasions. Priests used long-handled "frying-pan" incense burners whose straight hollow handles symbolized serpents. These censers were often depicted in drawings of priests and ceremonies, and archaeologists have excavated countless fragments around both temples and houses at Aztec sites. A second type of priestly duty was administration and caretaking. Priests managed the economy of the temples, including construction, personnel, and provisions. They took care of the idols and sacred objects, and they were constantly sweeping for cleanliness and symbolic purification. The third priestly duty was in the realm of education and learning. Priests ran the *calmecac*, supervised the *tlamacazton* and lay personnel, and kept the sacred books. Priests were literate, and they were the repositories of Aztec learning and knowledge concerning the gods and rituals, the calendar, and astronomy.

Above the *tlamacazqui* was a smaller group of elite priests called fire priests, *tlenamacac* or "Fireseller." These priests were responsible for the performance of the highest ritual, human sacrifice. Regular priests assisted at the stone of sacrifice, but only a fire priest could wield the lethal flint-knife. At the top of the priestly hierarchy were two high priests with the title *quetzalcoatl*. The holiest and most devout of all priests, one presided over each temple at the top of the Templo Mayor pyramid – the Tlaloc temple and the Huitzilopochtli temple.

Priests must have presented a terrible picture to outsiders. Their faces and bodies were dyed black. Much of their body was scarred and mutilated from constant bloodletting. Their unwashed hair, worn long, became matted with dried blood from their ears and tongue. The fire priests and their assistants were also covered with blood from sacrifices. Why so much blood?

Human Blood Offerings

The myths recounted above established the rationale for human blood offerings. The gods sacrificed themselves to create the world and sun, and they offered their own blood to create people. Humankind owed a tremendous debt to the gods, and this debt could only be discharged through frequent offerings of human blood. The Aztecs accomplished this duty through two practices: autosacrifice and human sacrifice.

Autosacrifice

The god Quetzalcoatl performed the first act of autosacrifice when he bled himself to give life to the bones of the ancients. Other gods also bled themselves, as shown in a carved stone relief from Tenochtitlan (figure 9.6A) in which Tezcatlipoca and Huitzilopochtli pierce their ears. All people engaged in autosacrifice at some point in their lives, usually to petition the gods for agricultural or human fertility. Human blood was linked to fertility in all Mesoamerican religions, and blood was the most valuable substance one could offer to the gods.

The most common act of autosacrifice was to pierce one's earlobes or upper ear with pointed *maguey* thorns. Sometimes other parts of the body were pierced, including the tongue, thigh, upper arm, chest, and genitals. The most devout practitioners (priests, for the most part) would pierce their flesh and then pull hollow straws or reeds through the hole. Priests engaged in autosacrifice nightly. They bathed and purified themselves, burnt incense, and proceeded to a secluded spot where they carried out the ritual. Friar Sahagún listed four different kinds of bloodletting practiced by the priests: "the drawing of straws," "the offering of thorns," "the bloodying," and "the cutting of ears"[15] (figure 9.6B).

Figure 9.6   Rituals of autosacrifice. A: The gods Tezcatlipoca and Huitzilopochtli pierce their ears with pointed bones (from a carved stone; image after Nicholson and Quiñones Keber 1983:31); B: Two priests pierce their tongue and ear with maguey thorns (After Codex Magliabechiano 1983:f.79r; drawings by Ellen Cesarski)

Although autosacrifice was an important and prevalent ritual, it was only a substitute for the more powerful human sacrifice. In the words of art historian Cecilia Klein, "autosacrifice from the beginning was viewed as a symbolic death substituted for the real thing and, as such, as a debt payment made in return for continued life."[16]

Heart Sacrifice

Friar Sahagún's Nahua informants described a heart sacrifice as follows:

> Thus was performed the sacrificial slaying of men, when captives and slaves died, who were called "Those who have died for the god."
>
> Thus they took [the captive] up [to the pyramid temple] before the devil,[17] [the priests] going holding him by his hands. And he who was known as the arranger [of captives], this one laid him out upon the sacrificial stone.

Figure 9.7 A heart sacrifice on a temple-pyramid. Next to the feather banner the heart is offered up to the sun. The body of the victim of a previous sacrifice rests at the base of the stairs, which are covered with blood (After Codex Magliabechiano 1983:f.70r; drawing by Ellen Cesarski)

And when he had laid him upon it, four men stretched him out, [grasping] his arms and legs. And already in the hand of the fire priest lay the [sacrificial] knife, with which he was to slash open the breast of the ceremonially bathed [captive].

And then, when he had split open his breast, he at once seized his heart. And he whose breast he laid open was quite alive. And when [the priest] had seized his heart, he dedicated it to the sun.[18]

After the heart was removed, the victims, "were sent rolling down the steps of the temple, and the steps were bathed in blood."[19] A priest then cut off the head for mounting on a skull rack next to the pyramid. Such a sacrifice was illustrated in the *Codex Magliabecchiano* (figure 9.7).

The victims of this ritual were not considered ordinary mortals. They were viewed as deities whose deaths repeated the original sacrificial deaths of gods described in myth. The key Aztec concept here was *ixiptla*, often translated as "deity impersonator." The preparations for a sacrifice began long before the actual cut of the knife, sometimes as much as a year in advance. A victim was chosen to become the god on a set date some time in the future. Through a series of rites, the human victim was transformed into the embodiment of the god on earth. The greatly-respected *ixiptla* spent his last days or months living as a god, and when the day of sacrifice arrived, he went with honor to meet his fate.

Most victims for sacrifice were enemy warriors captured in battle. The captor sponsored the sacrifice, thereby gaining prestige. The higher the rank of the victim, the greater the honor. Captives were brought back from the battleground and housed until the time for their ceremony of transformation. Victims were carefully chosen to match the requirements of the god to be honored. Most gods required warriors for their *ixiptla* although some were satisfied with slaves purchased for the occasion. Tlaloc required children for his *ixiptla*, either purchased as slaves or the secondary offspring of nobles. Women were sometimes sacrificed as *ixiptla* for female deities. The most stringent requirements were those of Tezcatlipoca for the sacrifice in the monthly ceremony of Toxcatl. His *ixiptla*, selected a full year in advance, had to be a handsome, well-bred youth with no bodily imperfections.

The transformation from human to *ixiptla* began with a physical and ritual cleansing. Slaves purchased for sacrifice in particular had to be bathed carefully to erase all traces of impurity. The cleansed victim was then dressed in the clothing and insignia of the god. Once fully attired, he became the god and was addressed and worshipped accordingly. The *ixiptla* carried out the rituals specified for that god, such as dancing, singing, and making special ceremonial processions through the city. He was attended by priests and given many luxuries, including delicacies to eat and women for sexual pleasure.

To be chosen as an *ixiptla* was considered a great honor. Warriors were prepared to die proudly and honorably if they were captured. The respect and admiration granted an *ixiptla* must have affected the victim greatly. According to the nobles who gave Friars Sahagún and Durán their information, sacrificial victims mounted the bloody steps of the pyramid with dignity and pride.

Not all sacrifices took place on top of a pyramid. The cult of Xipe Totec, whose priests dressed in the flayed skin of sacrificial victims (figure 9.5), included two spectacular forms of sacrifice. In the so-called "gladiator sacrifice," an especially brave captive warrior was tied to a large, carved, circular stone and forced to fight a mock battle with an experienced Mexica soldier. The victim was given a sword whose obsidian blades had been replaced by feathers, but his adversary was fully armed and dressed for battle. In the "arrow sacrifice," the victim was tied spread-eagled to a wooden frame and shot full of arrows so that his blood dripped on the ground. In addition to these sacrifices to Xipe Totec, some victims were sacrificed by burning in a large fire pit, and others simply had their necks slit.

Many sacrifices were followed by a ceremonial meal at which the family of the captor or sponsor ate a portion of the victim's body. This was a highly religious occasion designed to honor the victim's memory. The victim was viewed as a symbolic kin relation of his captor, and this act of cannibalism was a sacred part of the whole ritual of sacrifice. Only a portion of the body was eaten, for this meal had a symbolic not a nutritional significance.[20] The gods also partook of the blood of the victims. After some sacrifices, the sponsor gathered up the blood in a bowl and "placed upon the lips of all [the images of] the devils the blood of him who had died for the gods."[21]

Explaining Aztec Sacrifice

Many ancient peoples around the world practiced human sacrifice, from the Greeks and Hebrews to the Inca and Maya. But few cultures made sacrifice such a central part of their religion as the Aztecs, and few cultures carried out human sacrifice on the same scale as the Aztecs.[22] Over the years anthropologists have attempted to account for the importance and prevalence of human sacrifice in Aztec religion. Some very different hypotheses have been proposed to explain this phenomenon. The most obvious explanation, one that would have been given by the Aztecs themselves, is that the gods required sacrifices. Aztec religion held that sacrifices were needed to keep the universe going. Most Aztecs were deeply religious people, and they believed their myths and religious precepts. Simply put, priests practiced sacrifice, and people put up with sacrifice, because they believed that it was necessary for the continued existence of the universe.

This religious explanation for human sacrifice is fine as far as it goes. One cannot understand the existence or nature of such practices without reference to the beliefs behind them. Nevertheless, anthropologists know that a people's own rationalization for their behavior often provides only a partial explanation for their actions. Aztec myths may explain why people practiced human sacrifice, but not why they practiced it so frequently. Nor do they explain why sacrifice was so common among the many widely dispersed ethnic groups who made up Aztec civilization. Could not the Aztecs have held fast to their myths and paid their debt to the gods with only a few sacrifices a year and with far less elaboration in the means of killing victims? To understand the pervasive nature of Aztec human sacrifice one must consider not only religious belief, but also the other purposes human sacrifice may have served in Aztec society.

In the 1970s, anthropologist Michael Harner gained media attention for his suggestion that the prevalence of sacrifice among the Aztecs could be explained by a lack of protein in their diet. Compared to most cultures around the world, the Aztec diet contained very little meat. Certainly, the rapidly growing population had depleted the game resources of most areas and the Aztecs did not have large, domesticated herd animals on which they could rely for meat. Therefore, Harner argued, sacrifice was stepped up to provide meat in the diet. This theory is more noteworthy for its media attention than for its scholarly rigor.[23] As I discuss in chapter 3, the relatively small contribution of meat to the Aztec diet did not prevent people from getting adequate protein. Processed maize was complemented by beans to provide a complete protein source. Intensification of agricultural practices gave larger crop yields.

The Aztecs did not need to resort to cannibalism to meet their protein needs.

A third explanation for the extent of Aztec human sacrifice, the explanation most commonly accepted today, stresses political factors. Aztec politics and religion were closely entwined. Kings ruled with the blessing of the gods, and the priests and temples were under the protection of the state. Human sacrifices were carried out in the service of politics. They were used as a form of external propaganda to demonstrate to other kingdoms the awesome power of the gods and the state. Extensive sacrifices at major public ceremonies advertised this power to subjects, allies, and enemies alike. Enemy rulers who attended the coronation of a Mexica king, for example, and were forced to witness the sacrifice of their own captured soldiers received a potent message about the superiority and might of the Aztec empire.

Propaganda by terror also was directed toward commoner subjects. Sacrifices were public spectacles that took place in highly visible settings – on top of the pyramid and in the open city plaza. Witnessing the gruesome deaths of not only enemy soldiers but also local slaves, infants, and the occasional free commoner must have made most people think twice before engaging in any form of resistance against their king or local noble. Just as commoners paid tribute in goods and services to nobles, so humans paid sacred tribute in blood to the gods. Both practices were obligatory debt payments, and the analogy between tribute and sacrifice was not lost on the Aztec people. This political use of human sacrifice was a feature of all Aztec city-states, not just Tenochtitlan. The Mexica of Tenochtitlan, however, carried sacrifice to great lengths, particularly at the great central temple-pyramid, the Templo Mayor.

The Templo Mayor

The primary site of human sacrifices in Tenochtitlan was the huge temple-pyramid known as the Templo Mayor. This massive stone monument was located in the Sacred Precinct, a walled holy city that covered 25 hectares (about 35 acres) in the heart of Tenochtitlan.[24]

The Sacred Precinct of Tenochtitlan

Most Aztec cities had a central religious area whose pyramids and other monuments faced a public plaza where crowds gathered to witness ceremonies (chapter 8). At Tenochtitlan, the Mexica walled off this central sacred zone, which became an inner city of its own (figure 1.1). Priests and nobles could enter the Sacred Precinct, and commoners were probably invited in to attend key ceremonies. Friar Sahagún included only the most prominent temples, shrines, and halls in his illustration of the precinct (figure 9.8); Spanish eyewitness descriptions listed over 70 individual structures.

The Templo Mayor, with its blood-stained twin stairways, dominated the Precinct (figure 9.8). The artist who painted Sahagún's illustration wanted to make sure that he portrayed the Huitzilopochtli temple in sufficient detail, so he added an enlargement above the main temple. Huitzilopochtli (or his *ixiptla*) is shown wearing the god's characteristic feathered headdress and carrying his fire-serpent weapon. Standard-bearers (probably stone statues) flank the Templo Mayor. Just in front of the central temple is a low, circular platform dedicated to Ehecatl, the wind god who was one aspect of Quetzalcoatl. A priest with an incense burner and incense bag stands on the platform. Below the platform is the skull rack (*tzompantli*), with two skulls shown. One of Cortés's soldiers reported that the great skull rack in the Sacred Precinct held 136,000 skulls; this estimate is probably exaggerated. Below the *tzompantli* is a ball court.

To the right of the Ehecatl shrine, another low platform supports the circular stone used in the gladiator sacrifice ritual dedicated to Xipe Totec; notice the ropes used to tether the victim during his fatal battle, and the blood on the steps of the platform. Below the gladiator stone sits Xipe Totec's temple, complete with bloody stairs. Xipe Totec himself (or his *ixiptla*) is drawn upside-down, adjacent to the gladiator stone. The two buildings in the lower left are a warriors" hall for the jaguar and eagle warriors, and a *calmecac* school. The priest offering incense to Quetzalcoatl has just come from the *calmecac*, as shown by the series of footprints. Among the temples in the

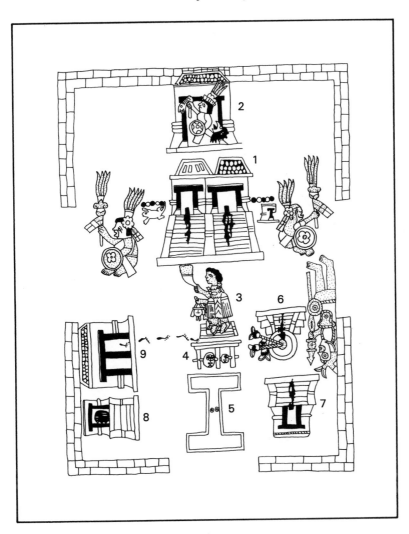

Figure 9.8 Early Spanish drawing of the Sacred Precinct of Tenochtitlan (after Sahagún 1905–07:v.6:39). Likely interpretations of the buildings are: 1: the Templo Mayor with Tlaloc and Huitzilopochtli temples; 2: magnification of the Huitzilopochtli temple; 3: circular shrine to Quetzalcoatl; 4: skull rack; 5: ballcourt; 6: stone for the gladiator sacrifice; 7: temple of Xipe Totec; 8: warriors' houses; 9: calmecac school. The two figures flanking the Templo Mayor are stone standard bearers and the upside-down figure on the right is probably a priest (Drawing by Ellen Cesarski)

Sacred Precinct that were not depicted in the Sahagún drawing were several dedicated to Tezcatlipoca; shrines to Tonatiuh and other gods; and the Coacalco temple, which housed foreign gods taken from conquered peoples. The captivity of foreign gods in the Coacalco "prison" symbolized both the subjugation of foreign peoples to the Aztec empire and the Aztecs" respect for the gods and beliefs of their subjects. This use of religious buildings as symbols of the empire's greatness was even more pronounced at the Templo Mayor itself.

The Templo Mayor

The heart of modern Mexico City was built over the ruins of the Sacred Precinct. Mexican archaeologist and architect Ignacio Marquina long ago determined where the Templo Mayor and other major structures were located in relation to modern streets and buildings, but no one suspected that the foundations of these buildings were still intact, nearly five centuries after their destruction. The chance find of the huge, carved Coyolxauhqui stone (figure 9.1), by power-company workers digging a trench in 1978, set off one of the largest excavation projects ever undertaken by the Mexican government. This project was directed by archaeologist Eduardo Matos Moctezuma. The Coyolxauhqui stone had been placed in front of the pyramid stairs as an offering, and Matos knew from Marquina's maps that the Templo Mayor was located immediately west of the find. When archaeologists extended the power-company's trench to the west, they came upon the lower steps of the pyramid. The combination of an undisturbed major offering and the intact stairs suggested that the Templo Mayor was in better condition than anyone had expected.

Unfortunately, in order to excavate the Templo Mayor, a number of sixteenth-century Spanish buildings had to be torn down. When the excavations were completed, however, the lowest levels of the Templo Mayor were open for all to see (figure 9.9). Like nearly all Mesoamerican pyramids, this structure was enlarged and rebuilt numerous times. The initial shrine, which probably dates to Tenochtitlan's early years, is located below the modern water table and could not be excavated. The second stage of construction consisted of a low platform with

*Figure 9.9   The Templo Mayor today. Stairways from several
construction stages are visible. The temples of the earliest
excavated stage are under the roof at right. The Coyolxauhqui
stone (figure 9.1) is visible under the scaffold in front of the stairs
(Photograph courtesy of Eduardo Matos Moctezuma; reproduced
with permission of the Instituto Nacional de Antropología
e Historia)*

two temples and two stairways. The platform and the lower
courses of the temple walls remain today. Up to five additional
stages of enlargement were carried out, but only the lowest
sections of the outer walls and the lowest steps for each stage
remain today. It seems logical to assume that each Mexica
tlatoani undertook a program to enlarge and improve the central temple, but it has proven difficult to correlate the construction stages with the reigns of individual kings.[25]

In addition to the foundations of the Templo Mayor itself,
some of the pavements and floors from various stages of construction have survived, and parts of several additional buildings have been excavated, including a hall for warriors just

*Figure 9.10   Offering 61 excavated in front of the Templo
Mayor. Among the contents of this buried chamber are stone deity
sculptures, incense burners, and diverse symbols of water and
fertility including a crocodile skull, coral, and seashells
(Photograph courtesy of Eduardo Matos Moctezuma; reproduced
with permission of the Instituto Nacional de Antropología
e Historia)*

north of the Templo Mayor. Numerous offerings were placed
under floors and below stairs at each stage of construction
(figure 9.10). These are interesting both for the fine objects
they contain and for the symbolism of the objects, which helps
us understand the meaning that the Templo Mayor held for the
Mexica.[26] The main temple was often referred to by the Aztecs
as Coatepec ("Serpent hill"), the place where Huitzilopochtli was
born and later killed his sister Coyolxauhqui. The 1978 find
of the Coyolxauhqui stone as a temple offering dramatically
confirmed this mythological association. Many of the human
sacrifices carried out at the Templo Mayor were reenactments
of Huitzilopochtli's victory over Coyolxauhqui.

Strangely enough, the Coyolxauhqui stone turned out to be one of only a few overt references to Huitzilopochtli that were uncovered by the Templo Mayor excavations. On the other hand, Huitzilopochtli's pyramid partner Tlaloc, the rain god, was glorified numerous times in the nearly 100 buried offerings that were excavated (figure 9.10). Most goods in these offerings were symbolically related to water and fertility. For example the organic remains of coral, seashells, and alligators were frequently included with offerings in the small, stone, sub-floor chambers, as were stone and ceramic depictions of seashells and other symbols of water and fertility.

Many of the offerings from the Templo Mayor contained other objects that served to glorify the Aztec empire and Tenochtitlan's role as its capital. From historical documents, we know that the Mexica were aware that they were the heirs to a tradition of central Mexican urban civilizations that stretched back to Teotihuacan and that they deliberately stressed their connections and continuity with these earlier cultures as a source of legitimacy for their own place as overlords of an expanding empire.[27] The offerings are archaeological confirmation of the importance the Mexica placed on this heritage. Fine objects from earlier Mesoamerican cultures were carefully guarded and some of these, such as Teotihuacan masks, were placed in the Templo Mayor offerings. Other objects, including stone sculptures and ceramic vessels, were deliberately fashioned in the styles of Tula and Xochicalco. In addition to offering something valuable to the gods, the Mexica of Tenochtitlan once again appear to be proclaiming themselves worthy of the mantle of Teotihuacan and Tula, powerful religious and political cities that ruled over large domains.

Another aspect of imperial symbolism in the Templo Mayor offerings was the predominantly foreign origin of the goods. Most of the objects in these offerings came from areas under Aztec control. The shells, alligators, and other maritime objects were from imperial provinces along the Pacific and Gulf of Mexico coasts. The numerous, fine-carved masks in the ancient Mezcala style originated in the Mezcala area of Guerrero, included in the southwestern provinces of the empire. Most of these items were probably received by the Mexica as tribute. Their burial in and around the Templo Mayor may have

Figure 9.11 Round pyramid at Calixtlahuaca, an Aztec city in the Toluca Valley. Round pyramids were dedicated to the wind god Ehecatl (Photograph by Michael E. Smith)

symbolized the subordination of their makers to the power of the mighty Tenochtitlan.

Other Pyramids, Other Sacrifices

Every city-state capital had its own major temple-pyramid facing the central plaza (chapter 8). The few of these that have survived are similar to the Templo Mayor in both form and function. The pyramids at Teopanzolco in Cuernavaca (figure 2.5) and Tenayuca in northern Mexico City are good examples of the twin-stair temple-pyramid style that was popular during the Early Aztec period. During Late Aztec times, many or most pyramids were built with a single stairway. The round pyramid at Calixtlahuaca in the Toluca Valley (figure 9.11) is an example of a temple dedicated to Quetzalcoatl in his guise as the wind god Ehecatl. Smaller towns, such as Coatetelco or Cuexcomate in Morelos, had smaller pyramids (figure 9.12).

Figure 9.12   Partially-restored small temple-pyramid at Coatetelco, an Aztec city in Morelos (Photograph by Michael E. Smith)

Although direct evidence is sparse, most of these smaller pyramids outside of Tenochtitlan probably were settings for rituals of human sacrifice. The Spanish conquerors noted sacrifices in many of the cities they encountered en route to Tenochtitlan, and local documents from throughout the Aztec empire mention extensive human sacrifices before 1519. At Teopanzolco a small platform across the plaza from the twin-stair pyramid (figures 2.5, 8.1) contained a burial chamber with many decapitated human skulls, the remains of a large sacrificial ritual.[28] Other rituals in addition to sacrifice took place at smaller temple-pyramids. At Cuexcomate, priests discarded ritual objects and other materials in a heap behind the pyramid. When we excavated this refuse pile, we found large numbers of long-handled incense burners and many broken ceramic bowls and plates, probably from offerings of food.[29] Such offerings were made during both private rituals of the priests and public ceremonies that involved the entire community.

Public Ceremonies

The Sacred Precinct was the stage for some of the most important rituals for the well-being of the empire and the city of Tenochtitlan. These included private rituals of penance and bloodletting by the many priests who lived in the Precinct, public sacrifices and pageants attended by priests and nobles, and the occasional major public spectacle attended by a wider audience. Most people, however, were more intimately involved in other types of ceremonies and rituals. First I discuss rituals of a public nature – those that occurred in open, public settings and permitted the participation of large numbers of people. Second I discuss rituals of a more private nature that were conducted within the confines of the home.

The Monthly Ceremonies

Each of the eighteen Aztec months had a distinctive series of ceremonies, which involved priests, rulers, nobles, and commoners alike. These ceremonies were devoted to particular religious themes, especially agricultural fertility. Many of the human sacrifices took place as parts of these monthly celebrations. Friars Durán and Sahagún left detailed records of the individual rituals carried out at each monthly ceremony.[30] I have drawn from their descriptions for the following example of the public ceremonies during the month of Toxcatl.

Toxcatl, May 4–23, fell at the height of the dry season. The days were hot and dusty; many streambeds were dry. Stores from the fall's harvest were running low, and farmers were anxiously awaiting rain so that new crops could be planted. The ceremonies of Toxcatl were dedicated to Tezcatlipoca in supplication for the start of the coming rainy season. The culminating event of the Toxcatl ceremonies was the sacrifice of Tezcatlipoca's *ixiptla* at the end of the month. This impersonator, selected by the priests a year in advance, had to be a young man of physical perfection:

> For he who was chosen was of fair countenance, of good understanding and quick, of clean body – slender like a reed; long and thin like a stout cane; well-built.[31]

The impersonator was trained in flute playing, speech, and flower carrying, and spent most of the year roaming the streets of Tenochtitlan with an entourage.

At the start of his last month, the *ixiptla* went to the *tlatoani*, who adorned him in the insignia and regalia of Tezcatlipoca. He was given four young women as wives; these women symbolized four fertility goddesses. The entire group visited all parts of the city during this final month, leading up to the sacrifice at the Templo Mayor. The "marriage" between Tezcatlipoca and the four goddesses occurred after nearly a year of abstinence and symbolized the coming of fertility following a long period of sterility or drought. The sacrifice itself symbolically marked the end of the dry period.

The theme of fertility after drought was also portrayed in the other rituals of Toxcatl. A large image of Huitzilopochtli was covered with amaranth dough, dressed in the god's insignia, and carried in procession to a temple where it was set up to receive offerings. Priests stoked the temple braziers into towering fires and offered incense. Quail were sacrificed to Huitzilopochtli's flames and later eaten by the king and nobles. The women of the city performed leaping dances to the music of drums and turtle-shell rattles. Warriors participated in an undulating "serpent dance," and young women performed a "popcorn dance" in which they were adorned with strings of popcorn that symbolized food and fertility. Toward the end of the feast, priests practiced bloodletting on all of the children, while other priests went around to people's homes, spreading incense.

Everyone, from the lowest commoner to the highest priests and king, was involved in some aspect of the Toxcatl ceremonies. Although the Toxcatl ceremony was "one of the most ostentatious and imposing known to the Indians,"[32] similar sets of rituals involving all ranks of society took place in each of the eighteen months.

The New Fire Ceremony

The New Fire ceremony, also known as the "binding of the years," was carried out upon the completion of each 52-year calendar cycle. The myth of the four suns predicted the destruction of the world by earthquakes at the end of a calendar cycle. Preparation for the possible end of the world began with major housecleaning: all household idols, cooking implements, clothing, and mats were discarded, and houses and yards were carefully swept and cleaned. During the last five unlucky days of the last year of the cycle, fires were extinguished, and the people climbed up on their roofs to await the fate of the world.

After dark on the final day of the calendar cycle, priests climbed the mountain Citlaltepec near Tenochtitlan to observe the heavens. Today Citlaltepec is called Cerro de la Estrella; both names mean "Star Mountain." The Pleiades constellation was the augury of the sunrise of the new cycle. The priest-astronomers anxiously followed this cluster of stars as it rose in the sky. If the constellation crossed the zenith as it normally does, they knew that the sun would rise again and the world would be spared for at least another 52 years. One hurdle remained, however. A new fire had to be kindled there on the mountaintop by a fire drill placed on the chest of a sacrificial victim:

> all were frightened and filled with dread . . . it was claimed that if fire could not be drawn, then [the sun] would be destroyed forever; all would be ended; there would evermore be night.[33]

Once a flame was lit, the victim was sacrificed, and his heart was thrown into the fire. The fire was carried to a temple in Tenochtitlan, where it was used to light many carefully-made torches. Warriors, messengers, and other swift runners took up the torches to carry the flame to all parts of the empire. Eventually, everyone's hearth was relit from the new fire. People everywhere rejoiced at the start of a new 52-year cycle, and they obtained new household goods to begin again. I suspect that the New Fire ritual was particularly appreciated by potters, obsidian knappers, mat makers, idol makers, and other artisans, although Sahagún and the other sources are silent on this issue.

We excavated two ritual dumps at Cuexcomate that contained the remains of household goods, most likely broken and discarded in a New Fire ceremony.[34] Unlike usual domestic refuse, which was spread around people's back yards and built

Figure 9.13   An Aztec ballcourt with a game in progress
(After Codex Magliabechiano *1983:f.80r; drawing by*
Ellen Cesarski)

up over a period of time, the materials in the ritual dumps
were placed into shallow pits in residential courtyards and
covered with a layer of rocks. We know that these deposits
were not simple trash pits because many pottery vessels could
be pieced back together, indicating that they were deliberately
broken at the pit. Vessels from ordinary trash deposits at this
site could almost never be reassembled because the pieces were
so widely scattered. These ritual dumps support Sahagún's
descriptions of such practices and confirm that celebrations
like the New Fire Ceremony took place in rural areas far from
Tenochtitlan.

The Ballgame

The Aztec ballgame *tlachtli* was a public ceremony with ancient roots that combined ritual, sport, and entertainment.[35]
The ballgame was played with a hard rubber ball on a large
I-shaped court (figures 9.13, 9.14). Carved stone rings were
mounted vertically in the center of the walls, often at the top
of a sloping ramp (see figure 9.14). Players could only hit the

Figure 9.14　A pre-Aztec ballcourt from the Epiclassic city of Xochicalco. Aztec ballcourts were very similar to this, although few examples survive (Photograph by Michael E. Smith)

ball with hips or knees, and they wore protective suits of deer-skin. If a player hit the ball through a ring, his team won the game. Goals were rare occurrences, however, and most games were probably won and lost on points gained for various maneuvers and skills. Sometimes the game was played between teams of players; at other times, individuals faced off against each other (see figure 9.13).

The ballgame was a sacred event charged with religious meaning. The ball was viewed as the sun that passed through the dark underworld (represented by the court) each night. The ballgame was a holy battle between the sun and the moon, between the sun and the planet Venus, or between the gods of youth and those of old age. The ballgame also had sacrificial connotations, and the ball was likened to a severed human head. In the ballcourt in figure 9.13, death is indicated by four human skulls and three death-heads, symbols of the god Mictlantecuhtli. Priests used the ballgame as a form of divination to predict the future and to help guide the actions of kings. A game would be commissioned and a possible future course of events assigned to each team. The results of the game were seen as an omen of the future.

The ballgame was significant not only as a religious event but also as one of the few organized athletic events in Aztec culture. The teams of neighboring cities played each other. Nobles both played the game and attended as spectators, gambling feathers and jade on the outcome. Some nobles could afford to gamble large sums at the ballcourt, but poorer nobles or commoners could find themselves in trouble. Of these latter individuals, Friar Durán said with scorn:

> These wretches played [the ballgame] for stakes of little value or worth, and since the pauper loses quickly what he has, they were forced to gamble their homes, their fields, their corn granaries, their maguey plants. They sold their children in order to bet and even staked themselves and became slaves.[36]

Private Domestic Rituals

Not all ritual was carried out in public ceremonies. Every Aztec home was also a setting for worship, much of which paralleled the actions that took place in temples and processions. Friar Durán described this domestic worship:

> All this food and drink was offered up in the temples, and each person offered the same in his domestic shrine . . . People made little hills of amaranth dough within their homes [and placed them] in shrines or special niches where the idols were kept, just as today they keep the [Christian] images.[37]

Most domestic rituals were carried out by women, who used sweeping and petitions to the gods to keep the spiritual world of the home and family in balance. Excavations of Aztec houses have turned up considerable evidence for domestic rituals that are barely suggested in the ethnohistoric sources.[38] Although no shrines like those mentioned by Durán have been found, domestic trash deposits do contain abundant, broken ritual objects, the most common of which are clay figurines (figure 9.15). Many figurines represent deities, and others depict people (women

*Figure 9.15 Ceramic figurines used in domestic rituals at
Yautepec (Photograph by Michael E. Smith)*

more commonly than men), animals, and other natural objects.
When archaeologists find figurines, the heads are rarely connected to bodies which suggests that they may have been broken deliberately before they were discarded. Figurines may have
been used in curing and other domestic rituals by women of
the family or by other women, who, as professional curers or
midwives, came into the home.

Remains of long-handled frying-pan incense burners or censers
of the sort used by priests are also common in Aztec domestic
trash deposits. Ethnohistoric sources described several occasions on which priests purified houses by censing them, but the
large numbers of fragments of such vessels suggest that the
commoners also must have used them in their homes to burn
incense. These domestic incense burners were identical to those
found at temples. Excavated deposits from temples, however,
have several times as many of these artifacts as the average
house. Other domestic rituals included rites associated with
childbirth, weddings, and burial after death.

The Christian priests, who worked hard to convert indigenous peoples following the Spanish conquest, were favorably impressed with the religiosity and devotion of the Nahua people, even though they objected to much of the content of native religion. Religious worship was well integrated into daily life at all levels of society. Beyond myths and rituals, religion was the context for the development of many of the intellectual and aesthetic accomplishments of the Aztecs.

10

Science and Art

> The philosophers and wise men had charge of recording all the
> sciences of which they had knowledge and of which they had
> achieved understanding, and of teaching from memory all the
> songs that preserved their sciences and histories.
>
> *Alva Ixtlilxochitl*[1]

The scientific and artistic achievements of the Aztec peoples
were considerable. I have already touched upon many of these
in the preceding chapters, for science and art were inextricably
bound up with other aspects of Aztec culture. The Aztecs, like
most ancient peoples, did not distinguish categories of "science" and "art" in the manner we do today. Many scientific
ideas were applied toward practical ends in areas such as agriculture, architecture, craft production, and medicine. Others
were applied toward religion and ritual, as in the cases of
astronomy and calendrics. Aztec art, too, was integrated into
religion, politics, and society. The Aztecs did not appear to
have had a concept of "art for art's sake," although they clearly
valued technical ability and aesthetic balance in many diverse
artistic media. Sculptures and paintings depicted gods and rituals, poetry dealt with humankind's place in the cosmos, and
dance and music were part of state ceremonies. Since religion
and politics were closely bound, much Aztec art also served
overt political ends. Monumental sculptures and large buildings proclaimed the glory of the city-state, and painted books
and wall murals recorded the great deeds of current and past
dynastic rulers. In this chapter I examine several aspects of
Aztec science and art that have not been treated in detail in
previous chapters: writing, calendars and astronomy, medicine,
and art in it various forms.

Figure 10.1   Modern reproduction of an Aztec folded book, the Codex Borgia *(1976) (Photograph by Mark Schmidt.* Codex Borgia *[Codex Vaticanus mess. 1] Facsimile-Edition by Akademische Drück u. Verlagsanstalt, Graz Austria, 1976)*

Writing

Paper

The Aztecs wrote on many media – stone sculptures, ceramic vessels, and other objects – but the most common medium was painted manuscripts. Most manuscripts consisted of long strips of paper folded accordion-style and painted on both sides (figure 10.1). Only a few of these books, or codices (singular, codex), survived the Spanish conquest, but they continued to be painted in much the same manner into the colonial period. Quite a few of these Aztec-style colonial documents have been preserved.

Some manuscripts were painted on deerskin and others on cloth, but most used paper made from the inner bark of the wild fig tree.[2] These trees were abundant in the Morelos area, where many towns specialized in papermaking. The Spanish

*Figure 10.2   Stone bark-beaters from Yautepec used to pound
bark fibers into paper (Photograph by Michael E. Smith)*

botanist Francisco Hernández observed papermaking in the
Morelos town of Tepoztlan in the mid-sixteenth century and
wrote a detailed description of the process. The papermaker
first stripped the bark off the tree with a stone knife, then
soaked it in running water to coagulate the sap. The sap was
scraped off, and the bark boiled in an alkaline solution to
loosen and separate the fibers. The wet fibers were arranged in
layers on a wooden drying board and pounded with a hammer
made from a flat, grooved pounder of basalt stone that was
bound to a wooden handle. These basalt tools, called bark-
beaters, are a commonly found artifact at Aztec sites in Morelos
(figure 10.2). Beating the fibers rendered them pliable and fused
them together into paper. The paper maker trimmed these sheets
to the size and shape desired and polished them with a stone.
Finally, a coating of white lime was applied to stiffen the paper
and produce a surface for painting. Contemporary Otomi Indians north of the Valley of Mexico still make paper this way
for rituals, and their methods have been adopted by peasants
from the state of Guerrero, who make paper for the colorful
paintings they sell to tourists and collectors.[3]

Books and Scribes

The Aztecs produced codices and other manuscripts or books for a variety of purposes.[4] *Religious books* such as the *Codex Borgia* contained depictions of gods and rituals, along with much information on the 260-day ritual calendar (see figure 10.5). These books were used by priests for divination and to keep track of rituals. *Historical books* (described briefly in chapter 1) typically consisted of a list of years in the year-count calendar accompanied by representations of key events in the history of a dynasty. Section one of the *Codex Mendoza* (figure 1.6) and the *Tira de la Peregrinación* (figure 2.4) are important examples of historical books. There were several types of *administrative books*, including tribute lists such as section two of the *Codex Mendoza* (figure 7.5), maps of city-state territories, and records of landholdings. The conqueror Bernal Díaz del Castillo made a note of Motecuhzoma's tribute books:

> he [Motecuhzoma's steward] kept an account of all the revenue that was brought to Montezuma in his books, which were made of paper – their name for which is *amal* [*amate*] – and he had a great house full of these books.[5]

Books and manuscripts were painted by trained scribes, *tlacuilo*, who were themselves nobles or were commoners in the service of nobles and priests. Priests and philosophers also learned to write. Friar Sahagún described the scribe as follows:

> The scribe: writings, ink [are] his special skills. [He is] a craftsman, an artist, a user of charcoal, a drawer with charcoal; a painter who dissolves colors, grinds pigments, uses colors.

> The good scribe is honest, circumspect, far-sighted, pensive; a judge of colors, an applier of the colors, who makes shadows, forms feet, face, hair. He paints, applies colors, makes shadows, draws gardens, paints flowers, creates works of art.[6]

Professional scribes often specialized in one of the various types of books. The occupation of scribe was hereditary, and the *Codex Mendoza* illustrates a scribe teaching his trade to his son (figure 4.8). The central symbol in the figure, two diagonal scrolls within a rectangular frame, is the Aztec glyph that signifies writing or scribal activity.

*Figure 10.3   Rock carving of a scribe from the Yautepec Valley.
He is painting five glyphs that signify writing or scribal activity
(Photograph by Michael E. Smith)*

During a regional survey of the Yautepec Valley in 1994, my
field crew was surprised to find this same glyph for writing
carved on a boulder in the middle of the countryside, far from
any sites. The relief depicts a scribe in the act of carving or
painting several of these scroll glyphs (figure 10.3). The location of this find may be a major clue to the purpose of the
carving. Situated just off the Aztec road that once connected
Yautepec with Cuauhnahuac, near the border between these
city-states, this boulder may have marked the boundary. The
figure of the scribe and the writing glyph probably were meant
to indicate that the boundary had been recorded by a scribe of
the type that specialized in paintings of boundaries and markers.[7]

Mesoamerican Background to Aztec Writing

The Aztec writing system was one of five distinct writing systems developed in ancient Mesoamerica; the others are the
Maya, Mixtec, Zapotec, and Epi-Olmec. Although each of these
scripts expressed a different language and had its own patterns

of writing, they shared common preoccupations with ruling dynasties, elite affairs, ritual, and calendrics. During the Classic period (AD 200–900), the Maya carved inscriptions on buildings, stelae, and other stone monuments, many of which still survive today. Classic Maya writing was the most complete of the Mesoamerican scripts, capable of recording anything that could be said in the Maya languages. A pre-Maya writing system, the Epi-Olmec script, recently was discovered in the Olmec area of the Mexican Gulf Coast. Although only a limited number of carved inscriptions have been found, linguists John Justeson and Terence Kaufman already have deciphered many of the glyphs.

Two different writing systems were developed by the ancient cultures of Oaxaca. Toward the end of the Formative period (around the time of Christ) Zapotec speakers in the Valley of Oaxaca invented a script that today is known through carved stone inscriptions at Monte Alban and other sites in that area. During the Early Postclassic period (ca. AD 900–1200), Mixtec speakers in the mountainous zone north of the Valley of Oaxaca worked out a pictographic writing system that survives in a number of painted prehispanic manuscripts such as the *Codex Nuttall*. Most existing Mixtec books are historical accounts of the ruling dynasties of the Mixtec city-states. Compared with Classic Maya writing, Mixtec writing was limited in scope, capable of expressing only a narrow range of historical and ritual events. The origins of Aztec writing may reach back to early systems of signs and symbols at Teotihuacan and Xochicalco, but the many stylistic and iconographic similarities between Mixtec and Aztec writing suggest that the Mixtec script, too, played an important role in the development of Aztec writing.[8]

The Aztec Writing System

Aztec manuscripts usually included two types of elements – pictures and glyphs – blended together so that it is sometimes difficult to separate them. Many events, places, people, and things were depicted by straightforward pictures that could be interpreted easily by the reader. With a little practice scholars today can "read" many of these pictures without any knowledge of Nahuatl. This very generalized form of communication had the advantage of not being tied to a particular language. Speakers of Nahuatl, Otomi, Tarascan, or Maya could all have read the pictorial parts of Aztec written texts.

Aztec hieroglyphs, on the other hand, were far more precise in their meanings. A hieroglyph, or glyph, is a sign that stands for a word, sound, or concept in a specific language. Aztec writing made use of several hundred glyphs.[9] The *calendrical date* was a common type of glyph, and historical accounts were based upon the year-count. According to the *Codex Mendoza*, for example, the reign of the Mexica king Chimalpopoca began in the year 4 tochtli or AD 1415 (see figure 1.6). Ritual books most frequently used day names from the 260-day ritual calendar (see below). *Numerical glyphs* were also common. In Aztec writing, a dot stood for one; a flag meant 20; a feather meant 400; and a priestly incense bag indicated 8,000 (see figure 7.5).

Personal names and titles were another category of glyph. Chimalpopoca's glyph, for example, was a direct translation of his name "Smoking shield" (figure 1.6). Glyphs for *actions and events* were less frequent, but examples do exist. *Place-names* were the most common type of Aztec glyph, and several hundred were included in the first two sections of the *Codex Mendoza* – the conquest list and the tribute list. Hundreds of *objects* also were depicted in the *Codex Mendoza*, as well as other sources, but these illustrations are better described as pictorial representations, not glyphs.

This rather small repertoire of hieroglyphs limited the scope of what Aztec writing by itself could express. As I discuss in chapter 1, however, written texts were not meant to be used alone. They were mnemonic devices that listed important people, events, or places, the remaining information to be filled in from the memory of the reader. The telling of history, for example, was primarily oral in format, with books serving only to outline the main events. Nevertheless, the principles of Aztec hieroglyphic writing were sophisticated, and the glyphs were much more than simple pictures of people and things.

Types of Hieroglyphs

Aztec writing employed three types of signs or hieroglyphs of increasing complexity and abstraction – pictographs, ideographs, and phonetic elements.

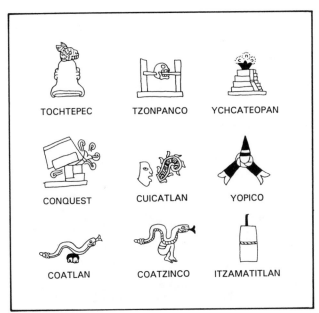

Figure 10.4   Place-name glyphs from the Codex Mendoza
*illustrating the principles of Aztec writing (see box
for explanation) (Drawing by Ellen Cesarski)*

Glyphs from the Codex Mendoza

1   Pictographic Glyphs

A   Tochtepec, "On the hill of the rabbit" (*Codex Mendoza*
1992:v.4:97; folio 46r)

toch(tli):	rabbit
tepe(tl):	hill, or place of
c:	on, or in

B   Tzonpanco, "On the skull rack" (*Codex Mendoza* 1992:v.4:40;
folio 17v)

tzonpan(tli):	skull rack
co:	on, or in

C   Ychcateopan, "On the temple of cotton" (*Codex Mendoza*
1992:v.4:79, 83; folio 37r, 39r)

ichca(tl):	cotton
teopan(tli):	temple
pan:	on

2   Ideographic Glyphs
D   Military conquest (*Codex Mendoza* 1992:v.4:26; folio 10v) (depiction of a burning temple)
E   Cuicatlan, "Place of song," or "Place of the Cuicateca" (*Codex Mendoza* 1992:v.4:91; folio 43r)

cuica(tl):	song
tlan:	abundance of, or place of

F   Yopico, "In the place of the Yopes" (*Codex Mendoza* 1992:v.4:45; folio 20r)

yopi(tzontli):	Xipe Totec's cap
Yopi(me):	a group living on the southwest edge of the Aztec empire

3   Glyphs with Phonetic Elements
G   Coatlan, "Where there are many snakes" (*Codex Mendoza* 1992:v.4:51; folio 23r)

coa(tl):	snake
tlan:	where there is an abundance of
tlan(tli):	teeth (phonetic)

H   Coatzinco, "On the small snake" (*Codex Mendoza* 1992:v.4:89; folio 42r)

coa(tl):	snake
tzin:	small
tzin(tli):	rump (phonetic)
co:	on, or in

I   Itzamatitlan, "Near the Ceiba trees" (*Codex Mendoza* 1992:v.4:54; folio 24v)

itzama(tl):	ceiba tree
titlan:	near or among
itz(tli):	obsidian (phonetic)
ama(tl):	paper (phonetic)

NOTE: These etymologies are from Berdan (1992b).

Pictographs are straightforward depictions of objects and people. In Aztec writing, a picture of a rabbit on a hill meant Tochtepec ("On the hill of the rabbit"). Tzonpanco ("On the skull rack") was represented by a drawing of a skull rack (see figure 10.4 and box). Pictographs were the most common type of Aztec glyph.

Ideographs are conventionalized representations of ideas or meanings. Their interpretation depends upon a certain level of cultural understanding, since the way in which a concept is depicted is usually culturally specific. The burning temple ideograph (figure 10.4D), for example, meant military conquest. In the glyph for Cuicatlan ("Place of song"), the song was represented by a flowery speech scroll, a common Nahuatl metaphor for song. The Yopico glyph ("In the place of the Yopes") was a depiction of Xipe Totec's peaked cap, an association based upon the importance of this god to the Yope people.

Phoneticism is the use of signs to represent words, syllables, or sounds. Phonetic glyphs were the most complex type of Aztec sign. Many examples of Aztec phonetic writing employed the "rebus principle," in which a word difficult to depict in writing was replaced by a word or words with the same sound (homonyms) that were easier to depict.[10] In figure 10.4, the glyph for Coatlan ("Where there are many snakes") uses a pictograph for the snake (*coatl*), but the sound "tlan" is depicted by teeth, *tlantli*; in the case of Coatzinco ("On the small snake"), the "tzinco" sound is signalled by a pictograph for rump (*tzintli*); Itzamatitlan ("Near the Ceiba tree") is written with two phonetic parts – *itztli* (obsidian) and *amatl* (paper).

Calendars and Astronomy

Calendars and timekeeping were a major concern of most Mesoamerican civilizations, which used several distinct calendrical systems for different purposes. The most widespread of these systems was a 260-day ritual calendar used for divination, astrology, and religious record-keeping. Annual calendars were used to keep track of events within the solar year, and various larger cycles of time were developed to keep track of events across the years. Use of these calendars hinged on careful observations of the stars and planets, so astronomy was a well-developed science. The Aztecs inherited a rich tradition of calendrics and astronomy from earlier Mesoamerican cultures, and from this tradition they focused their attention on three types of calendar: the ritual calendar, the annual calendar, and the 52-year calendar round.[11]

Table 10.1   The twenty day names

Day name	Meaning	Associated numbers in the 260-day ritual calendar				
Cipactli	Alligator	1	8	2	9	etc.
Ehecatl	Wind	2	9	3	10	
Calli	House	3	10	4	11	
Cuetzpallin	Lizard	4	11	5	12	
Coatl	Snake	5	12	6	13	
Miquiztli	Death	6	13	7	1	
Mazatl	Deer	7	1	8	2	
Tochtli	Rabbit	8	2	9	3	
Atl	Water	9	3	10	4	
Itzcuintli	Dog	10	4	11	5	
Ozomatli	Monkey	11	5	12	6	
Malinalli	Grass	12	6	13	7	
Acatl	Reed	13	7	1	8	
Ocelotl	Jaguar	1	8	2	9	
Cuauhtli	Eagle	2	9	3	10	
Cozcacuauhtli	Vulture	3	10	4	11	
Ollin	Movement	4	11	5	12	
Tecpatl	Flint knife	5	12	6	13	
Quiahuitl	Rain	6	13	7	1	
Xochitl	Flower	7	1	8	2	

Glyphs for the day names are portrayed in figure 10.5.

The 260-Day Ritual Calendar (tonalpohualli)

Mesoamerican peoples used a cycle of 260 days to keep track of rituals, to forecast the future, and to determine which days would be lucky or unlucky for the outcome of various events and actions. This calendar comprised two repeating, meshed cycles: a cycle of twenty day names and a cycle of thirteen numbers. The twenty day names are listed in table 10.1; their glyphs are depicted in figure 10.5. The cycle of day names began at the top with cipactli (alligator) and runs through xochitl (flower); it then returns to cipactli to repeat again. The cycle of numbers similarly repeats itself, running from one to

Figure 10.5 Page from the Codex Borgia, *a ritual almanac. Each panel depicts a deity and several day names in the lower band. The page is read in a zig-zag pattern, starting in the lower right and following the direction of the footprints. The deities in order are as follows: lower right: Tonatiuh (the sun god); lower left: Tlazolteotl (moon goddess; note the rabbit in the moon); middle left: Yacatecuhtli (god of merchants); middle right: the Black Tezcatlipoca; upper right: the Red Tezcatlipoca; upper left: Mixcoatl (a fire god). The day name glyphs, following the same zig-zag pattern, are listed in their correct order; see Table 10.1 for their names (Codex Borgia 1993:pl.55; reproduced courtesy of Alan Rogers)*

thirteen over and over. Each day in this calendar is identified by a number and a day name. Given twenty day names and thirteen numbers, there are 260 unique combinations.

Table 10.1 shows the first few cycles of the 260-day ritual calendar. The first three days, for example, are 1 cipactli, 2 ehecatl, and 3 calli. When the first cycle of thirteen numbers is completed, the number one is paired with the fourteenth day name (1 ocelotl), which is followed by 2 cuauhtli, and so forth. When the final, twentieth day name is reached (7 xochitl), the day name cycle starts over with the next number in sequence, 8 cipactli, 9 ehecatl, and so on. After 260 days, thirteen cycles of day names have been coupled with twenty cycles of numbers, and the final, unique combination (13 xochitl) is reached. The calendar then comes back to its starting point, 1 cipactli, and a new cycle begins. The 260-day calendar is probably the calendrical form with the greatest antiquity in Mesoamerica. No one, however, is sure just how a period of 260 days was selected for this important ritual cycle.

In Aztec culture, this simple calendrical cycle was the foundation for a complex series of ritual associations. For example, each group of 13 days was a unit named by its first day (1 cipactli, 1 ocelotl, 1 mazatl, and so on). These groups were thought to have special symbolic significance, and each was presided over by a different deity. In addition, each of the twenty day names had its own patron deity. The 260-day calendar also included thirteen deities known as the "Lords of the Day", thirteen holy birds, and nine "Lords of the Night" deities.

The 260-day calendar was used to predict the fate of individuals (based upon their birth date), and to determine days to hold important events, both ritual and practical. Individual days were considered to be either lucky, unlucky, or neutral, as were each of the numbers, day names, groups of 13 days, and the gods associated with any of them. Important ceremonies were tied to specific days in the 260-day calendar, and people arranged their affairs around the lucky and unlucky associations of particular days. For example the *pochteca* merchants made sure that the day they set out on a long journey was a lucky day. Much of the complex, esoteric meaning of this calendar and its symbolism have been lost, and the content of the ritual books based upon it, such as the *Codex Borgia* (figure 10.5), are only partially understood today.

The Annual Calendar

The annual solar calendar consisted of 365 days arranged into eighteen months of twenty days, with five unlucky days to finish out the year. The actual solar year is closer to 365.25 days long, and earlier Mesoamerican peoples had calculated its precise length. The Aztecs had this knowledge, but we do not know how they resolved the discrepancy, whether they added days (as in our leap years) or used some other means to keep the calendar in tune with the seasons.

The annual calendar was used for both practical and religious purposes. It kept track of the seasons and the monthly public ceremonies, and it may have had a role in agriculture.[12] Each twenty-day month was divided into four weeks of five days, and this period structured everyday life much as the seven-day week organizes our lives today. Weekly markets, for example, were held every five days, and smaller markets convened every twenty days.

The Calendar Round and Year Count

When the 260-day ritual calendar was combined with the 365-day annual calendar, the result was a major cycle of 18,980 days, or 52 years. Each day in this cycle, called the calendar round, had a unique combination of entries in the two calendars. For example, the Spaniards first entered Tenochtitlan on November 8, 1519. This was the ninth day of the month Quecholli in the annual calendar, and the day 8 ehecatl in the ritual calendar. This same designation (9 Quecholli, 8 ehecatl) reappeared every 52 years.

The year-count, a simplified version of the calendar round, was used to keep track of the years. Each year within the 52-year calendar round was assigned its own designation of a name with numeral. Four of the day names were used for this purpose, and they were referred to as the year bearers: calli, tochtli, acatl, and tecpatl. They were combined with the numbers one through thirteen following the same principle of repeating cycles as the 260-day calendar. The combination of four day names with thirteen numbers produced a 52-year cycle that matched the cycle of the calendar round.

The events recorded in Aztec native historical accounts were dated using the year-count. Since we know that the Spaniards entered Tenochtitlan in the year 1 acatl, or AD 1519, we can correlate the European and Aztec calendars to assign European

Table 10.2   The year-count calendar and its correlation with
the European calendar

Aztec Year	European Year	Aztec Year	European Year
1 Tochtli	1506	10 Acatl	1515
2 Acatl	1507	11 Tecpatl	1516
3 Tecpatl	1508	12 Calli	1517
4 Calli	1509	13 Tochtli	1518
5 Tochtli	1510	1 Acatl	1519
6 Acatl	1511	2 Tecpatl	1520
7 Tecpatl	1512	3 Calli	1521
8 Calli	1513	4 Tochtli	1522
9 Tochtli	1514	5 Acatl	1523

Source: Caso (1971)

dates to the events of Aztec history. Table 10.2 lists the years
from 1 tochtli (1506) to 5 acatl (1523) in the year-count. Each
year name reoccurs every 52 years, however, which causes
great problems for the reconstruction of Aztec history from
native historical sources. It is impossible to tell from the year
name alone which cycle an event belongs to. According to the
sources, for example, Tenochtitlan was founded in the year 2
calli, but 2 calli could be AD 1273, 1325, 1377, 1429, or 1481
(to name only five possibilities). We have ascertained that 1325
is the correct date only by carefully cross-checking with other
events.

Astronomy

The Aztecs, like all peoples of ancient Mesoamerica, were avid
astronomers who carefully tracked the stars and planets at
night. Most observations and calculations were made by priests
and nobles. In the *Codex Mendoza*, for example, a priest was
depicted observing the stars in order to keep track of the schedule for nightly rituals (figure 10.6). Friar Torquemada described
king Nezahualpilli of Texcoco as a great astronomer:

> It is said that he was a great astrologer; that he was much con-
> cerned with understanding the movement of the celestial bodies.

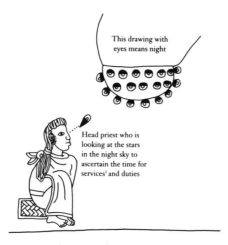

This drawing with
eyes means night

Head priest who is
looking at the stars
in the night sky to
ascertain the time for
services¹ and duties

Figure 10.6   A priest tracks the stars at night
(Codex Mendoza 1992:v.4:131; folio 63r)

Inclined to the study of these things, he would seek in his kingdom
for those who knew of such things, and he would bring them to his
court. He would communicate to them all that he knew. And at
night he would study the stars, and he would go on the roof of his
palace, and from there he would watch the stars, and he would
discuss problems with them.[13]

The archaeoastronomer Anthony F. Aveni has worked out many
of the details of Aztec astronomy.[14] Mesoamerican astronomers typically used fixed locations in temples and other buildings to observe the heavens. They tracked the rising and setting
of the sun, moon, planets, and stars at the horizon by placing
sets of crossed sticks along the line of sight. The precise direction of the sun at sunrise was a particularly important orientation in Mesoamerican cosmology. The position where the
sun rises in the east varies throughout the year. The sun rises
at its northernmost point on the summer solstice (June 21) and
at its southernmost point on the winter solstice (December 21).
In valleys surrounded by high mountains, such as the Valley of
Mexico, astronomers tracked the direction of the sunrise by
noting the point of the sun's appearance over specific mountain
peaks and other features on the eastern horizon. The length of
the solar year was easily calculated by noting the direction

where the sun rose on a solstice and counting the number of days until it returned to the same position.

Important astronomical alignments and orientations were recorded and used by surveyors and architects to lay out cities and buildings. For example, the Templo Mayor was designed so that on the spring equinox (March 21) the sun rose directly between the Huitzilopochtli and Tlaloc temples. The monthly ceremony of Tlacaxipehualiztli, dedicated to Xipe Totec, a god with solar associations, was held at this time. Friar Motolinía noted that the ceremony took place "when the sun was in the middle of [the temple of] Huitzilopochtli, which was the equinox, and because this was a little twisted, Motecuhzoma wished it torn down and straightened."[15] Aveni measured the alignment of the Templo Mayor, and found that its orientation, 7 degrees south of east, matched precisely the direction of the sun when it rose over the massive platform in the notch between the two temples on March 21 in Late Aztec times.

Aztec astronomers tracked many other celestial bodies in addition to the sun. The New Fire ceremony, which celebrated the start of a new 52-year calendar round was signalled not by sunrise but by the passage of the Pleiades constellation across the zenith of the midnight sky. Astronomers calculated to great accuracy the length of the solar year, the lunar month, the period of revolution of the planet Venus (584 days), and other celestial cycles. They noted and predicted solar and lunar eclipses and paid close attention to comets and shooting stars. Although some of this great body of astronomical knowledge was put to practical use in the calibration of calendars, most functioned more in the realm of divination and ritual. The emphasis on astronomical alignment was related to the important role of the cardinal directions in Aztec symbolism; rituals were choreographed to conform to key alignments and directions, and heavenly bodies from the stars and planets to comets were thought to have religious significance.

Medicine

The Aztecs had an extensive body of knowledge and belief concerning health and sickness. Their overall level of health

was quite good for a preindustrial population, but many illnesses and injuries were common.[16] The Aztecs attributed illnesses to one of three types of causes: supernatural, magical,
or natural. Supernatural ailments were sent by the gods as
punishment for various transgressions. They were treated
by making religious offerings and undergoing confession to a
priest. Magical illnesses were caused by a sorcerer known as a
tlacatecolotl, literally "owl man." These malevolent individuals cast spells on others, causing them to become ill or even
die. Such spells were diagnosed through divination. In a common form of divination, the healer or priest would toss twenty
corn kernels onto a cloth to observe the pattern they made.
Treatment of magical ailments involved the use of precious
stones (e.g., jade, quartz crystals), and often the consumption
of exotic substances (e.g., worms, skunk blood and skunk
spray).

More practical diagnoses and cures were carried out by
physicians, who treated naturally-caused illnesses and injuries.
Physicians were learned and experienced men and women.
Female curers worked mostly within people's homes, and the
chroniclers, who were mostly males and priests, unfortunately
provide little information on these important women. Friar
Sahagún's Nahua informants described the qualities of a good
physician as follows:

> The true doctor.
> He is a wise man [*tlamatini*];
> he imparts life.
> A tried specialist,
> he has worked with herbs, stones, trees, and roots.
> His remedies have been tested;
> he examines, he experiments,
> he alleviates sickness.
> He massages aches and sets broken bones.
> He administers purges and potions;
> he bleeds his patients;
> he cuts and he sews the wound;
> he brings about reactions;
> he stanches the bleeding with ashes.[17]

This description probably applied equally well to male and female
physicians.

In the realm of naturally-caused ailments and injuries, Aztec medicine was highly empirical and practical. Snake bites were treated by cutting the wound and sucking out the poison. Fractured bones were set successfully, and cures for wounds were very effective. Sahagún described in detail the treatment for a head wound.[18] The blood was washed away and the wound cleansed, first with urine, then with *maguey* sap (known for its curative properties). Next, an ointment of *maguey* sap and herbs was applied, and the wound bound tightly to keep out the air. If inflammation (infection) occurred, the medicine was applied several times; if not, the wound was kept bandaged until it healed.

The Aztecs used hundreds of medicinal herbs, and modern studies have shown that these had true pharmaceutical value in curing ailments and injuries. Many Aztec medical practices were more effective than those used by early Spanish doctors, and the Spanish emperor soon sent physicians and other scientists to study Aztec medicine and herbs. The priest Motolinía was quite impressed with Aztec physicians:

> They have their own skilled doctors who know how to use many herbs and medicines which suffices for them. Some of them have so much experience that they were able to heal Spaniards, who had long suffered from chronic and serious diseases.[19]

Fractured bones were healed by setting the limb with a plaster cast strengthened by a splint. Although fractures were known to be caused by simple injuries, on a symbolic level they were attributed to the mythological quail who caused Quetzalcoatl to drop and break the bones of the ancestors in Mictlan. As a physician set a fracture, he recited a chant acknowledging this mythological association:

> Well now,
> O Quail,
> O One from the Place of Disturbance,
> What harm are you doing
> To the bone from the Land of the Dead [Mictlan],
> Which you have broken,
> Which you have smashed? . . .
> I am the Priest,
> I am the Plumed Serpent [Quetzalcoatl]

I go to the Land of the Dead . . .
There I shall snatch up
The bone of the Land of the Dead.
They have sinned –
The priests,
The dust-birds;
They have shattered something,
They have broken something.
But now we shall glue it,
We shall heal it.[20]

Art

The Mixteca-Puebla Style

Aztec paintings and sculptures were executed in a distinctive style that was one expression of a more widespread phenomenon scholars call the "Mixteca-Puebla style." The Mixteca-Puebla style evolved out of an earlier tradition of painted pottery produced in coastal Mesoamerica in the Epiclassic and Early Postclassic periods (AD 750–1150). Standardized religious symbols, such as feathered serpent designs and the step-fret motif, were painted on ceramic vessels in many areas of Mesoamerica outside of central Mexico. In the Early Aztec period, peoples of the Mixteca-Puebla region of southern Puebla and northwestern Oaxaca adopted many of these symbols and created a painting style that used vivid colors and a standardized, precise, geometric depiction of images. H. B. Nicholson and Eloise Quiñones Keber describe several characteristics of the style: "Imaginative exaggeration of prominent features, strong black outlines, and bright, flat colors, resulted in images of striking boldness and visual impact."[21] Even without the use of color, as in sculptural reliefs or tracings from painted manuscripts, the vivid Mixteca-Puebla images stand out (see figures 9.3, 9.6).

Artists in the city of Cholula, in the heart of the Mixteca-Puebla region, probably participated in the creation and elaboration of the Mixteca-Puebla style during the Early Aztec period. Cholula had long been a holy city and pilgrimage center (its central pyramid was the largest in Mesoamerica), and its renowned Cholula Polychrome ceramics (figure 5.6) were painted in the Mixteca-Puebla style. Other examples of the style include Postclassic polychrome ceramics from Puebla, Tlaxcalla, and the Mixtec region; mural paintings from the Mixteca-Puebla area; and the Mixtec codices. In the Late Aztec period, Artists throughout central Mexico adopted the Mixteca-Puebla style for their painted manuscripts, such as the *Codex Borgia* (figure 10.5), and sculptural reliefs (figures 9.1, 9.3, and 10.3).

Aztec manuscripts and sculptures in the Mixteca-Puebla style were produced by scribes and artists for the use of the nobility. The widespread adoption of this style throughout central Mexico was facilitated by the network of interaction within the Aztec nobility described in chapter 6. The use and enjoyment of objects decorated with the Mixteca-Puebla style was not limited to the nobility, however. Commoners had ready access the polychrome ceramics of Cholula and other areas through the market system, and fragments of these vessels are not uncommon in commoner contexts at Aztec sites. This style was so popular in Late Aztec Mesoamerica that it spread far beyond the central Mexican highlands. Manuscripts and murals painted in the Mixteca-Puebla style have been found in several of the distant, outer provinces of the Aztec empire. Similar murals were also painted on the Caribbean coast of Yucatan and in highland western Guatemala, Maya-speaking areas outside of the empire. The Aztecs were part of the Mesoamerican world system, a social universe far more extensive than the territory of their empire. The distribution of the Mixteca-Puebla style is graphic evidence for the economic and cultural integration of Postclassic Mesoamerica.[22]

The Art and Politics of Imperial Sculpture

Stone sculpture was a major medium of Aztec art,[23] and Aztec sculptors far surpassed their earlier Mesoamerican ancestors in technical and aesthetic abilities. A sculpture of the goddess Tlazolteotl giving birth (figure 9.4) shows the realism of many Aztec pieces, as does a depiction of a man carrying a cacao pod (figure 10.7). Animals were frequent subjects of the sculptors, and snakes were the most often portrayed. Some snakes were carved naturalistically (figure 10.8); others were stylized representations of Quetzalcoatl, the feathered serpent god.

*Figure 10.7 Sculpture of a man holding a cacao pod
(Height: 35 cm; photograph courtesy of the Brooklyn Museum,
40.16, Museum Collection Fund)*

Jaguars were the next most commonly carved animal, and many
of these images convey a sense of power (figure 10.9) befitting
the importance of the jaguar in Aztec thought. Jaguar warriors
were the elite troops, Tezcatlipoca had jaguar associations, and
kings sat on jaguar skin thrones. Deities were another popular
subject of sculptors, and ritual objects such as stone boxes,
bowls, and panels were also common. These small- and medium-
size sculptures of humans, animals, deities, and ritual objects,
were carved in many city-states throughout the Aztec heartland. We found numerous small stone sculptures at Cuexcomate,
which shows that their use was not limited to cities. After the
Triple Alliance empire came to power a new school of monumental imperial stonecarving developed in Tenochtitlan.

Mexica sculptors drew on the stylistic elements and iconography of the Mixteca-Puebla style to create huge, relief-
covered, stone monuments that glorified the state and empire.

Figure 10.8　Sculpture of a snake (Diameter: 61 cm; photograph courtesy of Dumbarton Oaks Research Library and Collections, Washington, DC)

Figure 10.9　Sculpture of a jaguar (Length: 28 cm; photograph courtesy of The Brooklyn Museum, 38.45, Carl de Silver Fund)

*Figure 10.10   "Temple of Sacred Warfare" sculpture
(Height: 1.22 m; photograph by Michael E. Smith, reproduced
with permission of the Instituto Nacional de Antropología
e Historia)*

Teams of carvers, who worked for the king and other state
officials, created some of the most dramatic monuments of the
ancient New World. Through their size, composition, and iconography, these huge sculptures were intended to communicate
deliberate messages about the might and legitimacy of the
empire. The basic themes or messages of Mexica imperial sculpture were that the Mexica possessed the religious and political
right to rule the world, that they had inherited this right from
the ancient civilizations of Teotihuacan and the Toltecs, and that
the empire enjoyed a cosmic significance beyond mere politics.

Imperial stone monuments portrayed the cosmic structure of
the universe, and they associated the empire with cosmic principles in order to legitimize the actions of its imperial leaders.
The "Temple of Sacred Warfare" was a powerfully symbolic
monument that brought the political content of Aztec sculpture to the forefront (figure 10.10). A massive model of a temple-
pyramid, it was decorated with relief carvings on all sides that

Figure 10.11   The so-called "Aztec calendar stone"
(Diameter: 3.58 m; photograph by Michael E. Smith, reproduced
with permission of the Instituto Nacional de Antropología
e Historia)

illustrated the themes of warfare, human sacrifice and death,
autosacrifice, the sun, and the founding of Tenochtitlan. The
overarching message portrayed on this sculpture was that war
was a sacred obligation because it was waged to capture victims
for sacrifice and that just as human sacrifice and autosacrifice
were carried out for the sun to ensure the rising of the sun, so
too were they required for the continuing glory of the imperial
capital Tenochtitlan.

The so-called "Aztec calendar stone," the best-known Aztec
monument, was another imperial sculpture that proclaimed the
glory and legitimacy of Mexica rule (figure 10.11). Research
by art historian Richard Townsend suggests that this colossal
monument (3.6 meters in diameter, 25 tons in weight) was
originally set horizontally, not vertically as it now stands in the
Museo Nacional de Antropología in Mexico City. The central
figure, Tlaltecuhtli ("Earth Lord"), was a death god in the
Mictlantecuhtli complex who represented the surface of the

Figure 10.12   The so-called "Aztec calendar stone"
(Drawing by Emily Umberger; reproduced with permission)

earth as described in the myth of Quetzalcoatl and the Bones of the Ancestors (figure 10.12). The creation of the earth was symbolized by glyphs for the four previous suns or creations. The date 13 acatl, prominently displayed at the top of the disk, was the year of the creation of the present sun, and it also marked the year of the accession of Itzcoatl, the Mexica king who created the Aztec empire. This correspondence of dates was significant, for it gave the temporal political event a cosmic importance.

The twenty day names arranged in a circle around the central figures account for the popular name of the monument, but it did not function as a calendar. The day names merely indicated the passage of time and the link between time and power. Around the perimeter of the disk were carved two fire-serpents, *xiuhcoatl*, that related to Huitzilopochtli and sacred warfare. The eight triangular pointers were directional indicators. The four larger pointers indicated the four cardinal directions and served as a symbol for the entire earth. In short, the "Aztec calendar stone" conveyed the message that the Aztec empire covered the whole earth (territory in all four directions), and that it was founded upon the sacred principles of time, directionality, divine warfare, and the sanction of the gods.

Literature and Poetry

Literature and poetry were oral arts practiced by priests and members of the nobility.[24] The Aztecs greatly valued oratorical skill, and fine speakers and poets had high reputations. The Acolhua king Nezahualcoyotl, for example, was widely revered as a great poet. The Nahua informants of Friar Sahagún had this to say about orators:

> The good narrator:
> pleasing words, joyful words,
> he has flowers on his lips.
> His speech overflows with advice,
> flowers come from his mouth.
> His speech, pleasing and joyful as flowers;
> from him come noble language
> and careful sentences.[25]

Fortunately, many poems, histories, and formal speeches by such narrators were recorded in Nahuatl soon after the Spanish conquest. Ethnohistorian Miguel León-Portilla divides Aztec literature into four categories: myths, sacred hymns, lyric poetry, and histories. I explore myths in chapter 9 and histories in chapter 1; here my discussion focuses on sacred hymns and poetry.

Sacred Hymns

Sacred hymns were chanted at ceremonies to honor the gods. Most were exhortations to the highest and most powerful deities, such as Ometeotl, Tlaloc, and Huitzilopochtli. The majority of hymns were dedicated to Tezcatlipoca, who was often addressed as "Giver of Life." In the following hymn, the Giver of Life is invoked in his roles as both the creator and destroyer of the world:

> With flowers you write,
> Oh Giver of Life!
> With songs you give color,
> with songs you shade
> those who must live on the earth.
>
> Later you will destroy
> eagles and tigers [jaguars];
> we live only in your painting
> here, on the earth.
>
> With black ink you will blot out
> all that was friendship,
> brotherhood, nobility.
>
> You give shading
> to those who must live on the earth.
>
> Later You will destroy
> eagles and tigers [jaguars];
> we live only in your painting
> here, on the earth.[26]

Tezcatlipoca, the Giver of Life, is described here as both a poet ("with flowers you write;" see below) and a scribe (the black ink, colors, and painting).

Lyric Poetry

The Nahuatl phrase for poetry was *in xochitl, in cuicatl*, which translates as "flower and song." Flowers and the beauty of the world were important themes of lyric poetry, as was the celebration of the singer or poet:

> The flowers sprout, they are fresh, they grow;
> they open their blossoms,
> and from within emerge the flowers of song;
> among men You scatter them, You send them.
> You are the singer![27]

Many poems dealt with the transience of life and the ability of poetry to transcend mortal limitations. The great Acolhua king Nezahualcoyotl expressed these ideas as follows:

> My flowers shall not cease to live;
> my songs shall never end:

I, a singer, intone them;
they become scattered, they are spread about.[28]

This concern for life's impermanence and the inevitability of
death was a major preoccupation of Aztec literature and
poetry. Nezahualcoyotl's poem quoted in chapter 1 is a good
example: "Not forever on earth, only a little while." But if our
lives are short we should enjoy them while we can:

One day we must go,
one night we will descend into the region of mystery.
Here, we only come to know ourselves;

only in passing are we here on earth.
In peace and pleasure let us spend our lives; come let
    us enjoy ourselves.
Let not the angry do so; the earth is vast indeed!
Would that one lived forever; would that one were
    not to die![29]

Music and Dance

Music and dance were holy arts, performed mainly at rituals
and ceremonies.[30] Drums were the instruments most commonly
mentioned in written sources and most often depicted in drawings. In figure 10.13, the instrument on the right is a large
upright wooden drum known as a *huehuetl* that was played with
the hands. On the left is a horizontal "slit gong" (*teponaztli*)
made of a single piece of wood that produced two tones when
struck in different places with mallets. Other instruments included trumpets of cut conch shells, pottery flutes and whistles,
and rattles.

These instruments were used to accompany the ritual dances
at public ceremonies. A warriors' dance is illustrated in figure
10.13. It included eagle and jaguar warriors as well as regular
soldiers carrying swords. The feather bundles and elaborate
rattles carried by the warriors in this drawing were used in
most dances. Many dances included both men and women,
and the participants often moved in a circular pattern around
the musicians in the center. Friar Durán was very interested in

*Figure 10.13   Ritual dance of warriors accompanied by drums
(After Durán 1994:pl.39; drawing by Ellen Cesarski)*

Aztec dance and song, although he was scandalized by some of
the dances of young people:

> Young people took great pride in their ability to dance, sing, and
> guide the others in the dances. They were proud of being able to
> move their feet to the rhythm and of following the time with their
> bodies in the movements the natives used, and with their voice the
> tempo. The dances of these people are governed not only by the
> rhythm but by the high and the low notes in the chant, singing and
> dancing at the same time.

> Thus these differences in songs and dances existed: some were
> sung slowly and seriously; these were sung and danced by the lords
> on solemn and important occasions and were intoned, some with
> moderation and calm, [while] others [were] less sober and more
> lively. These were dances and songs of pleasure known as "dances
> of youth," during which they sang songs of love and flirtation,
> similar to those sung today on joyful occasions. There was also
> another dance so roguish that it can almost be compared to our
> own Spanish dance the saraband, with all its wriggling and grim-
> acing and immodest mimicry. It is not difficult to see that it
> was the dance of immoral women and fickle men . . . it is highly
> improper.[31]

11

Final Glory and Destruction

> Nothing but flowers and songs of sorrow
> are left in Mexico and Tlatelolco,
> where once we saw warriors and wise men.
>
> We wander here and there
> in our desolate poverty.
> We are mortal men.
> We have seen bloodshed and pain
> where once we saw beauty and valor.
>
> We are crushed to the ground;
> we lie in ruins.
> There is nothing but grief and suffering
> in Mexico and Tlatelolco,
> where once we saw beauty and valor.
>
> Have you grown weary of your servants?
> Are you angry with your servants,
> O Giver of Life?
>
> *Aztec poem*[1]

Aztec civilization reached the height of its development in the years following AD 1500, only to be cut short by a band of Spanish conquerors between 1519 and 1521. The coming of the Europeans in the aftermath of Christopher Columbus's voyages spelled doom for many hundreds of native cultures in North and South America. Some peoples, including the Aztecs, were conquered by force, others submitted peacefully, and still others resisted European advances for centuries. Some were wiped out by epidemic disease before they were able to choose resistance or submission. The Aztecs were the first state-level society encountered by the European invaders, and the means of their conquest – military defeat combined with decimation by epidemics – were to be repeated many times across the New World.

The Final Century: 1428–1519

Most of this book describes Aztec civilization during the 91 years between the formation of the Triple Alliance empire in 1428 and the arrival of the Spaniards in 1519. In many ways this interval, the Late Aztec B period, represented the pinnacle of cultural development in ancient Mesoamerica. The expansion of the empire brought peace and law to central Mexico. The explosive growth of markets and craft production joined diverse regions and sectors together in a burgeoning economy that brought prosperity and opportunity to many people. Cities flourished, and rural pioneers opened up new land to cultivation to feed a growing population. Political and economic successes were aided by a vigorous state religion, which in turn allowed learning and the arts to thrive. Important intellectual advances were made in the diverse fields of history, poetry, philosophy, medicine, astronomy, and engineering. Painting, sculpture, and other visual arts were elevated to new aesthetic heights under the patronage of the state and religion. These developments came at a cost, however.

Aztec society was sharply divided by class. Economic and cultural rewards were not evenly distributed. Human sacrifice was used by the state to terrorize the commoners, who had no voice in the arena of politics. Nobles controlled most of the wealth and had more freedom than did commoners. Prosperity benefitted all classes in some way (except perhaps the slaves), but ultimately, the economy rested upon the backs of the peasants in the field. As the empire expanded, some of this burden was shifted from the Valley of Mexico to more distant provinces through the system of imperial tribute. Nevertheless, the tribute system was not productive enough to fully compensate for the rapid growth of the Aztec population.

Population growth stimulated the growth of markets, commerce, and craft production, but economic prosperity, in turn, encouraged people to have larger families. Demographic growth was a major factor pushing the expansion of cities, city-states, and the empire, which furthered the evolution of religion and intellectual life. The most immediate and direct effect of the Aztec population explosion was the intensification of agriculture.

During the Late Aztec B period, however, society began to show signs of stress. Feeding the three million Aztecs was increasingly difficult, and famines occurred with more frequency. Archaeological reconstructions of life at rural sites point to sharp declines in the standard of living of Aztec peasants under the empire owing most likely to declining agricultural productivity, increased tributary exploitation by city-states and the empire, or both.

Aztec civilization during the final century thus illustrates the two-headed results of demographic, economic, and political expansion: prosperity and cultural florescence coupled with growing hardship for the commoner class, and impending crises for society as a whole. This was the situation that Hernando Cortés and his army encountered in 1519.

Conquest by Spain

Cortés and Motecuhzoma

In the decades after Columbus's first voyage of 1492, the Spaniards colonized the Caribbean islands and set up a base in Cuba.[2] Several expeditions explored parts of the Mexican and Central American coasts, where the Spaniards heard rumors of a rich and powerful kingdom in Mexico. In February of 1519, Hernando Cortés set sail from Cuba with eleven ships and 500 men to explore the Mexican coast. Funding for the expedition was split between the Spanish crown, represented by governor Diego de Velásquez in Cuba, and Cortés himself. At the last minute, Velásquez had second thoughts about the ambitious Cortés and withdrew permission for the trip, but Cortés sailed anyway. Later the governor tried unsuccessfully to recall and imprison Cortés. On the island of Cozumel, off the east coast of the Yucatan peninsula, Cortés came upon Gerónimo de Aguilar, a Spaniard who had survived shipwreck several years earlier. Aguilar had learned to speak Yucatec Maya, and he joined the expedition as an interpreter.

The group then rounded the peninsula and stopped at Potonchan on the Gulf Coast. A local army came out to meet the Spaniards, but after a brief battle, the natives withdrew.

Their leaders offered Cortés gifts, including several young women. Among the women was Malintzin, a noblewoman, bilingual in Nahuatl and Maya, who had been sold into slavery. The combined linguistic abilities of Malintzin and Aguilar enabled Cortés to communicate with the Aztecs. Malintzin (also called Marina or Malinche) proved to be a useful assistant to the Spaniards. She later became Cortés's mistress and bore him a son, Martín.

When the Spaniards landed in the territory of the Totonac peoples, near what is today the city of Veracruz, they were greeted by messengers from Motecuhzoma. The Mexica king had been following their progress, and he sent Cortés gifts of precious feathers and gold. This offering was made in part to ascertain who these strange foreigners were. Some thought that the Spaniards could be gods, and their reactions to the gifts would help to clarify their nature. But the Spaniards did not respond like gods. In the words of Friar Sahagún's Nahua informants:

> They laid before them golden streamers, quetzal feather streamers, and golden necklaces.
> And when they have given them the gift, they appeared to smile, to rejoice exceedingly, and to take great pleasure. Like monkeys they seized upon the gold. It was as if then they were satisfied, sated, and gladdened. For in truth they thirsted mightily for gold; they stuffed themselves with it, and starved and lusted for it like pigs.[3]

Cortés imprisoned the messengers and forced them to witness the firing of a cannon, which terrified them. He then released them to return to Motecuhzoma with a frightening account of the strangers. The Mexica king was perplexed. He summoned his wise men and magicians, but they, too, were unable to fathom the nature of the Spaniards. Cortés and his army did not behave like gods, nor did they behave like a Mesoamerican invading army. Motecuhzoma chose to wait before taking any action against the strangers. His hesitation contributed to the rapid Spanish victory.

Hernando Cortés set up camp and spent several months exploring the area in the vicinity of his landfall. He engaged the local Totonac rulers in skirmishes and negotiations. The Totonacs soon came to respect the military abilities of the Spaniards, whose swords, guns, armor, horses, fighting dogs, and military tactics held great advantage over Mexican obsidian swords and the one-on-one fighting style of Mesoamerican armies. Local rulers complained bitterly about the heavy burden of imperial tribute, and Cortés responded by taking some haughty Mexica tribute-collectors prisoner. The audacity of this action astonished the Totonac nobles, who quickly came over to the side of the Spaniards when Cortés offered to free them of Mexica domination.

By this time, Cortés had heard descriptions of the great imperial capital Tenochtitlan and its incredible riches. His army set out for central Mexico accompanied by hundreds of allied Totonac troops. The Spaniards did not head directly for the Valley of Mexico, however. Cortés had learned that Motecuhzoma could field armies of many thousands of soldiers, and his small group of Spaniards and Totonacs was no match for such forces. Instead, the expedition headed for Tlaxcalla, the powerful Aztec state that still resisted conquest by the Triple Alliance. At first Cortés's soldiers were challenged by the Tlaxcallan armies, but Cortés soon convinced the rulers to join him in his march to Tenochtitlan. Motecuhzoma was increasingly worried about the Spaniards' intentions. Several times he sent precious gifts (including objects of gold) to Cortés, accompanied by the suggestion that there was no need for Cortés to visit the capital city. His troops were welcome to take the gifts and simply return across the water. The gold, of course, made the Spaniards more anxious than ever to see the city. Gold was what they sought.

The Spaniards and their Totonac allies left Tlaxcalla with several thousand additional soldiers. The party first visited the nearby holy city of Cholula. There they were welcomed by the nobles. Cortés, however, fearing an ambush, ordered his armies to massacre thousands of unarmed Cholulan warriors. Then, the people of Cholula were compelled to declare their loyalty to Spain. Cortés and his forces now struck out for Tenochtitlan. Motecuhzoma continued to send gifts and messages urging Cortés to head back to Spain, but the Spaniards and their allies pressed on. At last, they entered the Valley of Mexico and approached the lake. The Spaniards were awed by the sight of the great cities with their monumental buildings (see the quotation that begins chapter 1).

Figure 11.1   Motecuhzoma welcomes Cortés and gives him gifts of jewelry (After Durán 1994:pl.58; drawing by Ellen Cesarski)

Cortés proceeded along the causeway toward Tenochtitlan, and Motecuhzoma went to greet him. In the words of Friar Durán:

> When Motecuhzoma heard that the Spanish captain was approaching, he again ascended his litter and then, carried on the nobleman's shoulders in the same way he had come, he went out to meet him. On seeing Cortés, he descended. When Cortés saw this, he climbed down from his horse and went to embrace the Aztec sovereign, treating him with much reverence. Motecuhzoma did the same, paying homage to the other with humility and words of welcome. From one of his noblemen he took a splendid necklace of gold, inlaid with precious stones, and placed it around Cortés's neck.[4]

This dramatic scene is depicted in figure 11.1. Great crowds had gathered to witness the meeting and gawk at the Spaniards. The soldier Bernal Díaz later recalled:

> Who could now count the multitude of men, women, and boys in the streets, on the roof-tops and in canoes on the waterways, who had come out to see us? . . . So, with luck on our side, we boldly entered the city of Tenochtitlan or Mexico on 8 November in the year of our Lord 1519.[5]

Motecuhzoma made the Spaniards welcome and put them up in the sumptuous palace compound of his father, the great Mexica *tlatoani* Axayacatl. Cortés repaid this courtesy by taking

Motecuhzoma prisoner on the pretext that a group of Spaniards on the coast had been attacked by native warriors. Cortés began to govern Tenochtitlan through the fiction that Motecuhzoma was still in authority. The Spaniards tried to suppress sacrificial rituals, with only partial success. This tense situation continued for several months. Then, in April of 1520, Cortés received news that an expedition had landed on the coast with orders from Velásquez to arrest him. He set off at once with half of his forces, leaving Pedro de Alvarado in charge of the capital.

Cortés managed to defeat the newly arrived Spanish force and won them over to his side. Meanwhile, Alvarado was having serious difficulties in Tenochtitlan. When he heard that human sacrifices were to be performed at a ceremony honoring Huitzilopochtli, Alvarado had the defenseless participants massacred in the temple courtyard. Outraged by the slaughter, the Mexica armies attacked the Axayacatl palace. At this point Cortés returned with his troops and new recruits, who managed to fight their way back into the palace. The ruling council of Tenochtitlan had long opposed Motecuhzoma's cooperation with the Spaniards and voted to depose the king. They elected his brother, Cuitlahuac, to replace Motecuhzoma as *tlatoani*. Hostilities continued, and at some point Motecuhzoma was killed. Spanish sources stated that he was killed by a stone thrown by one of his own people, whereas native accounts related that he was murdered by the Spaniards.

Cortés and his group were besieged. Amidst the fighting they made plans to flee the city (figure 11.2). On the night of June 30, 1520, they attempted to slip out of Tenochtitlan. Many of the Spaniards had laden themselves with heavy loads of gold, which slowed down their escape. This night has since been called the *noche triste* ("night of sorrows") due to the heavy casualties of the bloody battles that took place. Eventually Cortés and his army made it across the causeway and retreated over the mountains to regroup in Tlaxcalla. Additional Spanish soldiers arrived to fortify the positions on the coast and to reinforce Cortés's army. The general kept busy recruiting new native allies and organizing his troops.

Several months later, Cortés set off for Tenochtitlan once again. This time he was supported by over 700 Spaniards and

Figure 11.2   Aztec warriors attack the Spaniards, who try to flee Tenochtitlan (After Durán 1994:pl.60; drawing by Ellen Cesarski)

close to 70,000 native troops. The army split into two parts, and each fought its way to the edge of the lakes by a different route. The combined Spanish and Tlaxcallan armies successfully defeated many local city-states that had been fortified with Mexica soldiers (figure 11.3). Numerous *tlatoque* declared their allegiance to Spain. When the armies met up, they laid siege to the island capital. The fighting was fierce, with many casualties on both sides, but the invaders' wreaked the greatest devastation with an unintentional weapon: disease. Friar Sahagún's native informants described the situation as follows:

> While the Spaniards were in Tlaxcala, a great plague broke out here in Tenochtitlan. It began to spread during the thirteenth month [the month of Tepeilhuitl, October 11–30] and lasted for seventy days, striking everywhere in the city and killing a vast number of our people. Sores erupted on our faces, our breasts, our bellies; we were covered with agonizing sores from head to foot.
>
> The illness was so dreadful that no one could walk or move. The sick were so utterly helpless that they could only lie on the beds like corpses . . . If they did move their bodies, they screamed with pain.
>
> A great many died from this plague, and many others died of hunger. They could not get up to search for food, and everyone else was too sick to care for them, so they starved to death in their beds.[6]

*Figure 11.3   Battle between the Mexica and Spaniards
(with their Tlaxcallan allies) (After Muñoz Camargo 1981:f.277r;
drawing by Ellen Cesarski)*

The siege of Tenochtitlan went on for several months, during which time many who were not injured became seriously ill. At some point before or during the siege, Cuitlahuac died of smallpox. He was replaced by Cuauhtemoc, a nephew of Motecuhzoma and a fierce warrior. The Spaniards blocked shipments of food into the city and cut off the fresh water supply by destroying the aqueduct from Chapultepec. The Mexica warriors fought bravely, but the outcome of the siege was inevitable. On August 13, 1521, Cuauhtemoc was captured and the Spaniards claimed victory over the Mexica. The Tlaxcallan soldiers, however, went on to massacre many of the remaining inhabitants of Tenochtitlan. The defeat and destruction of the city was remembered in the following elegy:

> Broken spears lie in the roads;
> we have torn our hair in grief.

The houses are roofless now, and their walls
are red with blood.

We have pounded our hands in despair
against the adobe walls,
for our inheritance, our city, is lost and dead.
The shields of our warriors were its defense,
but they could not save it.[7]

Perspective

The question is sometimes asked, "How did 500 Spaniards manage to defeat the Aztec empire whose armies had tens of thousands of warriors?" As the above account should make clear, this question is not well phrased. The Aztec empire was defeated by 500 Spaniards, aided by tens of thousands of native allies and a disease epidemic of proportions never before seen in the New World. Much of the Spanish success was owed to the political astuteness of Hernando Cortés, who quickly divined the disaffection towards the Mexica that prevailed in the eastern empire. He turned that desire for rebellion to his own benefit through strategic alliances with the Totonacs and other Mexica subjects as well as with their traditional enemies, the Tlaxcallans. These indigenous troops deserve credit for a major part of the Spanish victory.

Motecuhzoma's hesitancy to attack the initial Spanish forces also contributed to the Aztec's defeat. Had the Mexica *tlatoani* challenged the Spaniards before they reached the Valley of Mexico, he almost certainly would have prevailed. Motecuhzoma's actions so puzzled and troubled the Nahua nobility that, after the conquest, they contrived a story to account for them. First, they created an "ancient" prophecy which stated that the god-king Quetzalcoatl would return from across the eastern sea to rule Mexico in the year 1 acatl, or 1519. Next, they invented a series of omens and signs that pointed to the coming of Quetzalcoatl. Finally, they claimed that Motecuhzoma truly believed Cortés to have been the deity himself. In the context of this story, Motecuhzoma's hesitation made sense; he thought that the arrival of the Spaniards was the second coming of Quetzalcoatl, not an invasion of strange foreigners.[8]

Ethnohistorian Ross Hassig has suggested a more reasonable

explanation for Motecuhzoma's indecision. He argues that at first, Motecuhzoma was unafraid of the Spaniards since the power of the Triple Alliance empire was great enough to awe most potential enemies. Nor did Cortés and the Spaniards behave like a Mesoamerican invading army. Their behavior was puzzling to the Mexica, but not initially threatening. In Mesoamerican warfare, invading forces did not arrive unannounced. Intentions were clearly broadcast in advance of actual hostilities, but Cortés professed friendly intentions. Furthermore, following his defeat of the Mexica's enemies, Tlaxcalla and Cholula, Cortés might have been approaching Tenochtitlan to propose an alliance. In Hassig's words, "So instead of meeting the Spaniards at some distance from Tenochtitlan and fighting them as they would have met an enemy force, the Aztecs permitted them to enter their capital, as they would have if they were peaceful."[9]

Hassig also points out that the Spaniards' arrival during the fall harvest season, a time rarely used for war in Mesoamerica, was another reason for Motecuhzoma initially to doubt the aggressive aims of Cortés. Moreover, had the emperor chosen to fight there were fewer Aztec troops available for battle, since most of the part-time forces were home working on the harvest. By the time the Spaniards were expelled from Tenochtitlan, and Motecuhzoma was replaced by more aggressive rulers, first Cuitlahuac and then Cuauhtemoc, it was too late for the Aztecs. The invading force had been heavily reinforced by both Spanish and native soldiers, and the dreaded smallpox virus had begun to decimate the population. Ultimately, this microorganism proved far more deadly than either Cortés's political shrewdness or Motecuhzoma's failure to attack.

The smallpox virus that devastated Tenochtitlan has been traced to a single soldier who arrived in Mexico in 1520 while Cortés was in Tlaxcalla preparing for his final assault.[10] Because many communicable diseases, such as smallpox, measles, and typhus, were absent in the New World, the Aztecs and other native peoples did not have any resistance to them. The situation was quite different in Europe (and in most of the world today), where a long history of exposure to these diseases had rendered them childhood ailments that were rarely fatal. When a disease such as one of these is unleashed on a new population, the resulting "virgin-soil epidemic" is usually catastrophic. The smallpox epidemic of 1520–21 was the first of many such virgin-soil epidemics to sweep through the New World in the centuries following European contact. According to one estimate, the population of the Valley of Mexico was reduced from 1.6 million in 1519 to 900,000 in 1521 as a result of this epidemic alone.[11]

The Nahuas under Spanish Rule

The Spanish conquest of the Aztecs and other Mesoamerican peoples was carried out for both economic and religious objectives. The conquerors initially sought gold (they "lusted for it like pigs" (Sahagún 1950–82:bk.12:31)), and later the colonists and the crown exploited Indian labor in silver mines and in agricultural endeavors. The conquest was also conducted in the name of God, with missionizing and conversion as major goals. Consequently the two institutions with the greatest immediate effect on people were the *encomienda*, which organized Indian labor for economic gain, and the church. I am switching here to the term Nahuas to describe the Aztecs and their descendants after the Spanish conquest, following the suggestion of ethnohistorian James Lockhart.[12] Central Mexican civilization as described in chapters 1 through 10 was greatly transformed after 1521, and I hesitate to use the term Aztec for the modified Colonial-period culture. This should not obscure the great continuity in many aspects of culture, particularly those related to the Nahuatl language. I use the term Indian to refer to native peoples after 1521, both Nahuas and others.

After 1521, boatloads of colonists began to arrive from Spain. Mesoamerica became a Spanish colony known as *Nueva España*, or New Spain, and its capital, Mexico City, was built over the ruins of Tenochtitlan. New Spanish towns and cities were founded throughout central Mexico, usually on the sites of existing Aztec towns. Some Spaniards moved to rural estates to become holders of *encomiendas*, but most remained in urban areas. As mining and sugarcane cultivation were established, the colonial economy of New Spain boomed, attracting ever more colonists. A few of the Nahua nobility learned Spanish and became involved in the Colonial economy, but most of the Nahua people who were not killed off by disease remained in their native communities and continued to speak Nahuatl. They were now subjects of the Spanish empire, which replaced the Aztec empire, and they were rapidly adopting the Christian religion of their conquerors. Nevertheless, in many respects, life continued much as it had before the Spanish conquest.

The Encomienda

By 1521 the dust had settled on the ruins of the Aztec empire and the remaining Nahuas began a process of accommodation to new masters. The *encomienda*, a grant of land and native labor made to an influential Spaniard, was a key institution of the early colonial period.[13] The Spanish crown had experienced earlier problems with *encomiendas* in the Caribbean, with the *encomenderos* assuming too much power and independence from the crown. Fearing that this would happen in New Spain as well, the crown forbid the establishment of the *encomienda* system there. But just as he had ignored Velásquez's order to halt his initial expedition, Hernando Cortés ignored the crown's wishes and proceeded to distribute *encomiendas* as rewards to his soldiers and associates. Once started, the institution received the support of the crown and soon spread throughout Spanish areas of Mesoamerica.

The Indians assigned to an *encomienda* were required to provide tribute goods and labor service to the *encomendero*, whose responsibility it was to protect them and to see to their religious conversion. The tribute goods paid to the *encomendero* usually consisted of daily necessities. For example, in the 1540s, one Spaniard was provided daily with the following goods: three chickens, one and a half loads of maize, 200 chiles, a loaf of salt, twelve loads of fodder, pine pitch, a load of charcoal, twelve loads of firewood, and the labor of eight Nahua servants. The Indians' obligations went far beyond supplying provisions, however. Their heaviest burden was labor, either on agricultural estates or in mines.

Although the *encomienda* system was a highly exploitative means of controlling Indian labor, it had the effect of permitting

Nahua local government and customs to continue under Spanish rule. *Encomiendas* were almost always allocated along the lines of preexisting political units. In most cases, an entire *altepetl* (city-state) was given to an *encomendero*, and many aspects of the prehispanic *altepetl* organization (such as the office of *tlatoani* and the *calpolli* system) continued to operate for more than a century after the Spanish conquest. These Colonial-period *altepetl* did not fight wars or sponsor sacrificial ceremonies, but they did regulate land allocations and mobilize tribute much as they had done in earlier times.[14]

As the sixteenth century wore on, waves of epidemics continued to wash over Mesoamerica. In 1531, measles swept through the land, followed by an unidentified disease in 1532, and yet another smallpox epidemic in 1538. The deadliest epidemic hit in the years 1545–48, when typhus wiped out 60 per cent or more of the Nahua inhabitants of central Mexico. It was followed by a mumps epidemic in 1550, another unknown disease in 1559–60, a second round of measles in 1563–64, and typhus once again in 1576–80. By that time the Nahua population in the Valley of Mexico numbered only 200,000 people, a reduction of 88 per cent from the size of the 1519 population. The decline in the Nahua population had reached its nadir.

The Church

The conversion of native peoples to Christianity was a fundamental goal of Spain's conquest and colonization of Mesoamerica.[15] Well-educated Spanish friars of the mendicant orders (Franciscans, Dominicans and Augustinians) were soon sent from Spain to attend to the religious conversion and welfare of the Nahuas and other peoples. Mass baptisms of thousands of individuals were carried out, and within a few decades of the Conquest, most Nahuas had been converted. The friars quickly realized that their preaching would be far more effective if delivered in Nahuatl (and other native languages), and so they learned the language and trained Nahua assistants and scribes to help them. Friars Sahagún, Durán, and others began the systematic study of Aztec religion in order to better understand people's beliefs and to enable the priests to convert the Nahuas

Figure 11.4   Sixteenth-century Christian church and convent at Xochimilco (Photograph by Louise Burkhart; reproduced with permission)

and to save their souls more successfully. Priests became the partisans and protectors of the Indians against their overexploitation by Spanish *encomenderos* and crown officials, and the Nahuas welcomed priests into their communities.

Churches were built throughout central Mexico, many associated with large convents and monasteries (figure 11.4). Like the great temple-pyramids of the Aztecs, these massive structures served not only as places of worship but also as symbols of the power and glory of God, deliberately built to impress the Indians.[16] A typical pattern in Nahua towns was to tear down the pyramid and erect a church on the elevated platform made by the rubble. This practice sent a strong message that the Christian God was supreme and was to be worshipped in place of Huitzilopochtli, Tezcatlipoca, and the rest. From the perspective of the Nahuas, the placement of the church on top of the former pyramid created continuity in the location and significance of sacred space. Indian communities took pride in their churches, which became symbols of local identity in New

Figure 11.5 Church built on top of the abandoned Cholula pyramid, an artificial mountain (Photograph by Michael E. Smith)

Spain. The Spaniards even built a church on top of the largest pyramid of ancient Mesoamerica, the artificial mountain of Cholula (figure 11.5). This pre-Aztec pyramid had been abandoned several centuries before the Spanish conquest, but Cholula had remained a holy city, and the friars were particularly concerned to make it a Christian city.

The friars encouraged the policy of *congregación*, designed by the Spanish colonial administration to gather together scattered Nahua settlements into new, larger towns with churches. The resulting *congregaciones* were partly a response to the continuing Nahua population decline of the sixteenth century. Gathering the Indians together in one place made it easier to preach to them, easier to protect them from overexploitation, and to the colonial officials, easier to collect imperial and *encomienda* taxes.

The Nahuas were quickly to become nominal Christians, but they did not entirely abandon the ways of their former religion:

they did not undergo a conversion experience, in the sense of responding to a personal spiritual crisis by consciously and intentionally replacing one entire belief system with another . . . [Aztec religion] was more a matter of collective, community rites and celebrations than of an individualized, personal faith . . . The native people interpreted Christianity in terms that were more or less compatible with their own cultures.[17]

The Nahuas did not have the concept of a "faith" or "religion" as a domain separable from the rest of culture, and their new religion is best seen as a syncretism or blend of Aztec beliefs and Christian beliefs. Conversion involved the adoption of essential Christian rites and practices while the basic mind set remained that of traditional Nahua culture. Rather than passively accepting a completely new and foreign religion, people created their own adaptation of Christianity, compatible with their colonial situation and with many of their traditional beliefs and values. Some of the early priests recognized the partial nature of these conversions, lamenting that in place of a thousand gods, the Indians now had a thousand and one. The pervasive influence of Nahua beliefs on central Mexican Christianity continues today and many aspects of modern folk Catholicism can be traced back to the Aztec past.[18] The syncretism of the Nahua and Spanish religions received concrete expression in the incorporation of Aztec religious symbols and objects into sixteenth-century churches and convents (figures 11.6 and 11.7).

Continuity and Change

What were the effects of the Spanish conquest on Aztec civilization? Clearly some things, such as human sacrifice, were eliminated immediately, whereas others, such as the Nahuatl language, have survived to the present day. Aztec imperial institutions and practices were the first to go. The Aztec empire ceased to exist in 1521, native warfare came to an end, the imperial trade and tribute systems closed down, and the outward signs of state religion were quickly suppressed.

Traditional patterns of community life, on the other hand, endured for several centuries in many rural areas. James Lock-

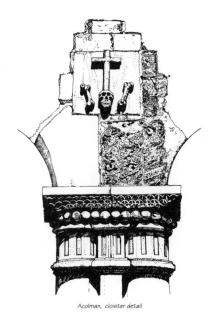

Acolman, cloister detail

Figure 11.6 Carving in the Augustinian convent at Acolman, ca. 1550 (Drawing by Richard Perry; reprinted with permission from Mexico's Fortress Monasteries *by Richard Perry, 1992, p. 45)*

hart's research with Nahuatl-language documents shows that the *altepetl* was allowed to carry on within the framework of the *encomienda* and colony, serving as a powerful force for the preservation of Nahua culture and practices. Within the Colonial-period *altepetl*, Nahuatl was still spoken and the *calpolli* remained the dominant unit of settlement.[19] Change came only gradually, with many practices continuing through the seventeenth and eighteenth centuries.

For the peasants in the field, it may have made little difference whether they were subjects of the Aztec empire or the Spanish empire. Men and women still produced goods for their family, for their *altepetl*, and for a distant foreign overlord. They remained tied to the land, rarely venturing far from their village, and social life revolved around the *calpolli* and *altepetl*, not some distant imperial city. These peasants were the carriers

*Figure 11.7   Aztec sacred stone box set into the wall of the
Dominican convent at Yautepec, ca. 1550. This box is used for
holy water today (Photograph by Michael E. Smith)*

of the Mesoamerican cultural tradition. It was through their
lives and actions, not the lives of nobles or priests, that many
aspects of Aztec culture were maintained despite the great
upheaval of the Spanish conquest.

This basic continuity in peasant life explains the seemingly
odd situation found by archaeologists at rural Nahua sites of
the early Colonial period. Although the Spanish conquest initiated the most dramatic and catastrophic cultural changes ever
to occur in Mesoamerica, there is little direct evidence of it at
rural sites. People continued to build the same types of houses,
and they continued to make and use traditional household goods,
such as unglazed Aztec orange pottery and obsidian tools, for
more than a century after 1521. Goods from Europe, or whose
manufacture used new European technologies, such as glazed
ceramics and iron nails, do not appear at rural sites until after
1650. This situation contrasts sharply with that of urban areas
where the introduction of Spanish material items was rapid.[20]

At first, new Spanish traits were simply incorporated into pre-existing Nahua cultural patterns. In the words of James Lockhart:

> In the economic realm as in the others, a strong indigenous base continued to provide the framework while Spanish items and modes quickly entered everywhere, not so much displacing as infiltrating, interpenetrating, and being assigned to niches already existing in the indigenous cultural scheme.[21]

Change eventually did come to peasant villages, however. Spanish replaced Nahuatl as the dominant language in most areas, although in isolated communities Nahuatl has survived. Spanish practices and culture gradually infiltrated Nahua villages, while Nahua practices had their own impact on the new colonial culture of New Spain. Considerable intermarriage between Indians and Spaniards took place, and by the time of the Mexican Revolution of 1910, most if not all Nahuas were of partial Spanish ancestry. Today Mexican culture is a true blend of Aztec traits, Spanish traits, and traits developed during the four and a half centuries of colonial and national rule. Similarly, the Mexican people are *mestizos*, their genetic heritage a combination of Indian and Spanish traits, with some African, Asian and other European genes contributed as well. The Spanish conquest may have put an end to the Aztec empire and it may have brought about the deaths of millions of people, but it did not extinguish Nahua culture. Today there are over one million Nahua Indians who speak Nahuatl, and Mexican national culture owes much of its distinctiveness and heritage to the contributions of Aztec civilization.

12

The Aztec Legacy Today

> Contemporary [Nahua] Indians have been placed in a contra-
> dictory position: while being preserved as living tribute to
> Mexico's noble indigenous past, they are also being discrimin-
> ated against for being Indians in a Mestizo-oriented society.
> *Anthropologist Judith Friedlander*[1]

What vestiges of Aztec civilization may be found in the cultures of central Mexico today? There are no full-blooded Aztecs alive today, and nowhere are there any villages that preserve
Aztec culture unchanged. Yet Nahuatl does survive as a living
language for over one million people, and modern Nahua Indian culture includes many traits preserved from the distant, pre-
Spanish past. Beyond the boundaries of contemporary Nahua
villages, Aztec traits have been interwoven into modern Mexican culture. Many Mexicans look to the Aztecs for the origin
of their cultural heritage and take pride in the achievements of
Aztec civilization. The Aztec heritage belongs to us all, however, and the Aztecs can teach us much about human society
and its diversity of lifeways and practices.

Modern Nahua Indian Culture

The category "Indian" in Mexico was invented with the arrival
of Hernando Cortés in 1519. At first, the term was used to
refer to the natives: Aztecs, Mayas, Zapotecs, and many other
peoples who were culturally and biologically distinct from the
invading Spaniards. As the Colonial period proceeded with its
extensive genetic and cultural mixing, Indian came to be a
social rather than a racial category. Today in Mexico, an "Indian" is someone who speaks a native language and lives in
rural poverty.[2] Judith Friedlander has lived in the traditional

Figure 12.1 A farmer in the village of Tetlama, Morelos, builds the stone foundation for a traditional-style house of adobe bricks. The resulting foundation walls are almost indistinguishable form nearby Aztec peasant house foundations; see figure 6.3 (Photograph by Michael E. Smith)

Nahua village of Hueyapan, Morelos, and she describes the nature of Indian identity as follows:

> To be Indian in Hueyapan is to have a primarily negative identity. Indian-ness is more a measure of what the villagers are not or do not have vis-a-vis the hispanic elite than it is of what they are or have . . . [To the villagers of Hueyapan], to be Indian, in other words, signified primarily that you were poor.[3]

Although characterized by the preservation of the Nahuatl language and rural poverty, Nahua Indian villages today also conserve many traditional practices that can be traced back to the Aztecs, most prominently in the sphere of domestic material culture. For example, when peasants construct traditional adobe-brick houses today, they often employ techniques and materials identical to those used by their Aztec ancestors five centuries ago (figure 12.1).[4] Traditional diet and food in modern Nahua villages exhibit many continuities with Aztec times. Maize and beans are still the mainstay of the diet, with tomatoes, avocadoes, chili peppers, and squash as important supplements. Today most villagers buy their tortillas ready-made from a special bakery called a *tortillería*, although on special occasions women still take out the *metate* and *comalli* to make tortillas by hand.[5]

Even in the most conservative Indian household, however, European-derived foods play a major role. Rice, onions, beef, pork, and chicken have become deeply-embedded parts of traditional cuisine. The principle feast dish today, mole, can be traced back to the Aztecs (the name is from *molli*, which means sauce in Nahuatl), but many of the ingredients of modern mole are derived from European cuisine, not Aztec. The example of diet is illustrative of the general situation in which Indian culture is an intermingling of Aztec and European traits. Cultural features or customs that are viewed as "traditionally Indian" today cannot necessarily be traced back to the Prehispanic past.[6]

Handwoven textiles are another example of a modern Indian tradition derived from both Aztec and Spanish origins. In Hueyapan, for example, women still spin thread by hand and weave cloth with a backstrap loom (figure 12.2) virtually identical to that used by the Aztecs (see figure 4.3). Although the technology is Prehispanic, the fiber they work is wool, not cotton or *maguey*, and the clothing that they make conforms to Spanish, not indigenous, traditions.[7]

The modern Nahua Indian peoples of Mexico are not Aztecs living in the twentieth century. The blending of Aztec and Spanish cultures was an active process in which people adopted some new traits and rejected others, just as they maintained some ancient practices and abandoned others. Modern village culture is not merely a static mixture of Aztec and medieval Spanish traits, however; it too has been evolving for several hundred years. The Nahua peoples have created their own dynamic, unique culture, and they continue to create it today, by meeting new challenges with the resources and knowledge available to them, of whatever origin. Some Nahuas have become completely integrated into the national culture, and others have kept to themselves in isolated villages. But in both

Figure 12.2   A modern Nahua woman, Doña Epifania of Hueyapan, Morelos, weaves cloth on a traditional backstrap loom. She is dressed in the traditional skirt and blouse of Hueyapan women (Photograph by Judith Friedlander; reproduced with permission from Being Indian in Hueyapan *by Judith Friedlander. Copyright (c) 1975; St. Martin's Press, Inc.)*

Indian villages and Mexico City, much of the distinctive flavor of modern Mexican culture derives from the Aztec past.

The Aztec Past and the Mexican Present

Mexican national culture today owes much to its heritage from the Aztecs and other ancient Mesoamerican peoples. This is perhaps most obvious in the realms of food and economics. The maize and bean duo is ubiquitous in the diet of urban Mexicans, if not as prominent as it is in that of rural Indians. The maize tortilla is the national staple, and *tortillerías* are found in just about every rural village and urban neighborhood today.[8] Many popular foods, from tacos and tamales to chili peppers and pulque, can be traced directly to the Aztecs. Today, families most often make mole and other sauces in an electric blender, but almost every central Mexican household also owns a stone mortar and pestle with the same form and called by nearly the same names as their Aztec predecessors (the modern term for mortar in Mexican Spanish, *molcajete*, derives from the ancient Nahuatl term, *molcaxitl*). The Spanish language as spoken in Mexico has been influenced by Nahuatl in several ways. Many Nahuatl terms have been borrowed into Spanish, and the characteristic lilting cadence that distinguishes the Spanish spoken in central Mexico from that of other areas can be attributed to Nahuatl influence.

Aztec markets continued to flourish after the Spanish conquest, and periodic markets are still a vibrant part of modern Mexican culture. Found in both rural and urban areas, the weekly market remains a major provider of food and other goods and has yet to be superseded by the expanding numbers of discount stores and supermarket chains. Most large Mexican towns and cities support one or more municipal marketplaces that are open daily, with the weekly markets serving individual neighborhoods. Traditional craft items, such as textiles, pottery, and carved wood, are widely used not only in Indian villages but also in many middle-class Mexican homes. Furthermore, they are also popular with the many tourists who visit Mexico each year. These craft items are rarely found in the chain stores but are commonplace in the municipal and periodic markets, as well as in special tourist markets.

In the middle of Mexico City, where the central precinct of Tlatelolco once stood, is the Plaza of the Three Cultures. These three cultures – Aztec, Spanish, and modern Mexican – together symbolize the Mexican nation and its heritage. In Tlatelolco, all three are physically present in close juxtaposition: Aztec pyramids, an early colonial church, and modern high-rise apartment buildings (figure 12.3). The symbolism of the Plaza of the Three Cultures is important for modern Mexicans, and in 1964, President Alfredo López Mateos dedicated a plaque in Tlatelolco that reads:

*Figure 12.3   Plaza of the Three Cultures in Tlatelolco
(Photograph by Louise Burkhart; reproduced with permission)*

On 13 August, 1521, Tlatelolco, heroically defended by Cuauhtemoc, fell into the power of Hernando Cortés. It was neither a triumph nor a defeat, but the painful birth of the Mestizo people that is Mexico today.[9]

The Mexican people have always looked back to the Aztecs with pride and admiration. Just as the Aztec dynasties used their Toltec heritage to establish their legitimacy, the Mexican government today turns to Aztec civilization as a source of authenticity and continuity with the past. The national symbol of Mexico is taken directly from Aztec history: the eagle holding a snake, perched on a cactus (figure 12.4). In the fourteenth century, this symbol marked the sacred place where Huitzilopochtli told the Mexica to build Tenochtitlan, and as the national capital, Mexico City remains a sacred place today.

One aspect of Mexico's veneration of the Aztec past is the attention given to archaeology by the national government. In Mexico, archaeologists do not just study ancient cultures; rather they uncover the national heritage for the benefit of the entire

*Figure 12.4   The national symbol of Mexico, from the Mexican
flag. This image is taken from the Mexica account of the
founding of Tenochtitlan (Drawing by Kori Kaufman)*

nation. Most archaeological research in Mexico is conducted
by the federal government, through the Instituto Nacional de
Antropología e Historia. The enormous resources poured into
the Templo Mayor excavations in the 1970s and 1980s show
the level of government commitment to documenting the Aztec
past. As the central monument of Tenochtitlan, the Templo
Mayor today symbolizes the grandeur of Aztec civilization.
The results of these and other excavations, and the results of
ethnohistoric research, have worth for people worldwide, however, not just for Mexicans. This information occupies a prominent place in the collective human story.

A Wider Perspective

Modern technology and communication have made the world
seem smaller and have greatly reduced the variety of cultures
on our planet. We are moving toward a single, homogeneous,
global commercial culture. This process began with the European age of exploration, and it continues at a rapid pace today.
In order to comprehend the nature of our species, our strengths

and weaknesses, it is essential to understand the great diversity of peoples and cultures that once lived on earth. The evolution from egalitarian farmers to state-level societies was perhaps the most momentous social transformation in human history. The appearance of kings, laws, writing, money, and unequal social classes marked a watershed in human affairs. Once this threshold was reached, at different times in different regions, there was no turning back.

We still live in states, the kind of society that first appeared with the Sumerians, Egyptians, Mayas and Teotihuacan. We can learn much about ourselves by studying how institutions of government and classes first arose, what life was like under the early states, how these civilizations adapted (or not) to their surroundings, and how they interacted with other peoples. With growing problems of ethnic conflict in the world today, the Aztecs provide an example of how states have dealt with issues of economic and political domination and ethnic interaction.

The Aztecs are a prime example of an early complex society. They forged a way of life suited to their conditions independently of Old World cultures, and they gained economic and political success through their own unique accomplishments. Study of the Aztecs provides us a glimpse of the past of all humanity and helps us to view the present and the past from a broader perspective. This wider perspective is the goal of modern anthropology, and it is no surprise that Aztec studies today form a crucial part of the discipline of anthropology.

The Nahua historian Fernando de Alvarado Tezozomoc was concerned that the history of the Aztecs never be forgotten. In Nahuatl he recorded the following passage shortly after AD 1600:

Thus they have come to tell it,
thus they have come to record it in their narration,
and for us they have painted it in their codices,
the ancient men, the ancient women.

Thus in the future
never will it perish, never will it be forgotten,
always we will treasure it,
we, their children, their grandchildren,
brothers, great-grandchildren,

great-great-grandchildren, descendants,
we who carry their blood and their color,
we will tell it, we will pass it on
to those who do not yet live, who are yet to be born,
the children of the Mexicans, the children of the Tenochcans.
Alvarado Tezozomoc, Crónica Mexicayotl [10]

After nearly five centuries we can answer Alvarado Tezozomoc confidently that the story of the Aztecs will never be forgotten. It lives on in their painted codices and the many other objects that survive; it lives on in the written descriptions of Spaniards and Nahuas; it lives on in the Mexican people today; it lives on in the ruins of Aztec houses and temples; and it lives on in the world of modern archaeological and historical scholarship.

Notes

1 The Aztecs of Mesoamerica

1 Díaz del Castillo (1963:214).
2 Cantares Mexicanos (1985:f.17r), translated from the Nahuatl by León-Portilla (1963:72).
3 Lockhart (1992).
4 The Nahuatl-language documents analyzed by Cline (1986, 1993) and Lockhart (1992) have less of these biases than do the more abundant Spanish-language documents.
5 For an overview of Mesoamerican cultures from ancient times to the present, see Carmack et al. (1996).
6 Kirchoff (1943) published the first list of Mesoamerican traits; see Weaver (1993) for a more recent example. The more common modern interaction approach is exemplified by Blanton and Feinman (1984) and Carmack et al. (1996).
7 The best treatment of Mesoamerican environments in historical and modern times is West and Augelli (1989). Paleoenvironmental research directed at reconstructing climate, land forms, and other features for the prehistoric past has only just begun in central Mexico; see O'Hara et al. (1994) and Metcalfe et al. (1994).
8 See the glossary at the back of the book for definitions of key Aztec terms.
9 In an influential article, Sanders (1956) first pointed out these unique features of central Mexico, which he called the "central Mexican symbiotic region." See also Sanders et al. (1979).
10 Not all scholars believe that the past can be studied objectively and scientifically. Those who follow the "construction" model of scholarship assert that the past is unknowable and the evidence is vague. The researcher is free to construct any interpretation that cannot be contradicted logically. Any interpretation of the past is as good as any other in this view. This model is unduly pessimistic. There are agreed-upon methods of scientific investigation and historical research that give us

powerful means to demonstrate that some interpretations of the past are far more reasonable and likely than others. On the other hand, an opposing "discovery" model of scholarship errs in the opposite direction by suggesting that researchers simply discover an objective and fixed truth that exists independent of a scholar's procedures or ideas.

11 Anales de Cuauhtitlan, folio 57 (Bierhorst 1992:116). I have modified the spellings of the Mexica kings to conform to the standard versions used in this book. Other published pictorial histories include the *Codex Telleriano-Remensis* (Quiñones Keber 1995) and the *Códice Aubin* (1963).

12 The standard edition of the *Codex Mendoza* is that of Francis F. Berdan and Patricia Reiff Anawalt; see *Codex Mendoza* (1992).

13 Cortés (1962); Díaz del Castillo (1963).

14 The standard Spanish version of his works is Durán (1967). The excellent English translations by Doris Heyden, Durán (1971) and Durán (1994), are volumes one and two of the Spanish original.

15 Fray Diego Durán, *Book of the Gods and Rites and the Ancient Calendar*, translated and edited by Fernando Horcasitas and Doris Heyden, copyright 1971 by the University of Oklahoma Press, pp. 79–80.

16 Durán (1994).

17 The English edition of the *Florentine Codex* was translated and edited by Arthur J. O. Anderson and Charles E. Dibble (Sahagún 1950–82). An earlier version of Sahagún's work, the *Primeros Memoriales*, is also important (Sahagún 1905–07); 1993; Baird 1993). There is a large body of scholarship on Sahagún and his work; useful collections include Klor de Alva et al. (1988) and Edmonson (1974).

18 See Alva Ixtlilxochitl (1975–77). This work has not been translated into English.

19 For example, the Aztec empire expanded greatly in the 1460s. According to Mexica histories, their king Motecuhzoma I was responsible for most of the conquests, with king Nezahualcoyotl of Texcoco merely providing some support. Alva Ixtlilxochitl's history of Texcoco, on the other hand, describes the conquests as Nezahualcoyotl's, with only minor aid from the Mexica. See chapter 2.

20 No complete edition of Chimalpahin's works exists. Several partial translations into Spanish and German have been published, and an excellent analysis by Susan Schroeder (1991) includes lengthy transcriptions and English translations. See Chimalpahin (1965).

21 Gerhard (1993), Gibson (1964), Kellogg (1995), and Lockhart (1992) review many of these documents. English translations of key administrative documents may be found in Anderson et al. (1976), Lockhart et al. (1986), and Cline (1993).

22 Acuña (1984–87). Central Mexico is covered in volumes 6–9. Cline's (1972) discussion of the *Relaciones Geográficas* includes an English translation of the original questionnaire.

23 Acuña (1984–87:v.6:201–202), author's translation.

24 The social archaeology approach is described in Renfrew and Bahn (1991). An influential application to Mesoamerica is Flannery (1976). Hodge (n.d.a.) reviews recent Aztec archaeological work from this perspective.

25 The results of the overall survey project are described in Sanders et al. (1979), who provide references to the individual survey reports.

26 Intensive site surface research at Aztec sites is described in Brumfiel (1980, 1991a, 1991b, 1992), Charlton et al. (1991), and Smith et al. (1994). See discussion in chapters 4 and 7.

27 See Boone (1987), Broda et al. (1987), and Matos (1988). The Templo Mayor excavations are discussed in chapter 9 below.

28 See Evans (1988, 1991), Smith (1992a, 1992b), and de Vega and Mayer (1991).

29 These projects are described in Parsons et al. (1982), Charlton et al. (1991), Brumfiel (1992), Hodge (n.d.b.), and Smith et al. (1994); see Hodge (n.d.a.).

30 Analytical techniques for archaeological materials are discussed by Renfrew and Bahn (1991).

31 Aztec cotton spinning is discussed in chapter 4. For the functional interpretation of spinning bowls, see Smith and Hirth (1988).

2 The Rise of Aztec Civilization

1 Fray Diego Durán, *The History of the Indies of New Spain*, translated by Doris Heyden, copyright 1994 by the University of Oklahoma Press, p. 20.

2 The most complete and up-to-date introduction to Mesoamerican archaeology is Weaver (1993). Other useful accounts include Blanton et al. (1993) and M. Coe (1993, 1994). For central Mexico before the Aztecs, Sanders et al. (1979) is the best single source.

3 The central Mexican Postclassic chronology is described in Sanders et al. (1979) and Smith (1992b). Division of the Late Postclassic period into two phases is described by Smith and Doershuk (1991).

4 For descriptions of Teotihuacan, see Millon (1973) or the articles in Berlo (1992) and Diehl and Berlo (1989).

5 Teotihuacan – Aztec continuities and disjunctions are discussed in the papers in Diehl and Berlo (1989) and Berlo (1992).

6 Epiclassic sites are discussed in Diehl and Berlo (1989) and Hirth (1996). Native historical accounts of Tollan and the Toltecs are discussed by Davies (1977), and archaeological research at Tula is described by Diehl (1983) and Healan (1989).

7 This contrasts greatly with earlier Teotihuacan ceramics and later Aztec ceramics, both of which have been found by archaeologists over large parts of northern Mesoamerica.

8 The Aztlan migrations, mentioned in most surviving native histories, are discussed by Davies (1973:3–22), Smith (1984), and van Zantwijk (1985:22–36).

9 Mesoamerican languages and their historical development are discussed in Suarez (1983) and Kaufman (1976). For Nahuatl historical linguistics, see Kaufman (1976) and Smith (1984).

10 This avoidance is reflected in archaeological settlement patterns, where there is little continuity of occupation between sites of the Early Postclassic (AD 950–1150) and Early Aztec (AD 1150–1350) periods. Most Early

Aztec sites were new foundations, although some of the small Early Post-classic sites continued to be occupied into the Aztec period.

11 Early Aztec city-states are discussed by Brumfiel (1983), Calnek (1978, 1982), Davies (1980), and Hodge (1984).

12 Twin-stair pyramids are described in Marquina (1951). Some scholars have suggested that this style was somehow spread by the Aztec empire, but most examples date to the Middle Postclassic period, long before the expansion of the empire (see Umberger and Klein 1993). Lockhart (1992:1) discusses the role of the Nahuatl language in uniting the peoples of central Mexico.

13 The main native accounts of Mexica history are found in Durán (1994), Alvarado Tezozomoc (1975), Torquemada (1975–83), and the Codex Chimalpopoca (Bierhorst 1992). The best current synthesis and presentation of these accounts is Davies (1973).

14 Alvarado Tezozomoc (1975:49–51), translated by Davies (1973:31).

15 Many scholars accept 1325 as a reasonable date for the founding of Tenochtitlan. Nevertheless, excavations near the Templo Mayor in Mexico City located Early Aztec deposits (AD 1150–1350) in the lowest levels (Vega Sosa 1979), leading Graulich (1992) and Smith (1992b) to suggest that there may have been an earlier settlement on the site that is not mentioned in the historical accounts.

16 This story is recounted in Alvarado Tezozomoc (1975:94–95). Marriage alliances as a form of diplomacy are described by Carrasco (1984) and Smith (1986).

17 León-Portilla (1963:155).

18 Fray Diego Durán, *The History of the Indies of New Spain*, translated by Doris Heyden, copyright 1994 by the University of Oklahoma Press, pp. 209–10. Not all of the laws are listed here.

19 See Pollard (1993) on Tarascan civilization.

20 These "rebellions" are described by Hassig (1988) and Davies (1973, 1987).

21 This is the view of Davies (1973:216).

3 People on the Landscape

1 Cruz y Moya (1954/55:Vol.2:133); author's translation.

2 The climate patterns are revealed by recent geophysical studies of changing lake levels in central Mexico. The start of dry conditions around AD 600 coincided with the fall of Classic-period Teotihuacan, and their end coincided with the Aztec population explosion. This temporal pattern is nearly the opposite of older views (based upon poor data) that posited a change to drier conditions in the eleventh and twelfth centuries. The new paleoenvironmental data are reported in Metcalfe et al. (1989, 1994) and O'Hara et al. (1994).

3 Larger families became economically beneficial to most people. Extra children contributed in the fields or the workshops to help meet increasing tribute demands, and to help families get ahead economically. City-state rulers had two good reasons to actively encourage larger families: they produced more tribute-payers, and more importantly, they produced more males to serve in the army. The relationship between popu-

lation growth and socioeconomic change was one of mutual encouragement, or, in the language of systems theory, positive feedback. Population growth stimulated social changes, some of which in turn encouraged further population growth. There are no detailed studies of Aztec demography; see the limited discussion in Brumfiel (1983), Sanders et al. (1979), or Smith and Heath-Smith (1994).

4 The literature on population pressure, agriculture intensification, and their relationships in ancient Mesoamerica and elsewhere is large. See Boserup (1965), Sanders et al. (1979), Blanton et al. (1993), Netting (1993).

5 The various Spanish estimates of the size of Aztec armies are discussed by Sanders (1970:403–404) and Hassig (1988; 1992).

6 See Borah and Cook (1963), Sanders (1970), and Whitmore (1992).

7 The results are described in Sanders et al. (1979:216–219), and their methods are discussed in Sanders et al. (1979:34–52). Charlton (1970) is one of the studies of modern settlements in the Valley of Mexico used for population estimates. The methods of archaeological demography are far from fool-proof, but comparisons with historical sources show that the archaeological population estimates are at least roughly correct. Similar patterns of rapid Late Aztec population growth have been found in recent and still unpublished regional surveys outside of the Valley of Mexico.

8 Aztec foods and diet are discussed by S. Coe (1994) and Ortiz de Montellano (1990).

9 Sahagún (1950–82:bk.6:235). Lewis (1951:137) describes modern peasant maize rituals with Aztec parallels.

10 Díaz del Castillo (1963:233). See discussion of the nutritional value of the algae in Furst (1978) and Ortiz de Montellano (1990:102–106).

11 Harner (1977). These arguments are countered by Price (1978) and Ortiz de Montellano (1990:85–94); see chapter 9.

12 Katz et al. (1974); Ortiz de Montellano (1990:98–102).

13 Cook and Borah (1979), Sanders et al. (1979), and Williams (1989) all argue that the Aztec population exceeded their carrying capacity, whereas Blanton et al. (1993:155–156, 201–203) and Ortiz de Montellano (1990:72–97) take an opposing stance. I favor the former interpretation. The nutritional status of individuals as determined from osteological analyses of skeletal remains could help clarify the situation, but to date very few Aztec burials have been excavated.

14 Johnson and Earle (1987); Trigger (1993).

15 Sahagún (1950–82:bk.10:41–42).

16 Aztec terracing is described by Charlton (1970), Donkin (1979), Evans (1990), Sanders et al. (1979:242–251) and Smith and Price (1994).

17 Doolittle (1990) and Sanders et al. (1979:252–273) describe the technology and archaeological evidence for Aztec canal irrigation. Ethnohistorical accounts are discussed in Palerm (1972) and Smith (1994).

18 Aztec *chinampas* are discussed by Armillas (1971), Calnek (1972, 1976), Parsons et al. (1982), Sanders et al. (1979:273–281), and Wilken (1987).

19 Evans (1990).

20 Netting (1993); Wilkin (1987).

21 Wilkin (1987); Sanders et al. (1979:252–273).

22 Smith (1994).

23 Parsons (1991) and Sanders et al. (1979:280) argue for centralized control of *chinampa* construction, although Wilken's (1987) research suggests that households could have built and maintained the system.

24 See discussion in Smith (1992a) and Smith and Price (1994). The continuous and dispersed nature of these settlement patterns calls into question the very concept of archaeological site as a discrete bounded unit of settlement.

25 Smith (1992a); Smith and Heath-Smith (1994); Smith and Doershuk (1991); Smith and Price (1994).

26 Random sampling is a mathematical method for selecting items to study. It is designed to ensure that the items selected – the sample – are representative of the larger collection of items – the population. By using random sampling, we could generalize from our sample of excavated houses to the entire population of houses at these sites.

27 All houses at Capilco and most houses at Cuexcomate were simple structures corresponding to the residences of peasants or commoners, so we applied a household size figure of 5.5 persons (taken from early colonial census documents). Cuexcomate also had seven small elite residences, and we used a household size of 11 persons, also from the census documents. The census figures are discussed in Carrasco (1976) and Cline (1993); our methods of population estimate are described in Smith (1992a) and Smith (1994).

28 These excavations were directed by T. Jeffrey Price, who conducted many of the technical analyses; see Smith and Price (1994). The example discussed in the text is unit 230.

29 Osvaldo Sterpone of the Instituto Nacional de Antropología e Historia made this discovery.

4 Artisans and their Wares

1 Fray Diego Durán, *Book of the Gods and Rites and the Ancient Calendar*, translated and edited by Fernando Horcasitas and Doris Heyden, copyright 1971 by the University of Oklahoma Press, p. 403. This description pertains to the 260–day ritual calendar discussed in chapter 10.

2 Brumfiel (1987) discusses patterns of craft production. See also Hodge (n.d.a.) and papers in Hodge and Smith (1994). The best ethnohistoric descriptions of artisans are in books 9 and 10 of Sahagún (1950–82).

3 Mesoamerican obsidian technology is discussed by Clark (1982, 1987) and papers in Gaxiola and Clark (1989).

4 Other major Mesoamerican obsidian sources are located in the mountains east of the Basin of Mexico, in the Tarascan territory of Michoacan, and in the highlands of Guatemala.

5 Archaeologist Don Crabtree was the first to perfect a method for prismatic blade removal. He used a wooden "chest-punch" from a standing position, with the core between his feet. John Clark (1982) later worked out an alternative method, probably closer to the Aztec technique, in

which the blade was produced from a sitting position, again with core between the artisan's feet.

6 Sahagún (1950–82:bk.10:83).

7 Descriptions of Aztec pottery are provided by Parsons (1966) and Séjourné (1983). Pottery production is discussed by Hodge et al. (1993) and Minc et al. (1994).

8 Anawalt (1981), Berdan (1987), and Hicks (1994) discuss the uses of cotton cloth. Cotton-spinning artifacts are described by Smith and Hirth (1988).

9 The term *maguey* refers to several closely-related species of the genus *Agave* that grow above 1,800 m elevation in central Mexico.

10 Hernández (1959:v.2:349), translated by Jeffrey R. Parsons and Mary H. Parsons (1990:276). Parsons and Parsons (1990) discuss the use of the *maguey* plant in both ancient and modern times.

11 Dorothy Hosler (1994) is the best source for information on copper and bronze metallurgy in Mesoamerica. My discussion is based upon that work plus numerous conversations with Hosler, who has analyzed copper/ bronze artifacts from my excavations in Morelos and from numerous other sites in Mesoamerica. Descriptions of copper objects for sale in the Tlatelolco market are found in Sahagún (1950–82:bk.8:67–69).

12 Sahagún (1950–82:bk.9:83–97). See also Berdan (1982:26–28, 154– 155) and Pasztory (1983:278–280).

13 *Codex Mendoza* (1992:f.70r). See also Rojas (1986:116,184) on the hereditary nature of Aztec crafts.

14 Aztec goldworking is described by Nicholson and Quiñones Keber (1983:152–161) and Saville (1920). Sahagún (1950–82:bk.9:73–78) de- scribes the goldsmiths of Tenochtitlan. Mixtec gold from Oaxaca is described and illustrated in Caso (1969).

15 Sahagún (1950–82:bk.9:80).

16 Aztec mosaics are described by Nicholson and Quiñones Keber (1983: 170–177) and Saville (1922). See ethnohistoric descriptions by Sahagún (1950–82:bk.8:80) and Durán (1994:417).

17 See Brumfiel (1980, 1987) and Hodge and Smith (1994).

18 My discussion of the Otumba project is based upon the following sources: Charlton et al. (1991), Otis Charlton (1993, 1994), Nichols (1994), and Hare (1994). Conversations with Thomas Charlton, Deborah Nichols, Cynthia Otis Charlton, and Timothy Hare have contributed greatly to my knowledge of this project, and I thank Charlton and Otis Charlton for tours of the Otumba site and labs in 1989 and 1993.

19 The Otumba project archaeologists have identified a central core area of the site that was probably an elite residential zone, and a number of the workshops were located in or near this area. This may suggest elite control over at least some craft production.

5   Merchants, Markets, and Money

1 Díaz del Castillo (1963:232).

2 For descriptions of contemporary traditional peasant markets in

Mesoamerica, see Cook and Diskin (1976), Carol A. Smith (1974), and Carmack et al. (1996).

3 The Inca of South America, contemporaries of the Aztecs, are an example of a civilization where trade and exchange were heavily controlled by the central imperial state. Both production and exchange were managed by state bureaucrats, and marketplaces only existed on the fringes of the Inca empire. See D'Altroy (1992).

4 Cortés (1962:87–89). For other first-hand descriptions of the Tlatelolco market, see Díaz del Castillo (1963:232–234), Sahagún (1950–82:bk.8: 67–69), Torquemada (1975–83:v.4:348–352), and Feldman (1978).

5 Torquemada (1975–83:v.4:345). Anderson et al. (1976:138–149) publish documents describing the Coyoacan market.

6 Fray Diego Durán, *Book of the Gods and Rites and the Ancient Calendar*, translated and edited by Fernando Horcasitas and Doris Heyden, copyright 1971 by the University of Oklahoma Press, p. 278. Durán (1971:277–279) also describes the Cholula market. See Berdan (1985: 346–349) for a discussion of specialized markets in general.

7 Carol A. Smith (1974).

8 Friar Motolinía (1950:59) described the specifics of the market schedules. Most ethnohistoric descriptions of markets pertain to the Valley of Mexico, but available evidence suggests that markets and market systems were similar throughout Aztec central Mexico. Areas outside the valley also had markets in most cities, towns and villages; market hierarchies; and periodic schedules with merchants travelling among markets (Smith 1994).

9 Fray Diego Durán, *Book of the Gods and Rites and the Ancient Calendar*, translated and edited by Fernando Horcasitas and Doris Heyden, copyright 1971 by the University of Oklahoma Press, pp. 274–275.

10 Sahagún (1950–82:bk.9:31).

11 Sahagún (1950–82:bk.9:17).

12 The reliance of Mesoamerican commerce on human carriers, made necessary by the lack of draft animals and wheeled transport, placed severe constraints on the nature of goods that could be traded over long distances. The human carriers could only carry limited loads over modest daily distances, and they had to be fed along the way. Although wealthy nobles could finance the transport of any type of good over any distance, merchants were limited to high-value, low-bulk goods if they were to profit from their ventures. See discussions of the economic and social conditions of Mesoamerican transport systems in Drennan (1984) and Sanders and Santley (1983).

13 Fray Diego Durán, *Book of the Gods and Rites and the Ancient Calendar*, translated and edited by Fernando Horcasitas and Doris Heyden, copyright 1971 by the University of Oklahoma Press, p. 138. Sahagún (1950–82:bk.9:1–19) lists the goods sold by the *pochteca*.

14 Berdan (1988:645–646).

15 Aztec money in the forms of cacao beans and cotton textiles resembled modern currency in several respects. These items served to store value in that they could be saved for use at a later occasion, and they functioned

as media of exchange in that they could be traded for a variety of other goods. Aztec money was not universally exchangeable like modern currency, however. One could use it to buy food, household items, or jewelry in the market, but land could not be purchased with cacao or textiles, and the use of money to pay for labor services was quite limited. Einzig (1966) discusses various types of nonwestern currency.

16 Anderson et al. (1976:208–213). Rojas (1986:261) presents additional information on prices and equivalents.

17 Molina (1972:f.37r), translated by Dibble (1988:72).

18 The only drawback is that the analytical techniques require expensive, specialized equipment, and the analyses can be quite costly. For this reason, only a few studies have been done to date on Aztec obsidian exchange. The success of chemical analyses of obsidian for other Mesoamerican cultures (e.g., Cobean et al. 1991; Pollard and Vogel 1994) augurs well for the future application of these methods to Aztec sites and artifacts. Smith (1990) discusses Aztec obsidian exchange in general.

19 This discussion is based upon Hodge and Minc (1990), Hodge et al. (1993), Minc et al. (1994), and Hodge (n.d.a.).

20 Díaz del Castillo (1963:226). For discussion of Cholula Polychrome ceramics, see papers in Nicholson and Quiñones Keber (1994).

21 The Valley of Mexico salt industry is discussed by Sanders et al. (1979:171–175) and Parsons (1994).

22 Economic changes in Early and Late Aztec times are described in Brumfiel (1980, 1991a, 1987), Charlton et al. (1991), Smith (1992a), and Smith and Heath-Smith (1994).

23 Molina (1972:f.39v, 36v), translated by Dibble (1988:73, 71).

6 Family and Social Class

1 Cline (1993:153).

2 By social class, I mean a category of people who stand in a similar relationship with respect to the basic resources of society. Among the Aztecs, nobles controlled most of the resources, particularly land and labor, and commoners had to work for nobles and pay them tribute. Some definitions of social class require the members to be conscious of their class membership and allegiance to one another (e.g., Mann 1986); in such an approach, Aztec nobility constituted a class, whereas commoners did not.

3 See the *Codex Mendoza* (1992). Modern discussion of the Aztec life cycle may be found in Berdan (1982:73–96), Clendinnen (1991a), and Soustelle (1961:163–202).

4 *Codex Mendoza* (1992:v.4:118).

5 *Codex Mendoza* (1992:v.4:120).

6 *Codex Mendoza* (1992:v.4:122).

7 These quotations are from the *Codex Mendoza* (1992:v.4:123, 122, and 124).

8 Information on these schools is found in Sahagún (1950–82:bks.3,8),

Durán (1971:289–295), and the *Codex Mendoza* (1992:v.4:126–135;v.3:f.60v–65r).

9 Fray Diego Durán, *Book of the Gods and Rites and the Ancient Calendar*, translated and edited by Fernando Horcasitas and Doris Heyden, copyright 1971 by the University of Oklahoma Press, p. 293.

10 Weddings and their preparations are described in Sahagún (1950–82:bk.8: 127–130). McCaa (1994) discusses the young age at which girls married.

11 Sahagún (1950–82:bk.8:130).

12 *Codex Mendoza* (1992:v.4:126).

13 Aztec women are discussed by Brumfiel (1991a), Burkhart (1996), Clendinnen (1991a), Kellogg (1995), and Klein (1994).

14 Aztec concepts of the afterlife are discussed by León-Portilla (1963:124–133) and Nicholson (1971).

15 Fray Diego Durán, *Book of the Gods and Rites and the Ancient Calendar*, translated and edited by Fernando Horcasitas and Doris Heyden, copyright 1971 by the University of Oklahoma Press, p. 122. For discussion of funeral practices and burials, see León-Portilla (1963: 134–133), Nagao (1985), and Smith (1992a).

16 Documentary sources such as the above quotation from Friar Durán mention the jars used to bury the charred bones from a cremation. Several of these urn burials, probably of Mexica kings or leaders, were recovered in the excavations at the Templo Mayor of Tenochtitlan (Matos 1988); they have not been found at other sites, however.

17 In what may be a similar situation, Sahagún (1950–82:bk.10:191–192) suggested that the Aztecs buried their dead at Teotihuacan, which of course was in ruins by that time. Excavations at Xochicalco are described by Hirth (1996).

18 Aztec social classes are discussed by Carrasco and Broda (1976), Hicks (1986), Lockhart (1992), and Smith (1986).

19 Preliminary data on these issues are assembled by Berdan (1987) and Hicks (1994).

20 Lockhart (1992) is the best source on the *calpolli*; see also Carrasco (1976) and Hicks (1982, 1986). These and other recent studies present a very different view of the *calpolli* than that found in many older works. In place of an egalitarian body that owned land unconnected to nobles, the new view points out inequalities within the *calpolli* and the position of members under the control of a lord. I am using the term "ward" for the subdivision of a *calpolli* sometimes called *tlaxilacalli* or *chinamitl* in the sources.

21 Lockhart (1992:154).

22 This discussion is based upon our excavations at Cuexcomate and Capilco. We used written documents from other settlements in Morelos to interpret aspects of social organization at these sites; see Smith (1992a, 1994) and Smith and Heath-Smith (1994). Other descriptions of Aztec village life may be found in Brumfiel (1991), Evans (1988), and Lockhart (1992).

23 Aztec kinship and household organization are discussed by Berdan (1982:66–72), Carrasco (1976), Kellogg (1995:160–212), and Lockhart (1992:59–93). The Aztec kinship system was of the bilaterial type, mean-

ing that individuals traced descent through both the maternal and paternal lines.

24 Sahagún (1950–82: bk.6:35–36). The Nahuatl term for potsherd, *tapalcatl*, is still used in central Mexico today, even among Spanish-speakers.

25 This argument is developed in Smith and Heath-Smith (1994). We used domestic artifact inventories to define quantitative measures of the standard of living at each excavated house.

26 Fieldwork at Yautepec is described in greater detail in chapter 8; see Smith et al. (1994) and Smith et al. (forthcoming).

27 Excavation of this palace is described in Smith (1992a). Susan T. Evans has done research on Aztec palaces in general; see Evans (1988).

28 This census, which dates to the 1530s, is published in Nahuatl and German in Hinz et al. (1983); much of the pertinent information is summarized by Carrasco (1972, 1976). The census quoted at the start of this chapter is a related document from another town.

29 Many works on the Aztecs state that nobles were exempt from tribute. This incorrect interpretation comes from an uncritical reading of early written sources. After the Spanish conquest, the Aztec nobility managed to convince the Spaniards (including many of the chroniclers) that they had not paid tribute in ancient times and therefore should not have to pay tribute to the Spanish crown. This misrepresentation is exposed by Lockhart (1992:106), who notes that "lords and nobles paid tribute to the altepetl [city-state] as a matter of course."

30 Initial preservation efforts were coordinated by the Sociedad Cultural Yautepec; later a new organization was formed to continue this work, the Patronato Pro-Restauración de la Zona Arqueológica de Yautepec, Morelos. Reports on the excavations include de Vega and Mayer (1991).

31 Alva Ixtlilxochitl (1975–77:v.2:92–100). My description is based on this source; see also Hicks (1982, 1984).

32 Calnek (1976). Unlike Tenochtitlan, Texcoco did not have a shortage of land, so Nezahualcoyotl's palace may have been larger than Motecuhzoma's. The large size of Alva Ixtlilxochitl's estimate for the compound (84 ha) suggests that he may have been describing the entire downtown area of Texcoco, including the palace area, central plaza, temples, and market, and not just the palace compound itself.

33 Townsend (1992:137–144). Agricultural terraces at Texcotzinco are shown in figure 3.4.

34 Brumfiel (1987), Carrasco (1984), and Smith (1986) discuss the social connections within the nobility.

35 Fray Diego Durán, *The History of the Indies of New Spain*, translated by Doris Heyden, copyright 1994 by the University of Oklahoma Press, p. 331.

7 City-State and Empire

1 Fray Diego Durán, *The History of the Indies of New Spain*, translated by Doris Heyden, copyright 1994 by the University of Oklahoma Press, pp. 206, 207.

2 Aztec city-states are discussed by Hodge (1984, 1994), Licate (1980), and Lockhart (1992). Lockhart (1992) and Schroeder (1991) analyze the native Nahua concept of *altepetl*.

3 Sahagún (1950–82:bk.10:15). See Davies (1973) and Lockhart (1992) on the *tlatoani*.

4 Zorita (1963:126).

5 Examples include Berdan et al. (1996), Hicks (1992), and Hodge (1984, 1994).

6 Acuña (1984–87).

7 The example is from Hodge (1994); see also Hodge (1984); Berdan et al. (1996).

8 Comparative city-states are discussed by Nichols and Charlton (1996). Renfrew and Cherry's (1986) model of "peer polity interaction" describes the dynamics of city-state systems in terms that are applicable to the Aztec and other Mesoamerican cases.

9 Fray Diego Durán, *The History of the Indies of New Spain*, translated by Doris Heyden, copyright 1994 by the University of Oklahoma Press, p. 406.

10 Hassig (1988) provides the most complete account of Aztec warfare; other sources include Davies (1987) and Isaac (1983a, 1983b). Clendinnen (1991a) discusses the effects of warfare on Aztec society and culture.

11 Davies (1973:110); this view is echoed by Conrad and Demarest (1984:53) and other authors.

12 Variations in ancient empires are discussed by Mann (1986). Hassig (1985) first applied the hegemonic empire model to the Aztecs, and Berdan et al. (1996) refined this approach. My discussion of the Aztec empire is based primarily upon Berdan et al. (1996).

13 Imperial control in the Valley is discussed in Berdan et al. (1996), Hodge (1994), and Hicks (1992).

14 The expansion of the empire outside of the Valley of Mexico is covered by Davies (1987) and Berdan et al. (1996).

15 *Codex Mendoza* (1992:v.3:f.43r).

16 Other unconquered enemy states included Metztitlan to the north of the Valley of Mexico, the Yope state and Tututepec along the Pacific coast, and various Maya polities south of the empire. See Davies (1968) and Berdan et al. (1996:chapter 6).

17 Acuña (1984–87:v.6:328); author's translation.

18 Berdan et al. (1996:142–143) discuss Oztoma and other fortresses.

19 Fray Diego Durán, *The History of the Indies of New Spain*, translated by Doris Heyden, copyright 1994 by the University of Oklahoma Press, p. 336. See Smith (1986) for further discussion of this passage and its implications.

20 Andrés de Tapia (1971), translated by Isaac (1983b:416).

21 Díaz del Castillo (1963:179) reports the Tlaxcallan viewpoint. The flowery war remains a controversial subject. In spite of its obviously propagandistic nature, many modern authors take the Mexica explanation at face value. See discussion in Davies (1987), Isaac (1983b), and Plunket and Uruñuela (1994).

8   Cities and Urban Planning

1   Chimalpahin, quoted by León-Portilla (1963:158).

2   Here I am following the functional approach to urbanism as outlined by Fox (1977) and Trigger (1972). Marcus (1983) applies this model to Mesoamerican cities. An alternative demographic approach is favored by Sanders and Price (1968) and Sanders and Santley (1983).

3   The city described in this fictionalized account is a composite picture of a typical city-state capital drawn from archaeological and ethnohistorical sources on various Aztec towns. Very little information survives on the city of Amecameca beyond its size (10,000 inhabitants in an area of 4 square km) and political status (see Hodge 1984, Parsons et al. 1982, and Schroeder 1991).

4   There is no single comprehensive study of ancient Mesoamerican urbanism and urban planning. Good introductions include Marcus (1983) and Sanders and Webster (1988). My discussion of Aztec urban planning is based upon my fieldwork at Cuexcomate (Smith 1992a) and Yautepec (Smith et al. 1994), visits to other Aztec towns in the Valley of Mexico and Morelos, and scattered references in the documentary and archaeological literature.

5   The *pochteca*, for example, lived in their own *calpolli*, as did many of the luxury artisans described by Sahagún (see chapter 4). The localized distribution of craft workshops at Otumba (see figure 4.11) also suggests *calpolli* organization (Charlton et al. 1991; Nichols 1994). Not all cities fit this model; for example, Huexotla does not appear to have had many craft specialists nor distinguishable *calpolli* divisions (Brumfiel 1980, 1987).

6   Alva Ixtlilxochitl (1975–77) describes Texcoco; see Hicks (1982, 1984). Davies (1973:40–78) presents some of the scattered documentary information on Azcapotzalco, and Angulo (1976) describes archaeological work in Cuauhnahuac (modern Cuernavaca).

7   Our six-month excavation at Yautepec uncovered particularly dense deposits of artifacts from which we recovered over 1.2 million potsherds. At the time of writing, our laboratory analyses are only partially done, and it will take some time to sort, describe, and analyze all of the ceramics, obsidian (tens of thousands of pieces), and other artifacts. Preliminary descriptions of our fieldwork at Yautepec may be found in Smith et al. (1994) and Smith et al. (n.d.); the palace excavations are described in de Vega and Mayer (1991).

8   We had planned to concentrate our efforts in a large open area just west of the palace (probably an elite residential neighborhood), but between the first and second field seasons this area was the setting for a planned invasion by squatters. Local government officials were unable to evict the squatters, so we changed our tactics and found other places to dig around town. Instead of an intensive study of one part of Yautepec, we ended up with a larger number of smaller excavations distributed more widely throughout the site.

9 An early colonial census permits the reconstruction of the population of Yautepec in 1519 at around 15,000 inhabitants (Smith 1994). When this figure is divided by the areal extent of the city – 210 hectares – the resulting population density of 71 persons per hectare is not too different from that of Cuexcomate (55 persons per hectare).

10 *Cantares Mexicanos* (f.19v–20r), translated by León-Portilla (1969:87).

11 The reconstruction painting of Tenochtitlan (figure 8.4) gives a fairly accurate idea of the look of the city. At this scale, however, the city would have been about twice as large as depicted in the painting. See figure 8.5 for a more accurate scale.

12 My discussion of Tenochtitlan is based on Calnek (1972, 1976), Marquina (1960), and Rojas (1986). Archaeological excavations are described by Berdan et al. (1996), Broda et al. (1987), Matos (1979, 1988), and Vega Sosa (1979).

13 Emily Umberger (1996) discusses these aspects of urban planning at Tenochtitlan. This model of the Mexica differentiating Tenochtitlan from other Aztec cities by drawing on their knowledge of ancient imperial capitals contrasts with previous discussions of Aztec urbanism, where smaller cities were considered to be small-scale copies of Tenochtitlan.

14 The conqueror Hernando Cortés said of the narrower southern causeway, "This causeway was as broad as two lances and very stoutly made such that eight horsemen could ride along it abreast" Cortés (1962:68).

15 I discuss the sacred precinct and Templo Mayor at greater length in chapter 9.

9 Creation, Sacrifice, and the Gods

1 Sahagún (1950–82:bk.3:1). See also Sahagún (1950–82:bk.7:4).

2 Good discussions of Aztec religion include Brundage (1985), Burkhart (1989), Carrasco (1990), Clendinnen (1991a), León-Portilla (1963, 1993), Miller and Taube (1993), and Nicholson (1971). There is a vast amount of ethnohistorical information on Aztec religion, thanks to the efforts of priestly chroniclers like Sahagún. Most of this material comes from Tenochtitlan, and therefore, my discussion of religion pertains primarily to the Mexica people unless otherwise noted.

3 Aztec myths are reviewed in León-Portilla (1963), Nicholson (1971) and Taube (1993).

4 From the *Leyenda de los Soles*; quoted in León-Portilla (1963:107–108).

5 Bierhorst (1992:148).

6 Sahagún (1950–82:bk.3:2).

7 Sahagún (1950–82:bk.3:4).

8 Jacques Soustelle (1961:115) observes that Aztec religion, "seems to us both complicated and contradictory, made up of different contributions which had not yet been assimilated and merged into a coherent system." Miguel León-Portilla (1963), on the other hand, finds more cohesiveness and integration in Aztec thought.

9 Several papers in Berlo (1992) discuss these deities.

10 Chimalpahin, quoted in León-Portilla (1963:161).

11 See Nicholson (1971). It should be stressed that this scheme is a great

simplification of a very complex situation. As Nicholson points out, the Aztecs themselves viewed the gods as more fluid and dynamic than this seemingly well-organized scheme might suggest.

12 Durán (1971:99).

13 Sahagún (1950–82:bk.6:5).

14 Priests are discussed by Alberti (1994), Brundage (1985), Clindinnen (1991a), and Nicholson (1971).

15 Sahagún (1950–82:bk.2:184–185).

16 Klein (1987:297).

17 The identification of Aztec deities with the devil, made by Sahagún and his assistants, is not a very accurate interpretation of their nature or role within Aztec religion.

18 Sahagún (1950–82:bk.2:184).

19 Durán (1971:81).

20 Aztec cannibalism in this respect was similar to other reported cases of cannibalism around the world. The eating of human flesh in most cases is a sacred act, done to close relatives in order to honor them and incorporate something of their essence into their living kin. This ethnographic reality contrasts sharply with the popular image of antagonistic cannibalism in which bloodthirsty tribes capture their enemies (or perhaps missionaries and anthropologists) to cook for dinner in a big stewpot.

21 Sahagún (1950–82:bk.2:185).

22 I should note that it is very hard to determine the actual frequency of human sacrifice. The Spanish conquerors deliberately exaggerated the extent of human sacrifice to make the Aztecs appear more barbaric; this helped justify their conquest and domination. Although we cannot make a quantitative estimate, however, most scholars agree that sacrifice was widespread and frequent in Aztec central Mexico.

23 See Harner (1977). Bernard R. Ortiz de Montellano (1978; 1990:85–94) published the strongest of several refutations of Harner's protein deficiency theory of cannibalism.

24 For the Sacred Precinct and Templo Mayor, see Boone (1987), Broda et al. (1987), López Luján (1994), Marquina (1960), Matos (1979, 1988), and Vega Sosa (1979).

25 Matos (1988) and Graulich (1992) propose alternative chronologies for the stages of construction of the Templo Mayor.

26 The offerings are described and analyzed by López Luján (1994). Artifacts and other objects excavated by the Templo Mayor project are on display at the Templo Mayor Museum, a stunning museum recently built at the site. Many of the objects are illustrated in Carrasco and Matos (1992).

27 Umberger (1987, 1996) discusses the way Aztec artists drew upon earlier imperial styles. See discussion in chapter 8.

28 Lagunas and Serrano (1972) describe the Teopanzolco skulls. We know that these were severed heads, rather than skulls removed from earlier graves and reburied, because they were accompanied by the top cervical vertebrae. This only occurs when the head is cut off at, or soon after, death. Severed skulls like this have also been found at other Aztec sites.

While we were excavating at Yautepec, for example, construction workers digging a trench near the excavations uncovered a large bowl containing a severed skull with cervical vertebrae. We know that the Teopanzolco sacrificial deposit dates to the Early Aztec period, contemporaneous with the large, double-stair pyramid at the site, from distinctive polychrome ceramic vessels included with the skulls.

29 Smith (1992a:327–333).
30 Durán (1971:412–470). Sahagún devoted an entire book of the *Florentine Codex* to the monthly ceremonies (1950–82:bk.2). The Toxcatl ceremonies are described in Durán (1971:426–429) and Sahagún (1950–82:bk.2:64–73); see also Doris Heyden's (1991) analysis.
31 Sahagún (1950–82:bk.2:64).
32 Durán (1971:426).
33 Sahagún (1950–82:bk.7:27).
34 Smith (1992a).
35 For the Mesoamerican ballgame, see Scarborough and Wilcox (1991).
36 Fray Diego Durán, *Book of the Gods and Rites and the Ancient Calendar*, translated and edited by Fernando Horcasitas and Doris Heyden, copyright 1971 by the University of Oklahoma Press, p. 318. People also gambled on the board game *patolli*, in which beans were moved around a course in a manner similar to the game pachisi.
37 Fray Diego Durán, *Book of the Gods and Rites and the Ancient Calendar*, translated and edited by Fernando Horcasitas and Doris Heyden, copyright 1971 by the University of Oklahoma Press, pp. 463, 452.
38 Burkhart (1996) explores the reasons why the early Spanish priests were usually quite ignorant of what happened within the confines of the house and home. Archaeological evidence for domestic ritual is discussed by Smith (1992a), Otis Charlton (1994), and Parsons (1972).

10 Science and Art

1 Alva Ixtlilxochitl (1975–77:v.1:527), translated by León-Portilla (1963:16).
2 The Nahuatl term for the wild fig is *amatl*; the trees are *Ficus benjamina* or *Ficus involuta*. Aztec books and paper are discussed in von Hagen (1944), Sandstrom and Sandstrom (1986) and Wyllie (1994).
3 Sandstrom and Sandstrom (1986) describe modern Otomi paper-making, and Stromberg (1976) describes the Guerrero tourist paper industry.
4 Important Aztec books mentioned in the text include the *Codex Borbinicus* (1974), the *Codex Borgia* (1976, 1993), the *Codex Telleriano Remensis* (Quiñones Keber 1995), the *Codex Magliabechiano* (1983), the *Codex Mendoza* (1992), and the *Tira de la Peregrinación* (1944). Robertson (1959) discusses Aztec books in general.
5 Díaz del Castillo (1963:227–228).
6 Sahagún (1950–82:bk.10:28). See also Alva Ixtlilxochitl (1975–77:v.1:527).
7 "Other [scribes] took care of the paintings of the boundaries, the limits, and the landmarks of the cities, provinces, and towns, and [recorded] to whom they belonged." (Alva Ixtlilxochitl 1975–77:v.1:527, quoted by León-Portilla 1963:157). León-Portilla (1992) provides an alternative

interpretation of the figure on the Yautepec relief as the god Cipactonal, patron of scribes and writing.

8 Classic Maya writing is discussed by Kelley (1976) and Coe (1992). Justeson and Kaufman (1993) describe their decipherment of Epi-Olmec writing. Marcus (1992) covers Maya, Aztec, Mixtec, and Zapotec writing, with an emphasis on the Oaxaca scripts. Systems of signs at Teotihuacan and Xochicalco are discussed in Berlo (1992) and Diehl and Berlo (1989).

9 Discussions of Aztec writing include Berdan (1992a), Marcus (1992), and Prem (1992). Berdan (1992b) is a catalog, description, and translation of all of the glyphs in the *Codex Mendoza* (1992), the single largest corpus of Aztec glyphs.

10 In English, rebus writing is often used in children's games. For example, the sentence "I saw Aunt Rose" can be written with four glyphs: an eye, a carpenter's saw, an ant, and a rose; similarly the word "belief" can be depicted by a bee and a leaf. Marcus (1992:20, 65) discusses the use of the rebus principle in Mesoamerican writing systems.

11 Aztec calendars are discussed by Aveni (1980), Caso (1971) and Marcus (1992).

12 A common misunderstanding concerning the use of ancient calendars in Mesoamerica and in other civilizations is that peasant farmers were dependent upon priests or other leaders to interpret the calendar in order to guide their farming. Unless instructed by leaders, peasants would not know when to plant their fields, which must be done just before the rainy season starts. This secret knowledge is said to have been the basis for the power of priests over peasants. Anyone familiar with traditional farmers in Mesoamerica or other parts of the world, however, knows that they do not need to consult priests or formal calendars to know when to plant and cultivate their fields. Peasants are very aware of weather and the seasons. They make decisions about planting based upon their observations, experience, and the benefit of many generations of accumulated practical knowledge of the environment and technology. Leaders achieve and maintain domination over subjects through their control over more tangible factors such as land and labor, not calendars.

13 Torquemada (1975–83:v.1:260 [bk.2:ch.64]), translated by León-Portilla (1963:142).

14 Archaeoastronomy is the study of ancient astronomy. Aveni's research provides the best introduction to the astronomical accomplishments of the Aztecs and other Mesoamerican cultures. See Aveni (1980, 1992) and Aveni et al. (1988).

15 Motolinía (1971:24; chap.16), translated by Aveni (1992:150).

16 Aztec medicine is discussed by Ortiz de Montellano (1990) and López Austin (1988). The Aztecs owed their good health in part to the lower levels of infectuous disease in the ancient New World when compared with the premodern Old World. With the exception of the llama of Andean South America, the New World lacked the large domesticated animals that were often vectors of disease transmission and contributors to poor sanitation in the Old World. Also, in the New World urbanism developed later and was less widespread than in the Old World. Dense,

urbanized populations are the prime breeding ground for infectious disease. The Aztecs and other native peoples, however, paid a heavy price for the lack of these diseases when Old World epidemics swept the New World in the sixteenth and seventeenth centuries (see Crosby 1972 and McNeil 1976).

17 Sahagún (1905–07:v.3:f.119r), translated by León-Portilla (1963:26).

18 Sahagún (1950–82:bk.10:161–162).

19 Motolinía (1971:160), translated by Ortiz de Montellano (1990:181).

20 Ruiz de Alarcón (1982:267–269).

21 Nicholson and Quiñones Keber (1994:vii). A number of authors have confused the Mixteca-Puebla style with the earlier coastal tradition, treating the two as manifestations of a single phenomenon. I have criticized this approach, however, because the coastal style occurred earlier in time and was not present in the Mixteca-Puebla area (see Smith and Heath-Smith 1980). The chapters in Nicholson and Quiñones Keber (1994) provide numerous examples and analyses of the Mixteca-Puebla style proper.

22 Mixteca-Puebla style murals are discussed in Smith and Heath-Smith (1980) and Nicholson and Quiñones Keber (1994), and manuscripts from the outer imperial provinces are discussed in Berdan et al. (1996). The Mesoamerican world system is discussed in Blanton and Feinman (1984).

23 Aztec stone sculpture is discussed in Pasztory (1983) and Nicholson and Quiñones Keber (1983). Monumental imperial sculptures and their religious and political significance are analyzed by Townsend (1979) and Umberger (1996).

24 The best introductions to Aztec literature and poetry are León-Portilla (1963, 1969). See also Cantares Mexicanos (1985) and Lockhart (1992).

25 Sahagún (1905–07:v.6:f.122), translated by León-Portilla (1969:27).

26 Aztec song, translated by León-Portilla (1969:68).

27 Cantares Mexicanos (1985:f.35v), translated by León-Portilla (1963:77).

28 Cantares Mexicanos (1985:f.16v), translated by León-Portilla (1963:78).

29 Cantares Mexicanos (1985:f.26r), translated by León-Portilla (1963:73).

30 Martí and Kurath (1964) discuss music and dance. Most information is from written sources, although a number of drums and other musical instruments have survived.

31 Fray Diego Durán, *Book of the Gods and Rites and the Ancient Calendar*, translated and edited by Fernando Horcasitas and Doris Heyden, copyright 1971 by the University of Oklahoma Press, p. 295.

11 Final Glory and Destruction

1 Cantares Mexicanos (1985), translated by León-Portilla (1962:149).

2 We are fortunate to have two views of the Spanish conquest of the Aztecs. The Spanish story was told by two of the participants, Hernando Cortés (1962), and Bernal Díaz del Castillo (1963), and summarized in the nineteenth-century account of Prescott (1843). The Aztec side of the story, contained in Sahagún (1950–82:bk.12), Durán (1994:483–563), and many scattered accounts, has been assembled by León-Portilla (1962)

and Lockhart (1993). Anderson and Dibble (1978) is another version of book 12 of Sahagún. Many modern books summarize the events of the conquest (e.g., Carmack et al. 1996:ch.4), and several recent works contain insightful analyses of the context and implications of the conquest (e.g., Clendinnen 1991b; Gillespie 1989:173–230; Hassig 1988:236–250). I base my discussion on these sources. See Lovell (1985) and Warren (1985) on the Spanish conquest of other Mesoamerican peoples.

3   Sahagún (1950–82:bk.12:31).

4   Fray Diego Durán, *The History of the Indies of New Spain*, translated by Doris Heyden, copyright 1994 by the University of Oklahoma Press. p. 529.

5   Díaz del Castillo (1963:218,219).

6   Sahagún (1905–07), translated by León-Portilla (1962:92–93). See also Sahagún (1950–82:bk.12:81).

7   Translated from the Nahuatl by León-Portilla (1962:137–138).

8   Many modern authors apparently believe this story, which is repeated in numerous accounts of the Spanish conquest. Gillespie (1989:173–201) provides a detailed historiographic analysis showing it to be a sixteenth-century fabrication, created in the attempt to make sense out of the cataclysm of the Spanish conquest.

9   Hassig (1988:242–244; the quotation is on p. 243).

10 Sixteenth-century epidemics are discussed by McCaa (1995), Prem (1991), Sanders (1970), and Whitmore (1992). McNeill (1976) analyzes the role of epidemics in world history, including the Aztec case.

11 Whitmore (1992). This initial epidemic reached Peru by 1526, where it killed the Inca emperor Huayna Capac long before any Europeans had arrived on the scene.

12 Lockhart (1992:1). For general treatments of Nahua culture in the century after the Spanish conquest, see Burkhart (1989), Cline (1986), Gibson (1964, 1966), Kellogg (1995), and Lockhart (1992). Gibson (1964) and Lockhart (1992) provide extensive overviews of the subject.

13 Early Mexican *encomiendas* are discussed by Gibson (1964, 1966) and Gerhard (1993). Gibson (1964:83) lists typical *encomienda* tribute goods.

14 Gerhard (1993); Gibson (1964); Lockhart (1992).

15 The role of the church is discussed by Gibson (1964, 1966). For the responses of the Nahuas to Christianity, see Burkhart (1989), Lockhart (1992), and Carmack et al. (1996:ch.5).

16 These early churches and monasteries, most of which still stand today, are fascinating structures. See Kubler (1948) and Perry (1992).

17 Carmack et al. (1996:165). See Burkhart (1989) for a detailed analysis of this situation.

18 Burkhart (1989), Ingham (1986).

19 Lockhart (1992); see also Cline (1986, 1993) and Kellogg (1995).

20 The archaeology of early colonial central Mexico is discussed by Charlton (1972), Charlton and Fournier (1993), Lister and Lister (1982), and González Rul (1988).

21 Lockhart (1992:201–202). See also Gibson (1964), Haskett (1991), and Kellogg (1995).

12 The Aztec Legacy Today

1 Friedlander (1975:130).
2 A few of the many excellent anthropological descriptions of modern Nahua peoples today are Friedlander (1975), Ingham (1986), Lewis (1951) Sandstrom (1991), and Taggart (1983). See also Carmack et al. (1996).
3 Friedlander (1975:71,75).
4 Modern traditional houses are discussed by Moya (1982), Sandstrom (1991), and Smith et al. (1992). The house being built in figure 12.1, when completed, resembled that shown in figure 6.5.
5 See Lewis (1951); Redfield (1929).
6 Foster (1960) discusses many examples of this phenomenon.
7 Friedlander (1975). For hand-spinning wool, the women of Hueyapan use large Aztec spindle whorls that they find in the fields. These whorls were originally used by the Aztecs to spin maguey fiber. Berdan and Barber (1988) also discuss modern Nahua textiles. Other modern Indian crafts and their historical development are discussed by Foster (1960), Friedlander (1975), Sandstrom and Sandstrom (1986), and Stromberg (1976). For modern use of Nahuatl, see Kaufman (1976).
8 The tortilla made of wheat flour is a northern Mexican food that originated well after the Spanish conquest. Wheat flour tortillas are available in central Mexican grocery stores, but they are not nearly as prevalent in the diet as the maize tortilla.
9 Plaque in the Plaza of the Three Cultures in Tlatelolco (see Fowler 1987:234).
10 Alvarado Tezozomoc (1975:4–5), translated by Marcus (1992:271–272).

Glossary of Nahuatl Terms

altepetl City-state or kingdom consisting of a town and surrounding rural area ruled by a *tlatoani* (chapter 7).

calmecac School for nobles or promising commoners (chapter 6).

calpolli A group of families who lived near one another and were subject to a single lord. Most *calpolli* had between 100 and 200 families. In cities *calpolli* formed neighborhood, whereas rural *calpolli* were either towns or collections of villages. The term *calpolli* is sometimes used in documents to designate a smaller residential unit, the ward (chapter 6).

chichimec Member of a hunting and gathering band of northern Mexico. The ancestors of the Aztecs were chichimecs who migrated south into central Mexico (chapter 2).

chinampa Raised field bed, a form of intensive agriculture used to cultivate swampy areas (chapter 3).

ixiptla God impersonator. Priests or planned sacrificial victims dressed in the regalia of a god and were venerated as that god during key ceremonies (chapter 9).

macehualli (plural, macehualtin) Commoner who was a member of a *calpolli* (chapter 6).

maguey Plant of the genus *Agave* with many economic and medicinal uses (chapter 3).

maquahuitl Sword made of a wood handle with two cutting edges of sharp obsidian blades (chapter 7).

metate Stone slab used to grind maize to make tortillas and tamales (chapters 3 and 6).

patolli   game of chance often played by gamblers (chapter 9).

pilli (plural, pipiltin)   Hereditary noble of a lower rank than a *tlatoani* or *tecuhtli* (chapter 6).

pochtecatl (plural, pochteca)   Professional merchant belonging to a specialized trading guild (chapter 5).

pulque   Fermented alchoholic beverage made from the sap of the *maguey* plant (chapter 3).

quachtli   Wonen cotton cape or blanket of a standard size used as currency and for tribute payments (chapters 4 and 5).

quauhpilli   Special social category of nobles by achievement created by Motecuhzoma I to reward outstanding commoner accomplishments in war (chapters 2, 7).

tecuhtli (plural, tetecuhtin)   High-ranking lord or noble who controlled a major estate and usually served in an important administrative or military position (chapters 6).

telpochcalli   School for commoner children (chapter 6).

teotl   Deity (chapter 9).

tequitl   Goods and labor service owed to lords by commoners (chapter 6).

tianquiz   Marketplace (chapter 5).

tlachtli   The Aztec ballgame, an event that combined ritual, sport, and entertainment (chapter 9).

tlacotli (plural, tlacotin)   Slave (chapter 6).

tlamama   Professional carriers or load-bearers, usually employed by merchants on trade expeditions (chapter 5).

tlatoani (plural, tlatoque)   King of a city-state. A *tlatoani*, literally "he who speaks," was always of the noble class (chapter 7).

tonalpohualli   260-day ritual calendar used for divination, astrology, and rituals (chapter 10).

tzompantli   Skull-rack for public display of the skulls of sacrificial victims (chapter 9).

Note: The best modern Nahuatl-English dictionary is Karttunen (1983). The most complete sources on sixteenth-century Nahuatl are Friar Alonso de Molina's Nahuatl-Spanish and Spanish-Nahuatl dictionary from 1571 (Molina 1970) and Friar Sahagún's *Florentine Codex* (Sahagún 1950–82).

References

Acuña, René, ed.
1984–87. *Relaciones geográficas del siglo XVI*. 9 vols. Universidad Nacional Autónoma de México, Mexico City. (Originally compiled 1578–1582).

Alberti Manzanares, Pilar
1994. Mujeres sacerdotisas Aztecas: Las cihuatlamacazque mencionadas en los manuscritos inéditos. *Estudios de cultura Náhuatl* 24:171–217.

Alva Ixtlilxochitl, Fernando de
1975–77 *Obras históricas*. 2 vols. Translated by Edmundo O'Gorman. Universidad Nacional Autónoma de México, Mexico City. (Originally written 1600–1640).

Alvarado Tezozomoc, Fernando
1975. *Crónica Mexicáyotl*. Translated by Adrián León. Universidad Nacional Autónoma de México, Mexico City. (Originally written 1609).

Anawalt, Patricia
1981. *Indian Clothing Before Cortés: Mesoamerican Costumes from the Codices*. University of Oaklahoma Press, Norman.

Anderson, Arthur J. O., Frances F. Berdan, and James Lockhart
1976. *Beyond the Codices: The Nahua View of Colonial Mexico*. University of California Press, Berkeley.

Anderson, Arthur J. O., and Charles E. Dibble
1978. *The War of Conquest: How It Was Waged Here in Mexico (The Aztec's Own Story as Given to Fr. Bernardino de Sahagún)*. University of Utah Press, Salt Lake City.

Angulo Villaseñor, Jorge
1976. Teopanzolco y Cuauhnahuac, Morelos. In *Los señoríos e estados militaristas*, edited by Román Piña Chán, pp. 183–208. Instituto Nacional de Antropología e Historia, Mexico City.

Armillas, Pedro
1971. Gardens on Swamps. *Science* 174:653–661.
Aveni, Anthony F.
1980. *Skywatchers of Ancient Mexico*. University of Texas Press, Austin.
1992. Moctezuma's Sky: Aztec Astronomy and Ritual. In *Moctezuma's Mexico: Visions of the Aztec World*, edited by Davíd Carrasco and Eduardo Matos Moctezuma, pp. 149–158. University Press of Colorado, Niwot, Colorado.
Aveni, Anthony F., Edward E. Calnek, and Horst Hartung
1988. Myth, Environment and the Orientation of the Templo Mayor of Tenochtitlan. *American Antiquity* 53:287–309.
Baird, Ellen T.
1993. *The Drawings of Sahagún's Primeros Memoriales: Structure and Style*. University of Oklahoma Press, Norman.
Berdan Frances F.
1982. *The Aztecs of Central Mexico: An Imperial Society*. Holt, Rinehart and Winston, New York.
1985. Markets in the Economy of Aztec Mexico. In *Markets and Marketing*, edited by Stuart Plattner, pp. 339–367. University Press of America, Lanham, MD.
1987. Cotton in Aztec Mexico: Production, Distribution, and Uses. *Mexican Studies / Estudios Mexicanos* 3:235–262.
1988. Principles of Regional and Long-distance Trade in the Aztec Empire. In *Smoke and Mist: Mesoamerican Studies in Memory of Thelma D. Sullivan*, edited by J. Kathryn Josserand and Karen Dakin, pp. 639–656. British Archaeological Reports, International Series, no. 402, Oxford.
1992a. Glyphic Conventions of the Codex Mendoza. In *The Codex Mendoza*, vol. 1, edited by Frances F. Berdan and Patricia Rieff Anawalt, pp. 93–102. University of California Press, Berkeley.
1992b. Appendix E: The Place-name, Personal Name, and Title Glyphs of the Codex Mendoza: Translations and Comments. In *The Codex Mendoza*, vol. 1, edited by Frances F. Berdan and Patricia Rieff Anawalt, pp. 163–239. University of California Press, Berkeley.
Berdan, Frances F., and Patricia R. Anawalt, eds.
1992. *The Codex Mendoza*. 4 vols. University of California Press, Berkeley.
Berdan, Frances F., and Russell J. Barber
1988. *Spanish Thread on Indian Looms: Mexican Folk Costume*. University Art Gallery, San Bernardino.
Berdan, Frances F., Richard E. Blanton, Elizabeth H. Boone, Mary G. Hodge, Michael E. Smith, and Emily Umberger

1996. *Aztec Imperial Strategies*. Dumbarton Oaks, Washington, DC.

Berlo, Janet C., ed.
1992. *Art, Ideology, and the City of Teotihuacan*. Dumbarton Oaks, Washington, DC.

Bierhorst, John, trans.
1992. *History and Mythology of the Aztecs: The Codex Chimalpopoca*. University of Arizona Press, Tucson. (Originally written sixteenth century).

Blanton, Richard E., and Gary Feinman
1984. The Mesoamerican World System. *American Anthropologist* 86:673–682.

Blanton, Richard E., Stephen A. Kowalewski, Gary M. Feinman, and Laura M. Finsten
1993. *Ancient Mesoamerica: A Comparison of Change in Three Regions*. 2nd ed. Cambridge University Press, New York.

Boone, Elizabeth H., ed.
1987. *The Aztec Templo Mayor*. Dumbarton Oaks, Washington, DC.

Borah, Woodrow, and Sherburne F. Cook
1963. *The Aboriginal Population of Central Mexico on the Eve of the Spanish Conquest*. Ibero-Americana, no. 45. University of California Press, Berkeley.

Boserup, Esther
1965. *The Conditions of Agricultural Growth: The Economics of Agrarian Change Under Population Pressure*. Aldine, Chicago.

Broda, Johanna, Davíd Carrasco, and Eduardo Matos Moctezuma
1987. *The Great Temple of Tenochtitlan: Center and Periphery in the Aztec World*. University of California Press, Berkeley.

Brumfiel, Elizabeth M.
1980. Specialization, Market Exchange, and the Aztec State: A View from Huexotla. *Current Anthropology* 21:459–478.
1983. Aztec State Making: Ecology, Structure, and the Origin of the State. *American Anthropologist* 85:261–284.
1987. Elite and Utilitarian Crafts in the Aztec State. In *Specialization, Exchange, and Complex Societies*, edited by Elizabeth M. Brumfiel and Timothy K. Earle, pp. 102–118. Cambridge University Press, New York.
1991a. Weaving and Cooking: Women's Production in Aztec Mexico. In *Engendering Archaeology: Women and Prehistory*, edited by Joan M. Gero and Margaret W. Conkey, pp. 224–251. Basil Blackwell, Oxford.
1991b. Tribute and Commerce in Imperial Cities: The Case of Xaltocan, Mexico. In *Early State Economics*, edited by Henri J. M.

Claessen and Pieter van de Velde, pp. 177–198. Transaction Publishers, New Brunswick.

1992. *Postclassic Xaltocan: Archaeological Research in the Northern Valley of Mexico (1991 Annual Report).* Unpublished field report. Albion College, Albion, MI.

Brundage, Burr C.

1985. *The Jade Steps: A Ritual Life of the Aztecs.* University of Utah Press, Salt Lake City.

Burkhart, Louise M.

1989. *The Slippery Earth: Nahua-Christian Moral Dialogue in Sixteenth-Century Mexico.* University of Arizona Press, Tucson.

1996. Mexica Women on the Home Front: Housework and Religion in Aztec Mexico. In *Indian Women of Early Mexico: Identity, Ethnicity, and Gender Differentiation,* edited by Susan Schroeder, Stephanie Wood, and Robert Haskett. University of Oklahoma Press, Norman. In press.

Calnek, Edward E.

1972. Settlement Pattern and Chinampa Agriculture at Tenochtitlan. *American Antiquity* 37:104–115.

1976. The Internal Structure of Tenochtitlan. In *The Valley of Mexico: Studies of Pre-Hispanic Ecology and Society,* edited by Eric R. Wolf, pp. 287–302. University of New Mexico Press, Albuquerque.

1978. The City-State in the Basin of Mexico: Late Pre-Hispanic Period. In *Urbanization in the Americas from Its Beginnings to the Present,* edited by R. P. Schaedel, J. E. Hardoy, and N. S. Kinzer, pp. 463–470. Mouton, The Hague.

1982. Patterns of Empire Formation in the Valley of Mexico. In *The Inca and Aztec States, 1400–1800: Anthropology and History,* edited by G. A. Collier, R. I. Roslado, and J. D. Wirth, pp. 43–62. Academic Press, New York.

Cantares Mexicanos

1985. *Cantares Mexicanos: Songs of the Aztecs.* Edited and Translated by John Bierhorst. Stanford University Press, Stanford. (Originally written sixteenth century).

Carmack, Robert M., Janine Gasco, and Gary H. Gossen, eds.

1996. *The Legacy of Mesoamerica: History and Culture of a Native American Civilization.* Prentice-Hall, Englewood Cliffs, NJ.

Carrasco, Davíd

1990. *Religions of Mesoamerica: Cosmovision and Ceremonial Centers.* Harper and Row, New York.

Carrasco, Davíd, and Eduardo Matos Moctezuma

1992. *Moctezuma's Mexico: Visions of the Aztec World.* University Press of Colorado, Niwot, CO.

Carrasco, Pedro
1972. La casa y hacienda de un señor Tlahuica. *Estudios de cultura Náhuatl* 10:235–244.
1976. The Joint Family in Ancient Mexico: The Case of Molotla. In *Essays on Mexican Kinship*, edited by Hugo Nutini, Pedro Carrasco, and James M. Taggert, pp. 45–64. University of Pittsburgh Press, Pittsburgh.
1984. Royal Marriages in Ancient Mexico. In *Explorations in Ethnohistory: Indians of Central Mexico in the Sixteenth Century*, edited by Herbert R. Harvey and Hanns J. Prem, pp. 41–81. University of New Mexico Press, Albuquerque.
Carrasco, Pedro, and Johanna Broda, eds.
1976. *Estratificación social en la Mesoamérica prehispánica*. Instituto Nacional de Antropología e Historia, Mexico City.
Caso, Alfonso
1969. *El tesoro de Monte Albán*. Instituto Nacional de Antropología e Historia, Memorias, No. 3. Instituto Nacional de Antropología e Historia, Mexico City.
1971. Calendrical Systems of Central Mexico. In *Archaeology of Northern Mesoamerica, Part 1*, edited by Ignacio Bernal and Gordon Ekholm, pp. 333–48. Handbook of Middle American Indians, vol. 10. University of Texas Press, Austin.
Charlton, Thomas H.
1970. Contemporary Agriculture in the Teotihuacan Valley. In *The Natural Environment, Contemporary Occupation and 16th Century Population of the Valley*, by Anton Kovar, Thomas H. Charlton, Richard A. Diehl, and William T. Sanders. The Teotihuacan Valley Project Final Report, Vol. 1, pp. 253–86. Occasional Papers in Anthropology, no. 3. Pennsylvania State University, Department of Anthropology, University Park.
1972. *Post-Conquest Developments in the Teotihuacan Valley, Mexico: Part I, Excavations*. Office of the State Archaeologist, Iowa City.
Charlton, Thomas H., and Patricia Fournier G.
1993. Urban and Rural Dimensions of the Contact Period, Central Mexico, 1521–1620. In *Ethnohistory and Archaeology: Approaches to Postcontact Change in the Americas*, edited by J. Daniel Rogers and Samuel M. Wilson, pp. 201–220. Plenum Press, New York.
Charlton, Thomas H., Deborah L. Nichols, and Cynthia Otis Charlton
1991. Aztec Craft Production and Specialization: Archaeological Evidence from the City-State of Otumba, Mexico. *World Archaeology* 23:98–114.
Chimalpahin, Francisco de San Antón Muñon

1965. *Relaciones originales de Chalco Amequemecan.* Translated by Silvia Rendón. Fondo de Cultura Económica, Mexico City. (Originally written 1606–1631).

Clark, John E.

1982. Manufacture of Mesoamerican Prismatic Blades: An Alternative Technique. *American Antiquity* 47:355–376.

1987. Politics, Prismatic Blades and Mesoamerican Civilization. In *The Organization of Core Technology,* edited by Jay K. Johnson and Carol A. Morrow, pp. 259–284. Westview Press, Boulder.

Clendinnen, Inga

1991a. *Aztecs: An Interpretation.* Cambridge University Press, New York.

1991b. "Fierceness and Unnatural Cruelty:" Cortés and the Conquest of Mexico. *Representations* 33:65–100.

Cline, Howard F.

1972. The Relaciones Geográficas of the Spanish Indies, 1577–1648. In *Guide to Ethnohistorical Sources, Part 1.* Howard F. Cline, ed. Handbook of Middle American Indians, vol. 12. Robert Wauchope, gen. ed., pp. 183–242. University of Texas Press, Austin.

Cline, S. L.

1986. *Colonial Culhuacan, 1580–1600: A Social History of an Aztec Town.* University of New Mexico Press, Albuquerque.

1993. *The Book of Tributes: Early Sixteenth-Century Nahuatl Censuses from Morelos.* U.C.L.A. Latin American Center, Los Angeles. (Originally compiled ca. 1540).

Cobean, Robert H., James R. Vogt, Michael D. Glascock, and Terrence L. Stocker

1991. High-Precision Trace Element Characterization of Major Mesoamerican Obsidian Sources and Further Analysis of Artifacts from San Lorenzo Tenochititlan, Mexico. *Latin American Antiquity* 2:69–91.

Codex Borbonicus

1974. *Codex Borbonicus: Bibliothèque del'Asemblée Nationale, Paris (Y120).* Edited by Karl Nowotny. Akademische Druck-u. Verlagsanstalt, Graz.

Codex Borgia

1976. *Codex Borgia (Cod. Gorg. Messicano 1).* Edited by Karl Nowotny. Akademische Druck-u. Verlagsansalt, Graz. (Originally composed pre-Conquest).

1993. *The Codex Borgia: A Full-Color Restoration of the Ancient Mexican Manuscript.* Edited by Gisele Díaz and Alan Rodgers, with Commentary by Bruce E. Byland. Dover Publications, New York. (Originally composed pre-Conquest).

Codex Magliabechiano
1983. *Codex Magliabechiano and the Lost Prototype of the Magliabechiano Group.* 2 vols. Edited with commentary by Elizabeth H. Boone. University of California Press, Berkeley. (Originally composed before 1566).

Codex Mendoza
1992. *The Codex Mendoza.* 4 vols. Edited by Frances F. Berdan and Patricia R. Anawalt. University of California Press, Berkeley. (Originally composed 1541).

Codex Telleriano-Remensis
1995 (see Quiñones Keber 1995).

Códice Aubin
1963. *Historia de la Nación Mexicana: Reproducción a Todo Color del Códice de 1576 (Códice Aubin).* Edited by Charles E. Dibble. José Porrúa Turanzas, Madrid. (Originally composed 1576–1608).

Coe, Michael D.
1992. *Breaking the Maya Code.* Thames and Hudson, New York.
1993. *The Maya.* 5th ed. Thames and Hudson, New York.
1994. *Mexico: From the Olmecs to the Aztecs.* 4th ed. Thames and Hudson, New York.

Coe, Sophie D.
1994. *America's First Cuisines.* Universitiy of Texas Press, Austin.

Conrad, Geoffrey W., and Arthur A. Demarest
1984. *Religion and Empire: The Dynamics of Aztec and Inca Expansion.* Cambridge University Press, New York.

Cook, Scott, and Martin Diskin, eds.
1976. *Markets in Oaxaca.* University of Texas Press, Austin.

Cook, Sherburne F., and Woodrow Borah
1979. Indian Food Production and Consumption in Central Mexico Before and After the Conquest (1500–1650). In *Essays in Population History,* edited by Sherburne F. Cook and Woodrow Borah, pp. 129–176. University of California Press, Berkeley.

Cortés, Hernando
1962. *Five Letters of Cortés to the Emperor.* Edited and translated by J. Bayard Morris. Norton, New York. (Originally written 1519–1526).

Crosby, Alfred W.
1972. *The Columbian Exchange: Biological and Cultural Consequences of 1492.* Greenwood Press, Westport, CT.

Cruz y Moya, Juan de la
1954/55. *Historia de la Santa y Apostólica Provincia de Santiago de Predicadores de México en la Nueva España.* 2 vols. Manuel Porrúa, Mexico City. (Originally written sixteenth century).

D'Altroy, Terence N.
1992. *Provincial Power in the Inka Empire*. Smithsonian Institution Press, Washington D.C.

Davies, Nigel
1968. *Los Señoríos Independientes del Imperial Azteca*. Instituto Nacional de Antropología e Historia, Mexico City.
1973. *The Aztecs: A History*. University of Oklahoma Press, Norman.
1977. *The Toltecs Until the Fall of Tula*. University of Oklahoma Press, Norman.
1980. *The Toltec Heritage: From the Fall of Tula to the Rise of Tenochtitlan*. Univeristy of Oklahoma Press, Norman.
1987. *The Aztec Empire: The Toltec Resurgence*. University of Oklahoma Press, Norman.

de Vega Nova, Hortensia, and Pablo Mayer Guala
1991. Proyecto Yautepec. *Boletín del Consejo de Arqueología* 1991:79–84.

Díaz del Castillo, Bernal
1963. *The Conquest of New Spain*. Translated by J. M. Cohen. Penguin, New York. (Originally written 1560s).

Dibble, Charles E.
1988. Molina and Sahagún. In *Smoke and Mist: Mesoamerican Studies in Memory of Thelma D. Sullivan*, edited by J. Kathryn Josserand and Karen Dakin, pp. 69–76. British Archaeological Reports, International Series, no. 402, Oxford.

Diehl, Richard A.
1983. *Tula: The Toltec Capital of Ancient Mexico*. Thames and Hudson, New York.

Diehl, Richard A., and Janet Berlo, eds.
1989. *Mesoamerica After the Decline of Teotihuacan, AD 700–900*. Dumbarton Oaks, Washington, DC.

Donkin, R. A.
1979. *Agricultural Terracing in the Aboriginal New World*. Viking Fund Publications in Anthropology, no. 56. University of Arizona Press, Tucson.

Doolittle, William E.
1990. *Canal Irrigation in Prehistoric Mexico: The Sequence of Technological Change*. University of Texas Press, Austin.

Drennan, Robert D.
1984. Long-Distance Transport Costs in Pre-Hispanic Mesoamerica. *American Anthropologist* 86:105–112.

Durán, Fray Diego
1967. *Historia de Las Indias de Nueva España*. 2 vols. Edited by Angel M. Garibay K. Porrúa, Mexico City. (Originally written 1581).
1971. *Book of the Gods and Rites and The Ancient Calendar*.

Edited and translated by Fernando Horcasitas and Doris Heyden. University of Oklahoma Press, Norman. (Originally written 1581).
1994. *The History of the Indies of New Spain*. Edited and translated by Doris Heyden. University of Oklahoma Press, Norman. (Originally written 1581).

Edmonson, Munro S., ed.
1974. *Sixteenth-Century Mexico: The World of Sahagún*. University of New Mexico Press, Albuquerque.

Einzig, Paul
1966. *Primitive Money*. Pergamon Press, New York.

Evans, Susan T.
1988. *Excavations at Cihuatecpan, an Aztec Village in the Teotihuacan Valley*. Vanderbilt University Publications in Anthropology, no. 36. Department of Anthropology, Vanderbilt University, Nashville.
1990. The Productivity of Maguey Terrace Agriculture in Central Mexico During the Aztec Period. *Latin American Antiquity* 1:117–132.
1991. Architecture and Authority in an Aztec Village: Form and Function of the Tecpan. In *Land and Politics in the Valley of Mexico*, edited by Herbert R. Harvey, pp. 63–92. University of New Mexico Press, Albuquerque.

Feldman, Lawrence H.
1978. Inside a Mexica Market. In *Mesoamerican Communication Routes and Cultural Contacts*, edited by Thomas A., Jr. Lee, pp. 219–227. New World Archaeological Foundation, Papers, no. 40, Provo, UT.

Flannery, Kent V., ed.
1976. *The Early Mesoamerican Village*. Academic Press, New York.

Foster, George M.
1960. *Culture and Conquest: America's Spanish Heritage*. Viking Fund Publications in Anthropology, no. 27. Wenner-Gren Foundation for Anthropological Research, New York.

Fowler, Don D.
1987. Uses of the Past: Archaeology in the Service of the State. *American Antiquity* 52:229–248.

Fox, Richard G.
1977. *Urban Anthropology: Cities in Their Cultural Settings*. Prentice-Hall, Englewood Cliffs.

Friedlander, Judith
1975. *Being Indian in Hueyapan: A Study of Forced Identity in Contemporary Mexico*. St. Martin's Press, New York.

Furst, Peter
1978. Spirulina. *Human Nature* 1:60–65.

334   *References*

Gaxiola, Margarita, and John E. Clark, eds.
1989. *La obsidiana en Mesoamérica*. Instituto Nacional de Antropología e Historia, Mexico City.

Gerhard, Peter
1993. *A Guide to the Historical Geography of New Spain*. Revised edition. University of Oklahoma Press, Norman.

Gibson, Charles
1964. *The Aztecs Under Spanish Rule: A History of the Indians of the Valley of Mexico, 1519–1810*. Stanford University Press, Stanford.
1966. *Spain in America*. Harper and Row, New York.

Gillespie, Susan D.
1989. *The Aztec Kings: The Constitution of Rulership in Mexica History*. University of Arizona Press, Tucson.

González Rul, Francisco
1988. *La cerámica en Tlatelolco*. Instituto Nacional de Antropología e Historia, Mexico City.

Graulich, Michel
1992. Mexico City's "Templo Mayor" Revisited. In *Ancient America: Contributions to New World Archaeology*, edited by Nicholas J. Saunders, pp. 19–32. Oxbow Books, Oxford.

Hare, Timothy S.
1994. *Lapidary Craft Specialists at Otumba (TA80): A Case Study in the Organization of Craft Production in Late Aztec Mexico*. Unpublished MA Thesis, Department of Anthropology, University of Iowa.

Harner, Michael
1977. The Ecological Basis for Aztec Sacrifice. *American Ethnologist* 4:117–135.

Haskett, Robert
1991. *Indigenous Rulers: An Ethnohistory of Town Government in Colonial Cuernavaca*. University of New Mexico Press, Albuquerque.

Hassig, Ross
1985. *Trade, Tribute, and Transportation: The Sixteenth Century Political Economy of the Valley of Mexico*. University of Oklahoma Press, Norman.
1988. *Aztec Warfare: Imperial Expansion and Political Control*. University of Oklahoma Press, Norman.
1992. *War and Society in Ancient Mesoamerica*. University of California Press, Berkeley.

Healan, Dan M., ed.
1989. *Tula of the Toltecs: Excavations and Survey*. University of Iowa Press, Iowa City.

Hernández, Francisco

1959. *Antiguedades de la Nueva España.* Universidad Nacional Autónoma de México, Mexico City. (Originally written 1571–1577).

Heyden, Doris
1991. Dryness Before the Rains: Toxcatl and Tezcatlipoca. In *To Change Place: Aztec Ceremonial Landscapes,* edited by Davíd Carrasco, pp. 188–202. University Press of Colorado, Niwot.

Hicks, Frederic
1982. Tetzcoco in the Early 16th Century: The State, the City and the Calpolli. *American Ethnologist* 9:230–249.
1984. Rotational Labor and Urban Development in Prehispanic Tetzcoco. In *Explorations in Ethnohistory: Indians of Central Mexico in the Sixteenth Century,* edited by Herbert R. Harvey and Hanns J. Prem, pp. 147–174. University of New Mexico Press, Albuquerque.
1986. Prehispanic Background of Colonial Political and Economic Organization in Central Mexico. In *Ethnohistory,* edited by Ronald Spores, pp. 35–54. Handbook of Middle American Indians, Supplement, no. 4. University of Texas Press, Austin.
1992. Subject States and Tributary Provinces: The Aztec Empire in the Northern Valley of Mexico. *Ancient Mesoamerica* 3:1–10.
1994. Cloth in the Political Economy of the Aztec State. In *Economies and Polities in the Aztec Realm,* edited by Mary G. Hodge and Michael E. Smith, pp. 89–111. Institute for Mesoamerican Studies, Albany.

Hinz, Eike, and Marie Heimann–Koenen, and Claudine Hartau
1983. *Aztekischer Zensus: Zur Indianischen Wirtschaft und Gesellschaft Im Marquesado Um 1540.* Verlag fur Ethnologie, Hanover. (Originally compiled ca. 1540).

Hirth, Kenneth G.
1996. *Ancient Urbanism at Xochicalco.* Book in preparation.

Hodge, Mary G.
1984. *Aztec City-States.* University of Michigan, Museum of Anthropology, Memoirs, no. 18. Ann Arbor.
1994. Polities Composing the Aztec Empire's Core. In *Economies and Polities in the Aztec Realm,* edited by Mary G. Hodge and Michael E. Smith, pp. 43–71. Institute for Mesoamerican Studies, Albany.
n.d.a. Archaeological Views of Aztec Culture, *Journal of Archaeological Research,* in press.
n.d.b. *Place of Jade: Society and Economy in Ancient Chalco.* Site report in preparation.

Hodge, Mary G., and Leah D. Minc
1990. The Spatial Patterning of Aztec Ceramics: Implications for Prehispanic Exchange Systems in the Valley of Mexico. *Journal of Field Archaeology* 17:415–437.

Hodge, Mary G., Hector Neff, M. James Blackman, and Leah D. Minc
1993. Black-on-Orange Ceramic Production in the Aztec Empire's Heartland. *Latin American Antiquity* 4:130–157.

Hodge, Mary G., and Michael E. Smith, eds.
1994. *Economies and Polities in the Aztec Realm.* Institute for Mesoamerican Studies, Albany.

Hosler, Dorothy
1994. *The Sounds and Colors of Power: The Sacred Metallurgical Technology of Ancient West Mexico.* MIT Press, Cambridge.

Ingham, John M.
1986. *Mary, Michael, and Lucifer: Folk Catholicism in Central Mexico.* University of Texas Press, Austin.

Isaac, Barry L.
1983a. Aztec Warfare: Goals and Battlefield Comportment. *Ethnology* 22:121–131.
1983b. The Aztec "Flowery War:" A Geopolitical Explanation. *Journal of Anthropological Research* 39:415–432.

Johnson, Allen W., and Timothy K. Earle
1987. *The Evolution of Human Societies: From Foraging Group to Agrarian State.* Stanford University Press, Stanford.

Justeson, John S., and Terrence Kaufman
1993. Decipherment of Epi-Olmec Hieroglyphic Writing. *Science* 259:1703–1711.

Karttunen, Frances
1983. *An Analytical Dictionary of Nahuatl.* University of Oklahoma Press, Norman.

Katz, S. H., M. L. Hediger, and Valleroy, L. A.
1974. Traditional Maize Processing Techniques in the New World. *Science* 184:765–773.

Kaufman, Terrence
1976. Mesoamerican Indian Languages. In *Encyclopedia Britannica, Macropedia*, vol. 11, pp. 956–63. Encyclopedia Britannica, New York.

Kelley, David H.
1976. *Deciphering the Maya Script.* University of Texas Press, Austin.

Kellogg, Susan
1995. *Law and the Transformation of Aztec Culture, 1500–1700.* University of Oklahoma Press, Norman.

Kirchoff, Paul
1943. Mesoamérica: Sus límites geográficas, composición étnica, y caracteres culturales. *Acta Americana* 1:92–107.

Klein, Cecelia F.
1987. The Ideology of Autosacrifice at the Templo Mayor. In *The*

Aztec Tempo Mayor, edited by Elizabeth H. Boone, pp. 293–370. Dumbarton Oaks, Washington, DC.

1994. Fighting with Femininity: Gender and War in Aztec Mexico. *Estudios de cultura Náhuatl* 24:219–250.

Klor de Alva, Jorge, H. B. Nicholson, and Eloise Quiñones Keber, eds.

1988. *The Work of Bernardino de Sahagún: Pioneer Ethnographer of Sixteenth-Century Aztec Mexico.* Institute for Mesoamerican Studies, Albany.

Kubler, George

1948. *Mexican Architecture of the Sixteenth Century.* 2 vols. Yale University Press, New Haven.

Lagunas, Zaid, and Carlos Serrano Sánchez

1972. Decapitación y desmembramiento corporal en Teopanzolco, Morelos. In *Religión en Mesoamérica. XII mesa redonda*, edited by Noemí Castillo Tejero and Jaime Litvak King, pp. 429–34. Sociedad Mexicana de Antropología, Mexico City.

León-Portilla, Miguel

1962. *The Broken Spears: The Aztec Account of the Conquest of Mexico.* Beacon Press, Boston.

1963. *Aztec Thought and Culture: A Study of the Ancient Nahuatl Mind.* University of Oklahoma Press, Norman.

1969. *Pre-Columbian Literatures of Mexico.* University of Oklahoma Press, Norman.

1992. *Los glifos toponímicos en la historia de Mesoamérica, siglos III A.C. a XVI D.C.* Instituto Nacional de Antropología e Historia, Mexico City.

1993. Those Made Worthy by Divine Sacrifice: The Faith of Ancient Mexico. In *South and Mesoamerican Native Spirituality*, edited by Gary H. Gossen, pp. 41–64. Crossroad, New York.

Lewis, Oscar

1951. *Life in a Mexican Village: Tepoztlan Restudied.* University of Illinois Press, Urbana.

Licate, Jack A.

1980. The Forms of Aztec Territorial Organization. In *Historical Geography of Latin America*, edited by James J. Parsons and William V. Davidson, pp. 27–45. Geosciences and Man, vol. 21. Louisiana State University, Baton Rouge.

Lister, Florence C., and Robert H. Lister

1982. *Sixteenth Century Majolica Pottery in the Valley of Mexico.* Anthropological Papers of the University of Arizona, no. 39, Tucson.

Lockhart, James

1992. *The Nahuas After the Conquest: A Social and Cultural History of the Indians of Central Mexico, Sixteenth Through Eighteenth Centuries.* Stanford University Press, Stanford.

1993. *We People Here: Nahuatl Accounts of the Conquest of Mexico*. University of California Press, Berkeley.

Lockhart, James, Frances F. Berdan, and Arthur J. O. Anderson, eds. 1986. *The Tlaxcalan Actas: A Compendium of the Records of the Cabildo of Tlaxcala (1545–1627)*. University of Utah Press, Salt Lake City. (Originally compiled 1545–1627).

López Austin, Alfredo
1988. *Human Body and Ideology*. 2 vols. Translated by Thelma Ortiz de Montellano and Bernard R. Ortiz de Montellano. University of Utah Press, Salt Lake City.

López Luján, Leonardo
1994. *The Offerings of the Templo Mayor of Tenochtitlan*. Translated by Bernard R. Ortiz de Montellano and Thelma Ortiz de Montellano. University Press of Colorado, Niwot.

Lovell, W. George
1985. *Conquest and Survival in Colonial Guatemala: A Historical Geography of the Cuchumatán Highlands, 1500–1821*. McGill-Queen's University Press, Kingston and Montreal.

Mann, Michael
1986. *The Sources of Social Power, Volume 1: A History of Power from the Beginning to AD 1760*. Cambridge University Press, New York.

Marcus, Joyce
1983. On the Nature of the Mesoamerican City. In *Prehistoric Settlement Patterns: Essays in Honor of Gordon R. Willey*, edited by Evon Z. Vogt and Richard M. Leventhal, pp. 195–242. University of New Mexico Press, Albuquerque.

1992. *Mesoamerican Writing Systems: Propaganda, Myth, and History in Four Ancient Civilizations*. Princeton University Press, Princeton.

Marquina, Ignacio
1951. *Arquitectura Prehispánica*. Instituto Nacional de Antropología e Historia, Mexico City.

1960. *El Templo Mayor de México*. Instituto Nacional de Antropología e Historia, Mexico City.

Martí, Samuel, and Gertrude Prokosch Kurath
1964. *Dances of Anahuac: The Choreography and Music of Pre-cortesian Dances*. Aldine, Chicago.

Matos Moctezuma, Eduardo
1979. *Trabajos Arqueológicos en el Centro de la Ciudad de México*. Instituto Nacional de Antropología e Historia, Mexico City.

1988. *The Great Temple of the Aztecs*. Thames and Hudson, New York.

1990. *Treasures of the Great Temple*. Alti Publishing, La Jolla, CA.

McCaa, Robert
1994. Child Marriage and Complex Families Among the Nahuas of Ancient Mexico. *Latin American Population History Bulletin* 26:2–11.
1995. Spanish and Nahuatl Views on Smallpox and Demographic Catastrophe in Mexico. *Journal of Interdisciplinary History* 25:397–431.
McNeill, William H.
1976. *Plagues and Peoples.* Academic Press, New York.
Metcalfe, Sarah E., F. Alayne Street-Perrott, Robert B. Brown, P. E. Hales, R. A. Perrott, and F. M. Steininger
1989. Late Holocene Human Impact on Lake Basins in Central Mexico. *Geoarchaeology* 4:119–141.
Metcalfe, Sarah E., F. Alayne Street-Perrott, Sarah L. O'Hara, P. E. Hales, and R. A. Perrott
1994. The Palaeolimnological Record of Environmental Change: Examples from the Arid Frontier of Mesoamerica. In *Environmental Change in Drylands: Biogeographical and Geomorphological Perspectives,* edited by A. D. Millington and K. Pye, pp. 131–145. Wiley, New York.
Miller, Mary, and Karl Taube
1993. *The Gods and Symbols of Ancient Mexico and the Maya: An Illustrated Dictionary of Mesoamerican Religion.* Thames and Hudson, New York.
Millon, René
1973. *Urbanization at Teotihuacan, Mexico, Volume 1, The Teotihuacan Map.* University of Texas Press, Austin.
Minc, Leah D., Mary G. Hodge, and James Blackman
1994. Stylistic and Spatial Variability in Early Aztec Ceramics: Insights Into Pre-imperial Exchange Systems. In *Economies and Polities in the Aztec Realm,* edited by Mary G. Hodge and Michael E. Smith, pp. 133–173. Institute for Mesoamerican Studies, Albany.
Molina, Fray Alonso de
1970. *Vocabulario en lengua Castellana y Mexicana, y Mexicana y Castellana.* Porrúa, Mexico City. (Originally written 1555–1571).
1972. *Confesionario mayor en la lengua Mexicana y Castellana (1569).* Edited by Roberto Moreno. Instituto de Investigaciones Bibliográficas, Mexico City. (Originally written 1569).
Motolinía, Fray Toribio de
1950. *History of the Indians of New Spain.* Edited and translated by Elizabeth A. Foster. The Cortes Society, Berkeley. (Originally written 1536–1543).
1971. *Memoriales, o libro de las cosas de la Nueva España y de los naturales de ella.* Edited by Edmundo O'Gorman. Universidad

Nacional Autónoma de México, Mexico City. (Originally written 1536–1543).

Moya Rubio, Victor José
1982. *La vivienda indígena de México y del mundo*. Universidad Nacional Autónoma de México, Mexico City.

Muñoz Camargo, Diego
1981. *Descripción de la ciudad y provincia de Tlaxcala*. Edited by René Acuña. Universidad Nacional Autónoma de México, Mexico City. (Originally written sixteenth century).

Nagao, Debra
1985. *Mexica Buried Offerings: A Historical and Contextual Analysis*. British Archaeological Reports, International Series, no. 235, Oxford.

Netting, Robert McC.
1993. *Smallholders, Householders: Farm Families and the Ecology of Intensive, Sustainable Agriculture*. Stanford University Press, Stanford.

Nichols, Deborah L.
1994. The Organization of Provincial Craft Production and the Aztec City-state of Otumba. In *Economies and Polities in the Aztec Realm*, edited by Mary G. Hodge and Michael E. Smith, pp. 175–193. Institute for Mesoamerican Studies, Albany.

Nichols, Deborah L., and Thomas H. Charlton, eds.
1996. *The Archaeology of City-States: Cross-Cultural Approaches*. Smithsonian Institution Press, Washington, DC. Forthcoming.

Nicholson, H. B.
1971. Religion in Pre-Hispanic Central Mexico. In *Archaeology of Northern Mesoamerica, Part 1*, edited by Ignacio Bernal and Gordon F. Ekholm, pp. 395–446. Handbook of Middle American Indians, vol. 10. University of Texas Press, Austin.

Nicholson, H. B., and Eloise Quiñones Keber
1983. *Art of Aztec Mexico: Treasures of Tenochtitlan*. National Gallery of Art, Washington, DC.
(eds) 1994. *Mixteca-Puebla: Discoveries and Research in Mesoamerican Art and Archaeology*. Labyrinthos, Culver City, CA.

O'Hara, Sarah L.; Sarah E. Metcalfe, and F. Alayne Street-Perrott
1994. On the Arid Margin: The Relationship Between Climate, Humans and the Environment: A Review of Evidence from the Highlands of Central Mexico. *Chemosphere* 29:965–981.

Ortiz de Montellano, Bernard R.
1978. Aztec Cannibalism: An Ecological Necessity? *Science* 200:611–617.
1990. *Aztec Medicine, Health, and Nutrition*. Rutgers University Press, New Brunswick.

Otis Charlton, Cynthia

1993. Obsidian as Jewelry: Lapidary Production in Aztec Otumba, Mexico. *Ancient Mesoamerica* 4:231–243.

1994. Plebians and Patricians: Contrasting Patterns of Production and Distribution in the Aztec Figurine and Lapidary Industries. In *Economies and Polities in the Aztec Realm*, edited by Mary G. Hodge and Michael E. Smith, pp. 195–219. Institute for Mesoamerican Studies, Albany.

Palerm, Angel

1972. *Agricultura y socieded en Mesoamérica*. Secretaria de Educación Pública, Mexico City.

Parsons, Jeffrey R.

1966. *The Aztec Ceramic Sequence in the Teotihuacan Valley, Mexico*. 2 vols. Unpublished Ph.D. Dissertation, Department of Anthropology, University of Michigan. University Microfilms, Ann Arbor.

1991. Political Implications of Prehispanic Chinampa Agriculture in the Valley of Mexico. In *Land and Politics in the Valley of Mexico: A Two-Thousand-Year Perspective*, edited by Herbert R. Harvey, pp. 17–42. University of New Mexico Press, Albuquerque.

1994. Late Postclassic Salt Production and Consumption in the Valley of Mexico: Some Insights from Nexquipayac. In *Economies and Polities in the Aztec Realm*, edited by Mary G. Hodge and Michael E. Smith, pp. 257–290. Institute for Mesoamerican Studies, Albany.

Parsons, Jeffrey R., Mary H. Parsons, David J. Wilson, and Elizabeth M. Brumfiel

1982. *Prehispanic Settlement Patterns in the Southern Valley of Mexico: The Chalco-Xochimilco Region*. University of Michigan, Museum of Anthropology, Memoirs, no. 14, Ann Arbor.

Parsons, Jeffrey R., and Mary H. Parsons

1990. *Maguey Utilization in Highland Central Mexico: An Archaeological Ethnography*. University of Michigan, Museum of Anthropology, Anthropological Papers, no. 82, Ann Arbor.

Parsons, Mary H.

1972. Aztec Figurines from the Teotihuacán Valley, Mexico. In *Miscellaneous Studies in Mexican Prehistory*, by Michael W. Spence, Jeffrey R. Parsons, and Mary H. Parsons, pp. 81–164. University of Michigan, Museum of Anthropology, Anthropological Papers, no. 45. Ann Arbor.

Pasztory, Esther

1983. *Aztec Art*. Harry N. Abrams, New York.

Perry, Richard

1992. *Mexico's Fortress Monasteries*. Espadaña Press, Santa Barbara.

Plunket, Patricia, and Gabriela Uruñuela
1994. The Impact of the Xochiyayotl in Southwestern Puebla. In *Economies and Polities in the Aztec Realm*, edited by Mary G. Hodge and Michael E. Smith, pp. 434–446. Institute for Mesoamerican Studies, Albany.

Pollard, Helen P.
1993. *Tariacuri's Legacy: The Prehispanic Tarascan State*. University of Oklahoma Press, Norman.

Pollard, Helen P., and Thomas A. Vogel
1994. Late Postclassic Imperial Expansion and Economic Exchange Within the Tarascan Domain. In *Economies and Polities in the Aztec Realm*, edited by Mary G. Hodge and Michael E. Smith, pp. 447–470. Institute for Mesoamerican Studies, Albany.

Prem, Hanns J.
1991. Disease Outbreaks in Central Mexico During the Sixteenth Century. In *"Secret Judgments of God:" Old World Disease in Colonial Spanish America*, edited by Noble David Cook and W. George Lovell, pp. 20–48. University of Oklahoma Press, Norman.
1992. Aztec Writing. In *Epigraphy*, edited by Victoria R. Bricker, pp. 53–69. Handbook of Middle American Indians, Supplement, vol. 5. University of Texas Press, Austin.

Prescott, William H.
1843. *History of the Conquest of Mexico*. Random House, New York.

Price, Barbara J.
1978. Demystification, Enriddlement, and Aztec Cannibalism: A Materialist Rejoinder to Harner. *American Ethnologist* 5:98–115.

Quiñones Keber, Eloise
1995. *Codex Telleriano-Remensis: Ritual, Divination, and History in a Pictorial Aztec Manuscript*. University of Texas Press, Austin.

Redfield, Margaret Park
1929. Notes on the Cookery of Tepoztlan, Morelos. *Journal of American Folk-Lore* 42:167–196.

Renfew, Colin, and John F. Cherry, eds.
1986. *Peer Polity Interaction and Socio-Political Change*. Cambridge University Press, New York.

Renfrew, Colin, and Paul Bahn
1991. *Archaeology: Theories, Methods and Practice*. Thames and Hudson, New York.

Robertson, Donald
1959. *Mexican Manuscript Painting of the Early Colonial Period: The Metropolitan Schools*. Yale University Press, New Haven.

Rojas, José Luis de
1986. *México Tenochtitlan: Economía e sociedad en el siglo XVI*. Fondo de Cultura Económica, Mexico City.

Ruiz de Alarcón, Hernando
1982. *Aztec Sorcerers in Seventeenth Century Mexico: The Treatise on Superstitions by Hernando Ruiz de Alarcón.* Edited and translated by Michael D. Coe and Gordon Whittaker. Institute for Mesoamerican Studies, Albany. (Originally written seventeenth century).

Sahagún, Fray Bernardino de
1905–07. *Historia de las cosas de la Nueva España. Edición parcial en facsimile de los Códices Matritenses.* 4 vols. Hauser y Menet, Madrid. (Originally written 1575–1577).
1950–82. *Florentine Codex, General History of the Things of New Spain.* 12 books. Translated and edited by Arthur J. O. Anderson and Charles E. Dibble. School of American Research and the University of Utah Press, Santa Fe and Salt Lake City. (Originally written 1575–1577).
1993. *Primeros Memoriales.* Facsimile edition, edited by Ferdinand Anders. University of Oklahoma Press, Norman. (Originally written 1575–1577).

Sanders, William T.
1956. The Central Mexican Symbiotic Region: A Study in Prehistoric Settlement Patterns. In *Prehistoric Settlement Patterns in the New World*, edited by Gordon R. Willey, pp. 115–27. Viking Fund Publications in Anthropology, no. 23. Wenner-Gren Foundation for Anthropological Research, New York.
1970. The Population of the Teotihuacan Valley, the Basin of Mexico, and the Central Mexican Symbiotic Region in the 16th Century. In *The Natural Environment, Contemporary Occupation and 16th Century Population of the Valley*, by Anton Kovar, Thomas H. Charlton, Richard A. Diehl, and William T. Sanders. The Teotihuacan Valley Project Final Report, vol. 1, pp. 385–452. Occasional Papers in Anthropology, no. 3. Pennsylvania State University, Department of Anthropology, University Park.

Sanders, William T., Jeffrey R. Parsons, and Robert S. Santley
1979. *The Basin of Mexico: Ecological Processes in the Evolution of a Civilization.* Academic Press, New York.

Sanders, William T., and Barbara J. Price
1968. *Mesoamerica: The Evolution of a Civilization.* Random House, New York.

Sanders, William T., and Robert S. Santley
1983. A Tale of Three Cities: Energetics and Urbanization in Pre-Hispanic Central Mexico. In *Prehistoric Settlement Patterns: Essays in Honor of Gordon R . Willey*, edited by Evon Z. Vogt and Richard Leventhal, pp. 243–291. University of New Mexico Press, Albuquerque.

Sanders, William T., and David Webster
1988. The Mesoamerican Urban Tradition. *American Anthropologist* 90:521–546.

Sandstrom, Alan R.
1991. *Corn is Our Blood: Culture and Ethnic Identity in a Contemporary Aztec Indian Village.* University of Oklahoma Press, Norman.

Sandstrom, Alan R., and Paula E. Sandstrom
1986. *Traditional Papermaking and Paper Cult Figures of Mexico.* University of Oklahoma Press, Norman.

Saville, Marshall H.
1920. *The Goldsmith's Art in Ancient Mexico.* Museum of the American Indian, Heye Foundation, Indian Notes and Monographs, no. 7, New York.

1922. *Turquoise Mosaic Art in Ancient Mexico.* Museum of the American Indian, Heye Foundation, Indian Notes and Monographs, no. 8, New York.

1925. *The Wood-Carver's Art in Ancient Mexico.* Museum of the American Indian, Heye Foundation, Indian Notes and Monographs, no. 9, New York.

Scarborough, Vernon L., and David R. Wilcox, eds.
1991. *The Mesoamerican Ballgame.* University of Arizona Press, Tuscon.

Schroeder, Susan
1991. *Chimalpahin and the Kingdoms of Chalco.* University of Arizona Press, Tucson.

Séjourné, Laurette
1983. *Arqueología e historia de valle de México: De Xochmilco a Amecameca.* Siglo Veintiumo, Mexico City.

Smith, Carol A.
1974. Economics of Marketing Systems: Models from Economic Geography. *Annual Review of Anthropology* 3:167–201.

Smith, Michael E.
1984. The Aztlan Migrations of the Nahuatl Chronicles: Myth or History? *Ethnohistory* 31:153–186.

1986. The Role of Social Stratification in the Aztec Empire: A View from the Provinces. *American Anthropologist* 88:70–91.

1990. Long-Distance Trade Under the Aztec Empire: The Archaeological Evidence. *Ancient Mesoamerica* 1:153–169.

1992a. *Archaeological Research at Aztec-Period Rural Sites in Morelos, Mexico. Volume 1, Excavations and Architecture.* University of Pittsburgh Monographs in Latin American Archaeology, no. 4. Pittsburgh.

1992b. Rhythms of Change in Postclassic Central Mexico: Archaeology, Ethnohistory, and the Braudellian Model. In *Annales, Ar-*

chaeology, and Ethnohistory, edited by A. Bernard Knapp, pp. 51–74. Cambridge University Press, New York.

1994. Economies and Polities in Aztec-period Morelos: Ethnohistoric Overview. In *Economies and Polities in the Aztec Realm*, edited by Mary G. Hodge and Michael E. Smith, pp. 313–348. Institute for Mesoamerican Studies, Albany.

Smith, Michael E., and John F. Doershuk

1991. Late Postclassic Chronology in Western Morelos, Mexico. *Latin American Antiquity* 2:291–310.

Smith, Michael E., and Cynthia Heath-Smith

1980. Waves of Influence in Postclassic Mesoamerica? A Critique of the Mixteca–Puebla Concept. *Anthropology* 4:15–50.

1994. Rural Economy in Late Postclassic Morelos: An Archaeological Study. In *Economies and Polities in the Aztec Realm*, edited by Mary G. Hodge and Michael E. Smith, pp. 349–376. Institute for Mesoamerican Studies, Albany.

Smith, Michael E., Cynthia Heath-Smith, Ronald Kohler, Joan Odess, Sharon Spanogle, and Timothy Sullivan

1994. The Size of the Aztec City of Yautepec: Urban Survey in Central Mexico. *Ancient Mesoamerica* 5:1–11.

Smith, Michael E., Cynthia Heath-Smith, and Lisa M. Cascio

(forthcoming) Excavations at the Aztec City of Yautepec, Morelos, Mexico. Unpublished Manuscript.

Smith, Michael E., and Kenneth G. Hirth

1988. The Development of Prehispanic Cotton-spinning Technology in Western Morelos, Mexico. *Journal of Field Archaeology* 15:349–358.

Smith, Michael E., and T. Jeffrey Price

1994. Aztec-Period Agricultural Terraces in Morelos, Mexico: Evidence for Household-Level Agricultural Intensification. *Journal of Field Archaeology* 21:169–179.

Smith, Michael E., Osvaldo Sterpone, and Cynthia Heath-Smith

1992. Modern Adobe Houses in Tetlama, Morelos. In *Archaeological Research at Aztec-Period Rural Sites in Morelos, Mexico, Part I: Excavations and Architecture*, by Michael E. Smith, pp. 405–418. University of Pittsburgh Monographs in Latin American Archaeology, no. 4, Pittsburgh.

Soustelle, Jacques

1961. *Daily Life of the Aztecs on the Eve of the Spanish Conquest.* Stanford University Press, Stanford.

Stromberg, Gobi

1976. The Amate Bark-Paper Painting of Xalitla. In *Ethnic and Tourist Arts*, edited by Nelson H. H. Graeburn, pp. 149–164. University of California Press, Berkeley.

Suárez, Jorge A.

1983. *The Mesoamerican Indian Languages.* Cambridge University Press, New York.

Taggart, James
1983. *Nahuat Myth and Social Structure.* University of Texas Press, Austin.

Tapia, Andrés de
1971. Relación hecha por el Sr. Andrés de Tapia, sobre la conquista de México. In *Colección de documentos para la historia de México,* vol. 2, edited by Joaquín Icazbalceta, pp. 554–594. Porrúa, Mexico City. (Originally written sixteenth century).

Taube, Karl
1993. *Aztec and Maya Myths.* University of Texas Press, Austin.

Tira de la Peregrinación
1944. *Tira de la Peregrinación Mexicana.* Librería Anticuaria G. M. Echaniz, Mexico City. (Originally composed sixteenth century).

Torquemada, Fray Juan de
1975–83. *Monarquia Indiana.* 7 vols. Edited by Miguel León-Portilla. Universidad Nacional Autónoma de México, Mexico City. (Originally written 1592–1613).

Townsend, Richard F.
1979. *State and Cosmos in the Art of Tenochtitlan.* Studies in Pre-Columbian Art and Archaeology, no. 20. Dumbarton Oaks, Washington, DC.
1992. *The Aztecs.* Thames and Hudson, New York.

Trigger, Bruce G.
1972. Determinants of Urban Growth in Pre-industrial Societies. In *Man, Settlement, and Urbanism,* edited by Peter J. Ucko, Ruth Tringham, and G. W. Dimbleby, pp. 579–599. Schenkman, Cambridge.
1993. *Early Civilizations: Ancient Egypt in Context.* The American University in Cairo Press, Cairo.

Umberger, Emily
1987. Antiques, Revivals, and References to the Past in Aztec Art. *Res* 13:62–105.
1996. Art and Imperial Strategy in Tenochtitlan. In *Aztec Imperial Strategies,* edited by Frances F. Berdan, Richard E. Blanton, Elizabeth H. Boone, Mary G. Hodge, Michael E. Smith, and Emily Umberger, pp. 85–106. Dumbarton Oaks, Washington, DC.

Umberger, Emily, and Cecilia Klein
1993. Aztec Art and Imperial Expansion. In *Latin American Horizons,* edited by Don S. Rice, pp. 295–336. Dumbarton Oaks, Washington, DC.

van Zantwijk, Rudolf
1985. *The Aztec Arrangement: The Social History of Pre-Spanish Mexico.* University of Oklahoma Press, Norman.

Vega Sosa, Constanza, ed.
1979. *El recinto sagrado de Mexico-Tenochtitlan: Excavaciones 1968–69 y 1975–76.* Instituto Nacional de Antropología e Historia, Mexico City.

von Hagen, Victor W.
1944. *The Aztec and Maya Papermakers.* J. J. Augustin, New York.

Warren, J. Benjamin
1985. *The Conquest of Michoacan: The Spanish Domination of the Tarascan Kingdom in Western Mexico, 1521–1530.* University of Oklahoma Press, Norman.

Weaver, Muriel Porter
1993. *The Aztecs, Maya, and Their Predecessors: Archaeology of Mesoamerica.* 3rd ed. Academic Press, San Diego.

West, Robert C., and John P. Augelli
1989. *Middle America: Its Lands and Peoples.* 3rd ed. Prentice-Hall, Englewood Cliffs.

Whitmore, Thomas
1992. *Disease and Death in Early Colonial Mexico: Simulating Amerindian Depopulation.* Westview Press, Boulder.

Wilken Gene C.
1987. *Good Farmers: Traditional Agricultural Resource Management in Mexico and Central America.* University of California Press, Berkeley.

Williams, Barbara J.
1989. Contact Period Rural Overpopulation in the Basin of Mexico: Carrying-capacity Models Tested with Documentary Data. *American Antiquity* 54:715–732.

Wyllie, Cherra
1994. *How to Make an Aztec Book: An Investigation Into the Manufacture of Central Mexican Codices.* Unpublished MA thesis, Department of Anthropology, Yale University.

Zorita, Alonso de
1963. *Life and Labor in Ancient Mexico: The Brief and Summary Relation of the Lords of New Spain.* Edited and translated by Benjamin Keen. Rutgers University Press, New Brunswick. (Originally written 1566–1570).

Index